ROCK THIS WAY

ROCK THIS WAY

CULTURAL CONSTRUCTIONS
OF MUSICAL LEGITIMACY

Mel Stanfill

UNIVERSITY OF MICHIGAN PRESS
Ann Arbor

Published in the United States of America by the
University of Michigan Press
Printed and bound by CPI Group (UK) Ltd, Croydon, CR0 4YY

First published August 2023

A CIP catalog record for this book is available from the British Library.

Library of Congress Control Number: 2023004276
LC record available at https://lccn.loc.gov/2023004276

ISBN 978-0-472-07628-4 (hardcover : alk. paper)
ISBN 978-0-472-05628-6 (paper : alk. paper)
ISBN 978-0-472-90362-7 (open access ebook)

DOI: https://doi.org/10.3998/mpub.12405073

The University of Michigan Press's open access publishing program is made possible thanks to additional funding from the University of Michigan Office of the Provost and the generous support of contributing libraries.

Cover illustration courtesy Shutterstock.com / thenatchdl

CONTENTS

ACKNOWLEDGMENTS

This book is better because of the advice, feedback, conversations, suggestions, and friendship of several people. The Race + IP conference, where I first took some of the ideas in this book for a test drive in 2017 and 2019, was tremendously welcoming of me—even when I couldn't remember off the top of my head that "thou shalt not steal" was used against Biz Markie (I can now, I swear). In particular, Bita Amani, Carys Craig, Betsy Rosenblatt, Madhavi Sunder, and Anjali Vats helped me feel included despite being only one of a few media scholars in a sea of law professors. Special thanks go out also to Stephanie Brown and Bill Fogarty for coming up with exactly the references I needed when I showed up in their inboxes with random questions about comedy studies and literary criticism, respectively.

My British Literature/Cool Kids writing group in the Department of English at UCF has been a source of both camaraderie and thoughtful critique. Many thanks to Anastasia Salter, Anna Jones, Bill Fogarty (again), James Campbell, Stephen Hopkins, and Tison Pugh for that and for being rad people I look forward to chatting with every month. Much love to faculty group chat (The Illegibles) for always being down for "Did I read this right?" or "Do I sound like a jerk in this email?" or (sometimes gallows) humor about the absurdity of life. Anastasia Salter (again), Anne Sullivan, Emily Johnson, and John Murray have been the best friends anybody could ask for.

The writing of this book took place in kind of a terrible couple of years. There was this global pandemic thing you may have heard of, and my mom, Jackie Stanfill, died. I could not have made it without my family—Daniel Stanfill, Burgandy Williams, Alyson, Honor, and Devon Giardini, and Don Stanfill—and the people who really came through when I was not quite keeping it together—Kristina Busse, JSA Lowe, and Anastasia Salter (again-again). I have tremendous gratitude for all of these people, for all of their help in ways big and small. This book (and I) wouldn't be the same without you.

Part of chapter 2 was previously published in an earlier version as Stanfill, Mel. 2021. "Can't Nobody Tell Me Nothin': 'Old Town Road,' Resisting Musical Norms, and Queer Remix Reproduction." *Popular Music* 40 (3–4): 347–63, https://doi.org/10.1017/S026114302100057X. Reprinted with permission. Parts of chapter 5 were previously published as "Blurred Lines oder: Das Gesetz spielt keine Rolle," in *100 Jahre Copyright*, edited by Lina Brion and Detlef Diederichsen, 138–47 (Berlin: Matthes & Seitz, 2019); and as "Blurred Lines, or: The Law Doesn't Matter," *100 Years of Now: Journal* (blog), November 13, 2019, http://journal.hkw.de/en/blurred-lines-oder-das-gesetz-spielt-keine-rolle/

Introduction

Rock This Way, or the Shape of Musical Norms

Fox television show *Glee* (2009–15), a musical comedy about a crew of lovable misfits and their high school glee club, was highly popular. The show had good ratings, attracted a large and intense fandom, enjoyed widespread merchandise sales—and produced huge music sales. Over the course of six seasons of cast recordings, *Glee* placed more than two hundred songs on the Billboard Hot 100, nearly twice as many as the second place artist, Lil Wayne, and far outstripping such heavy hitters as Elvis Presley and the Beatles.[1] By 2014, *Glee* had sold more than 60 million songs;[2] by 2015, sales had surpassed 11 million albums.[3] All in all, the *Glee* cast stands among the most successful music artists of all time—and they had all of this success with cover songs, some of which also combined more than one preexisting song in a mash-up. This success matters because musical works that build on other works, like cover songs and mash-ups, are often seen as lazy or uncreative—and sometimes illegal. Yet here *Glee* was, releasing multiple such works each week, 22 weeks a year for six years, and outselling many artists doing so-called "original" work.

This combination of factors makes the period inaugurated by *Glee*'s premiere particularly interesting to examine in terms of the popular understanding of what I call transformative musical works. With "transformative musical works," I mean to create a category that can hold in loose alliance multiple kinds of works that build from existing music—cover songs, remixes, mash-ups, parodies, and soundalike songs—that are *transformative*, meaning they rework the prior song in some significant way. The term "transformative" was developed in a 1990 law review article,[4] but came into broader use after it was invoked by the Supreme Court's decision in *Campbell v. Acuff-Rose* (1994), which centered on a parody song and found that courts considering whether a reuse of someone else's creative work infringes copyright should consider "whether and to what extent it is 'transformative,' altering the original with new expression, meaning, or message."[5] The concept has since been taken up broadly, both as a legal term and more descriptively to classify types of creative works.[6] Taking the transformative musical work as its focus, this book seeks to understand when music that builds from other music is or isn't positively received, the structures of the music industry that enable or resist such work, and its encounters with copyright law. This book understands race as central to the perception of transformative musical works, and thus looks at how these points of contact are shaped by the long history of overvaluing and overprotecting the work of white artists, undervaluing and underprotecting the work of Black artists (and other artists of color, but in the context of U.S. music, overwhelmingly Black artists), and treating Black artists under the rubric of what legal scholar Anjali Vats calls copyright thuggery—viewing them as thieves incapable of creativity.[7] Ultimately, I show that the extent to which a transformative musical work is seen as *having* new expression or meaning is contingent on cultural notions of creativity, legitimacy, and law, all of which are structured by white supremacy.

ONE NATION UNDER SOMEBODY ELSE'S GROOVE: PROBLEMATICS OF TRANSFORMATIVE MUSICAL WORKS FROM GLEE TO GEORGE CLINTON

As a preview of the kind of work this book does, I now turn to two examples that trace out some of the key issues. First, let's look at *Glee* more closely. In 2011, having heard good things about *Glee* and noticing that it was on Netflix, my household gave it a try one evening and enjoyed it enough to keep watching.[8] As I watched, one question sort of sat in the back of my mind: why did I find some of the show's cover songs good, and why did some of them seem boring or even bad? Examining how these musical works were discussed in the press, such bifurcated assessments are common. When *Glee*'s songs are positively received, one reason is that they demonstrate musical skill. One story praised a particular cover for "the pitch-perfect harmonies and the gorgeous undertone of beat-boxing and 'chik-ke-chik' beats that gave the song effortless buoyancy."[9] Another commented of the Glee Live! In Concert! tour that one song "may have been the best vocal number of the night. A smart arrangement. Grade: A-plus," emphasizing good execution of elements like vocals and arrangements to support the high grade awarded.[10]

While musical aptitude is probably a characteristic many people would find necessary for a good song, others focused on how the music made them feel. By the middle of the show's first season, one article insisted that "the way those sparkly kids burst into song—the dorkiness of it all—is so indelible and fun you could just explode with giddy amusement every time they light into Journey, or Van Halen, or Lily Allen, or the Police."[11] From the vantage point of the show's end, another writer hearkened back to those feelings evoked at the beginning: "Before the show had even aired, this rendition of the Journey hit ['Don't Stop Believin'"] had made its way online, and without any context, it was kind of electrifying."[12] What's seen as good about the music of *Glee*, that is, is often the emotion—specifically, in these instances, excitement—it evokes.[13]

Sometimes, there is praise for *Glee*'s fidelity to the previous version of the songs they cover. At other times, it's the way *Glee* reworks the source songs that people value, with one story praising the *Glee: The Power of Madonna* album for "an amped-up version of '4 Minutes' bolstered by the thrust of a marching band; a creative mash-up of 'Borderline' and 'Open Your Heart'; and the boys offering the gender-reversal 'What It Feels Like for a Girl.'"[14] Changing the arrangement (or even the genre) by adding the marching band, mashing up different songs, and boys taking on a woman's song about what it's like to be a girl—not faithful reproductions—are what garner praise here, which is also a frequent theme in how and when transformative musical works are praised more broadly.

However, *Glee* also had plenty of musical critics. Some artists, like Gorillaz, flatly said they wouldn't allow them to cover their songs.[15] Sometimes, far from the giddiness described above, the *Glee* versions of songs are considered "uninspired"[16] or "uninspiring."[17] Often, critiques show that there is a fine line to walk between fidelity (good) and a too-exact copy (bad). One critique noted that the Glee Live! show "didn't show much imagination."[18] Another provided the damningly faint praise that "as unnecessary as the faithful takes on 'Bust Your Windows' or 'Take a Bow' are, their candy-coated treatment keeps them sweet enough in this context."[19] One frequent complaint is that songs are overproduced, as in "over-produced and over-orchestrated"[20] or "overproduced and melodramatic."[21] This sense that the songs are gimmicky dovetails with arguments that there isn't enough feeling in them, as in "While the vocal arrangement on this song was interesting, [the singer] failed to summon enough emotion to make it memorable."[22] That is, Glee's covers are seen as bad when they're all style and no substance.

Despite this ambivalence, the show's music was, as noted at the beginning of this chapter, very popular. As one reviewer described it in 2009, "they storm the charts weekly with new songs."[23] One article argued that Glee "might be doing more for music than its fellow Fox juggernaut, 'American Idol'" (Fox 2002–16, ABC 2018–present),[24] another hugely popular musical show that generated significant music sales. After all, Glee not only sold many copies of its own cast recordings, but often increased sales for the source songs; for example, Journey's "Don't Stop Believin'" (1981) returned to the charts after they covered it.[25] This reinvigoration is much like how "the success of 'Walk This Way' put Run-DMC on the popular culture radar, and it landed Aerosmith—who was more or less washed-up at the time—*back* on that radar."[26] As we'll see, however, when hip-hop artists transform an existing song it's rarely met with the positive reception Glee got, regardless of its benefits to the source artist. Glee's cover may have similarly revitalized Sir Mix-a-Lot's 1992 song "Baby Got Back"—though, in a controversy that came to be known as #JoCoGleeGate, their arrangement exactly copied that of independent artist Jonathan Coulton's cover, without crediting or compensating him.[27] This copying was perfectly legal because by default, song arrangements that use what's called the mechanical license—a compulsory license to record someone else's composition if certain terms are met—are in the public domain; they are not recognized as creative works in their own right, "subjecting them to uniquely high creativity standards" compared to other kinds of reworking.[28] Moreover, "those who use copyrighted material without the authorization of the copyright owner, and outside the protections of fair use, are not eligible for copyright protection in their creations, however transformative they may be,"[29] so that without securing permission or litigating fair use, Coulton held no rights in his arrangement despite its innovation.[30] This incident foreshadows a central issue in this book—it is uneven and unpredictable which kinds of transformative musical works are valued, both socially and legally.

In the end, Glee's music was massively successful, and it managed its fantastic feats of record and download sales using other people's songs. However, unlike many other instances of success through transformative musical reuse found in hip-hop sampling or the mash-ups, remixes, parodies, and soundalike songs this book examines, the language of uncreative copying, freeloading on other people's work, or theft and copyright infringement did not appear in press discussion about *Glee*'s music. *Glee* therefore also raises some of this book's key questions: When is a transformative musical work perceived positively? When are questions of creativity and copyright invoked—and when are they not?

If, in one way, this book's story begins with me watching *Glee*, in another way, the story starts, as maybe all good ones should, with George Clinton. In 2013, popular culture scholar Francesca Royster, author of *Sounding Like a No-No: Queer Sounds and Eccentric Acts in the Post-Soul Era*, had come to campus to give a presentation, and I had a conversation with her about her book's chapter on funk music legend George Clinton. As Royster describes, Clinton's interrelated Parliament and Funkadelic groups, which she shorthands as the composite P-Funk, "sometimes dared to 'Doobie' its funk, taking on consummately 'white' pop standards and lending them a hard funk edge," reworking music from groups like the Doobie Brothers, a mostly white band associated with soft rock and blue-eyed soul. She argues that P-Funk's "relationship to white rock in some ways acknowledges cross-influence, as well as the borrowing and reborrowing of black sound" and calls Clinton's cover of Cream's "Sunshine of Your Love" (1967) "a form of (loving) revenge" for Cream having copied from Black artists for their sound.[31] What stood out to me about these examples was how Clinton openly built from other people's music as part of his own practice—borrowing, acknowledging influence, and reusing things he loved.

Royster also notes that "in answer to the high number of unacknowledged samples of his music, Clinton has both gone to the courts and produced an album of frequently sampled songs called *Sample Some of Disc, Sample Some of D.A.T.*, which includes an application form for the use of copyrighted materials."[32] Releasing this collection seemed like a contradiction to me alongside the freedom with which Clinton reused others' work. However, it turns out that this history is considerably more complex. While there have certainly been lawsuits over Clinton's catalog—including, (in)famously, *Bridgeport v. Dimension Films* (2005), in which the Sixth Circuit found that there is no *de minimis* defense for using just a tiny portion of a song as a sample, and that all samples, no matter how small, require licensing[33]—these suits were brought not by Clinton but by Bridgeport

Music, a rights aggregator. Bridgeport did so despite the fact that they, as Demers notes, "admitted to forging Clinton's signature on the copyright transfer documents." These suits were decidedly not for Clinton's benefit, as "a federal judge in Florida found against Clinton in a 2001 ruling that deprived the funk artist of songs valued at $210 million."[34] Clinton thus illustrates how Black artists' music has not tended to be protected by the law, a key issue for this book.[35]

While releasing *Disc/D.A.T.* might look like a power grab in which Clinton attempted to dictate how people could sample from him, it was in fact a move toward more equitable sampling. On one hand, it wasn't just any album of sampled songs, but a "collection of sounds and previously unreleased out takes and songs,"[36] meaning that it encouraged sampling from recordings that Clinton holds the rights to as opposed to those held by Bridgeport, returning benefit to the actual artist. On the other hand, it offers far better terms than are standard for samples, requiring royalty payments only when copies are sold rather than up front and setting the royalty using the statutory rate for the mechanical license (9.1¢ per copy), as opposed to thousands of dollars up front for a standard sample buyout.[37] Having worked for many years in fan studies, I initially approached *Disc/D.A.T.* from the position that everything should always be freely transformed into new works, but I came to realize that my focus on fans appropriating corporate culture didn't really translate to a situation steeped in the long tradition of white appropriation of Black people's music. From this relatively random encounter with another scholar and the conversations it provoked, I came away sure that I wanted to write this book, and George Clinton provided one of its key questions: who is able to transform whose music—both normatively and legally—and how does race matter to this acceptability?

Ultimately, this book explores the field of inquiry opened up by these two examples. I examine several key questions. What insight does the discourse around transformative musical works provide into social understandings of creativity? How do quotidian assessments of creativity and legitimacy in transformative musical works compare to what the law protects? How do social structures of inequality, especially race, affect all of these questions? These issues lead to overarching meta-questions: which transformative musical works are socially seen as legitimate, how do these assessments arise from structural factors, and what are the stakes of assessing appropriate musical reuse in the way it's currently done?

LAWYERS, RACE, AND MONEY:
TRANSFORMATIVE MUSICAL WORKS MEET CRITICAL RACE THEORY

Understanding social sensemaking around transformative musical works requires incorporating both cultural and legal understandings of what it means to create and how creative works relate to previous works, as well as recognizing that the cultural and the legal cannot be fully disentangled. To begin with the latter point, though the law is often thought of as objective, neutral, and consistent, in truth the commonsense story about law is just that—a story, and one that does cultural work. Fundamentally, it's most productive to understand the law as a tool, as legal scholar Madhavi Sunder does,[38] or, in the words of communications scholar Tarleton Gillespie, as a technology, "an artificial apparatus designed by man [*sic*] to intervene in and organize human activity."[39] Thinking of the law as something people created to serve certain purposes makes it possible to question both those purposes and whether the law succeeds in serving them. Through its delineation of legal and illegal, law makes "some behaviors less attractive, valuable, or permissible, and others more so"—even in the absence of formal legal action like a civil suit or criminal case.[40] However, it's also important to recognize that, as Susan Silbey and Austin Sarat point out, "'the law' is a fiction, but laws are real."[41] Law is a social construct with a great deal of material power.

Moreover, recognizing law as a social construct means recognizing how it is shaped by the society that constructed it. In particular, since the 1970s (though consciously framing itself as a movement dates to 1989), the scholarly project of Critical Race Theory (CRT) has shown how apparently neutral laws are in fact structured by the racial inequality endemic to U.S. society.[42] CRT interrogates how laws consistently both impact race as a social power system and are impacted *by* race as a social power system.[43] CRT requires understanding racism not as individual prejudice but a structure that positions some races as superior and others as inferior, with material effects.[44] As legal scholars Kimberlé Crenshaw, Neil Gotanda, Gary Peller, and Kendall Thomas describe in their introduction to the landmark volume *Critical Race Theory: The Key Writings That Formed the Movement* (1996), CRT seeks "to understand how a regime of white supremacy and its subordination of people of color have been created and maintained in America, and, in particular, to examine the relationship between that social structure and professed ideals such as 'the rule of law' and 'equal protection.'"[45] That is, the problem is not merely that law has not been neutrally applied to white people and people of color (though it hasn't), but rather that apparently neutral legal concepts are themselves structured by white supremacy. Accordingly, as legal scholar K. J. Greene notes, CRT scholars not only "reject the use of 'neutral' accounts of legal decision-making," but specifically "focus on the perspectives of subordinated peoples."[46]

Understanding racism as a structure makes it possible to see how it has been baked in to U.S. institutions and culture from the nation's inception—it's the baseline, not deviant.[47] Given this structure, Crenshaw notes that just doing away with formal inequality (such as through civil rights legislation), "though symbolically significant to all and materially significant to some," doesn't in itself get rid of exclusion and in fact can slow down progress given "the societal self-satisfaction engendered by the appearance of neutral norms and formal inclusion."[48] CRT, in thinking structurally and moving away from individual prejudice, highlights that "the injury of racial inequality exists irrespective of the decisionmakers' motives."[49] Racism doesn't require intent, and CRT calls for focus on effects. CRT thinks systemically across society; legal scholars Mari Matsuda and Charles R. Lawrence III argue that "as critical race theorists, we do not separate cross burning from police brutality nor epithets from infant mortality rates."[50] Accordingly, while much of CRT's attention tends to be on things like cross burning and police brutality, CRT has also made important interventions in property law. Cheryl Harris's classic essay "Whiteness as Property," for example, argues both that property in the United States has been structured by white supremacy—only white possession of land, not Indigenous people's use, was seen as the legitimate basis for property rights—and that notions from property law shape whiteness as a category. Both property and whiteness are premised on "the right to exclude."[51]

Thus, while inequality in copyright is experientially quite unlike cross burning or police brutality, it does reinstantiate these broader structures of racialized law in general and property in particular. The body of intellectual property scholarship that examines this intersection has been named "Critical Race IP" by legal scholars Anjali Vats and Deidre A. Keller, who define this field as an "interdisciplinary movement of scholars connected by their focus on the racial and colonial non-neutrality of the laws of copyright, patent, trademark, right of publicity, trade secret, and unfair competition using principles informed by CRT."[52] Accordingly, much as

CRT recognizes that law in general, and property law in particular, is not neutral but structured by white supremacy, Critical Race IP thinkers such as Vats point out that "whiteness and its attendant property interests structure intellectual property law, often in the guise of equality and race neutrality."[53] Formal inclusion in the IP regime, that is, has not fundamentally altered the fact that "intellectual property recognizes some authors and inventors, and misrecognizes others. In turn, law apportions the material spoils of creativity unequally,"[54] and particularly, in the U.S. context, does so by race.

Fundamentally, the "what" that law protects and doesn't is deeply and inevitably bound up in the "who." If, as legal scholar Rosemary Coombe rightly notes, the law drawing a protective boundary around some kinds of creation inevitably leaves other kinds unprotected,[55] transformative musical works can't be understood without interrogating which things fall into which category. This is where the George Clinton example discussed earlier becomes important. On one hand, Black artists have tended to be less protected. As legal scholar Olufunmilayo B. Arewa points out, "the ability to borrow from African-American sources was intimately connected to social and cultural hierarchies. These hierarchies were reflected in and reinforced by copyright frameworks that historically have permitted borrowings from certain categories and types of cultural expression, at times without compensation."[56] On the other hand, under assumptions of copyright thuggery, Black artists who attempt to borrow are often framed as uncreative thieves.[57] Building on what came before is unevenly available, and Black people are disproportionately likely to have the limits of law without its possibilities. Through CRT and Critical Race IP, it becomes clear that, if the law is a fiction that does cultural work, it is specifically *racialized* cultural work.

JUST MY IMAGINATION (PRODUCING CREATIVITY): THE ROMANTIC AUTHOR AND BELIEFS ABOUT ART

Beginning from this CRT frame that takes seriously how law and institutions are not neutral and *are* specifically racialized makes it possible to interrogate the other components of how transformative musical works are socially perceived—authorship and creativity, and the reuse of existing materials in new works. To begin with the construction of authorship and creativity, defining who counts as an artist or author and what it means to be an artist or author is enmeshed in both popular beliefs about authorship and legal questions about what rights and protections artists and authors have. The contemporary commonsense view of authors and artists has its roots in an 18th- and 19th-century aesthetic movement called Romanticism that valued individualism and emotion. During Romanticism, the individual came to be seen as the origin of art, which comes from his (usually his) internal genius,[58] disconnected from any exterior influence.[59]

This model of individual, isolated creativity is strongly represented in music. Media studies scholar Jack Hamilton notes that "rock music conceived of musical creativity in fiercely individualist terms, as matters of personal transcendence."[60] This ideology is pervasive throughout discourse around popular music; as communication scholar Thomas Schumacher argues, "most criticism of popular music remains firmly tied to the aesthetics and affects of rock music."[61] In particular, there is an idea of music as self-expression:

> rock ideology fetishizes "originalism," and frequently trumpets the fact that nearly all of the genre's greatest heroes wrote the vast bulk of their own material. This primacy of self-containment is, of course, conducive to the conviction that rock is above all a genre of authentic self-expression, and it helps tamp down anxieties about the music's relationship to mass culture and commerce's role in the artistic process.[62]

This model of music as authentic self-expression functions to suppress concerns that these works are merely for monetary gain—which would violate the norm of the Romantic author creating solely from internal drive. Media studies scholar Matt Stahl directly links rock norms of authenticity and the Romantic author, saying, "the presumed autonomy of the creative cultural-industry worker, exemplified in the figure of the rock star, is a function of mystification by the culture itself," adding that it "is a legacy of the proliferation in and appropriation of Romantic myths of the artist as rebel and outsider by our culture."[63] These social beliefs exist about musicians, that is, because they exist about authors generally.

When this notion of individual authorship then collides with the way that white people are seen as individuals, while racialized Others get defined by their group—a feature of white supremacy—it explains much about whose music is protected and valued. The combination of always being seen as representing a group and understanding creativity as disconnected from others is one route by which protection of creative works is uneven by race. Such beliefs give rise to situations like that of the song "Mbube," which was actually written in 1939 by South African composer Solomon Linda, but was perceived to be a traditional African song—part of the public domain and free to use in reworkings such as "The Lion Sleeps Tonight" (1961)—despite being a recent song with an identifiable author.[64] Even when artists of color are individual creators, their contents are often still assumed to be communal and unowned.

This idea that artists create as the expression of individual, internal talent is now hegemonic and therefore seems obvious or natural—but neither aspect of this model holds up in practice. As Hamilton's and Stahl's views discussed above begin to show, keeping authorship strictly separated from commerce is a fiction. In fact, the interaction of the two is exactly what copyright law regulates. At a basic level, the law assumes that creativity needs external incentives. In fact, literary scholar Martha Woodmansee argues that the invention of the Romantic author and of copyright law were intertwined, both serving to enable writing as a profession.[65] U.S. Copyright is legally rooted in Article I, Section 8, Clause 8 of the Constitution, known as the Copyright Clause, which identifies the purpose of copyright protection as "To promote the Progress of Science and useful Arts"; this purpose is accomplished "by securing for limited Times to Authors and Inventors the exclusive Right to their respective Writings and Discoveries." The underlying argument is that exclusive rights enable authors to benefit from their creativity, which encourages them to create, enabling more progress of science and arts for everyone. Legal scholar Jessica Litman identifies copyright as "a bargain between the public and the author, whereby the public bribed the author to create new works in return for limited commercial control over the new expression the author brought to her works."[66] That is, copyright includes commercial incentives, and it does so to encourage people to create, and this is a relationship between the public and the author that is mediated by the law. Thus, while copyright is often framed as rooted in what is *fair*, the originating force is the promotion of progress of science and arts through commercial incentives—not what a creator deserves.

Creativity doesn't happen without influence either. The concept of the author writing in a vacuum has been contested since the late 1960s in literary theory by writers like Roland Barthes (1967), who argued against seeing the author as the source of a text's meaning, and Michel Foucault (1969), who argued that the author was a social construct that should be interrogated rather than assumed.[67] While these French theorists may not be widely known outside some corners of academia, questioning the Romantic individualist author is considerably more widespread. As Michael Awkward, a scholar of African American culture, points out, "analyses of writers' echoes of the compelling words, ideas, images, and themes of their predecessors are among the most common and, hence, most rigorously investigated forms of literary study."[68] This tendency is even stronger in legal scholarship; Sunder argues that "it is by now a commonplace observation in copyright scholarship that all creativity is derivative."[69] That is, new works are widely (though certainly not universally) understood to build from previous works.

The Romantic author is even further from reality given that the rights and benefits of authorship often end up in the hands of corporations, not the actual creative individuals who make the artistic works. Stahl, who wrote a book-length study of these artist-industry relationships, notes that recording artists:

> work under unequal contacts and must hand over long-term control of the songs and albums they produce to their record companies. Typically, these contracts are exclusive, meaning that without getting special permission to do otherwise the recording artist is allowed to record only for the company with whom he has a contract. The contracts are also typically assignable, meaning that they (and hence, in a certain sense, the artists) can be bought and sold, most often along with the companies who hold them.[70]

Not only do artists not control the products of their work, that is, but they also don't necessarily control who they work for. Moreover, as hip-hop scholar Tricia Rose points out, "if an employee creates a work, then in the absence of a contract to the contrary, work for hire alienates the work from the employee-creator. The employee is the employer's instrument or medium of creation, the work is the employer's."[71] Putting these aspects of music industry practice side by side, it becomes clear that these models are not only disempowering but dehumanizing, reducing artists to property and tools. Such facts of contracts are why the legal concept of authorship is important to interrogate—a work is actually created by one or more people, but through legal structures like contracts or work for hire status, a corporation may come to be the legal author.[72] As Stahl notes, "understood in common sense as an act of original creation, authorship appears to underwrite ownership. However, in practice it often seems that ownership establishes authorship—as a set of rights—retroactively."[73] For such reasons, legal scholar Jane Ginsburg argues, authorship is more about control than creation.[74] This reorientation to recognize authorship as a legal category rather than a creative one is essential to understanding how creative works get made, and understanding authorship as a cultural category is essential to this book.

However, like the law itself, the hegemonic understanding of what artists do is a construct that has powerful effects. These effects demonstrate what Foucault calls the "author function," emphasizing that the concept of the author does a particular kind of work that's rooted in, and shifts according to, the legal and social context.[75] Authors are constructed by law and other institutions, and therefore have different contours in different contexts. The Romantic author does cultural work; as legal scholars Chander and Sunder argue, "the trope of the 'romantic author' has served to bolster the property rights claims of the powerful."[76] As Toula and Lisby point out, "even as the concepts of authorship and originality are destabilized in literary studies, they are still a bedrock justification for strengthening copyright protections."[77] Indeed, as critical legal studies scholar Boatema Boateng argues, "the law exists to specify and police a sharp demarcation around the work of each creator. It is, in effect, a system for organizing knowledge and cultural production so that their social and temporal contexts are deemphasized and devalued in order to uphold the fiction of an individual creator."[78] Seeing artists as individuals expressing their creative genius encourages protecting their works. The idea of the suffering individual author is often cynically deployed by corporate rightsholders for their own benefit, with record companies appealing to the need to pay musicians fairly in order for music to be made at the same time that artists already create without fair compensation, under what legal scholar James Boyle calls "a system of contracts . . . that makes feudal indenture look benign."[79] However, the culturally inculcated reverence for the author is often still effective regardless of whether it is invoked sincerely.

The role of reuse in creativity is the third major site of cultural contestation this book examines. Transformative reuses "employ the quoted matter in a different manner or for a different purpose from the original" such that "the secondary use adds value to the original—if the quoted matter is used as raw material, transformed in the creation of new information, new aesthetics, new insights and understandings."[80] This is where the creative works in this book come in: they draw from existing music to make new music, which many scholars argue should be understood as more like quoting than stealing. However, transformative musical works aren't always understood as building on what came before, but rather are treated as theft. For example, actions that are possible in analog production are forbidden when they are digital. As Kembrew McLeod and Rudolf Kuenzli explain, singing a bit of existing song in a new song probably would not be considered infringement, but sampling the recording itself tends to be understood as infringing.[81] The two are the same action under different technological conditions, but understood very differently.

However, as legal scholar Julie Cohen points out, there's a fundamental tension in copyright law: if authors get control to encourage them to create because creating benefits the public, that very control also diminishes the benefit to the public.[82] That is, if and as copyright protection results in control of creative works, treating them like property, and especially propertizing disproportionately for corporate gain, there are costs for creativity. As Boyle asks, "given that we all learn from and build on the past, do we have a right to carve out our own incremental innovations and protect them by intellectual property rights?"[83] Lewis Hyde argues that intellectual property is a public good, "the intangible equivalent of the tangible *res publicae* (roads, bridges, harbors) or of the Republic itself."[84] In particular, they are public goods that enable making more goods. By closing off existing creativity, the ability to build on it is removed, diminishing the benefit the public is supposed to get from copyright.

After Romanticism and the isolated author model, Euro-American norms of music production changed: alluding to and building on the work of others was a norm, until it wasn't. As beliefs shifted, Western classical music, which had formerly been part of everyday life, became "rarefied and untouchable," with the result that "practices such as borrowing and improvisation, which gave performers authority to change music, became increasingly disfavored."[85] This isn't to say that these practices of musical reuse ceased to happen after the Romantic author; as musicologist J. Peter Burkholder shows, they remain common.[86] However, their prevalence has been suppressed and denied under the Romantic author regime. With this normative view of authorship, the understanding of creativity as involving relationships to other work is downplayed. Creators have to disavow their influences, refuse transformativity, and pretend to be that Romantic author—sincerely or not—to avoid accusations of copying or theft.

But these kinds of creativity are not suppressed in other cultural traditions, particularly, in the context of U.S. popular music, the work of Black artists. Music rooted in African American traditions, for example, often involves repeating and reworking what has gone before as a routine part of making new art. As Arewa describes, "blues and other forms of African-American cultural production have involved creation through collaboration and repetition[,] and in blues, repetition, revision, and synthesis of varied musical influences has often been a core aspect of creation and innovation."[87] In this model of creativity, engaging with particular creative forebears situates an artist in a tradition and is not viewed negatively. However, such music's tendency to rework previous songs, alongside its use of improvisation, puts it outside the norm—a norm that must be recognized as not neutral or universal, but particular and white.

This is not to say that all creativity should always freely be treated as public goods. Even when Black artists do comply with hegemonic norms of creativity, for example, the regular protections still don't seem to apply, as with "innovative black composers, whose ground-breaking work was imitated so widely that it became the 'idea' and thus impossible to protect."[88] That is, though there is a common distinction in copyright between an idea (which is not protected) and an expression (which is protected), expressive features of Black people's music often end up treated as ideas. Through such acts of extraction, "while individual black artists without question have benefited from the IP system, the economic effects of IP deprivation on the black community have been devastating."[89] The devalued status of these works is often overdetermined as devalued people participate in devalued forms of creativity. Ultimately, these examples tend to boil down to artists of color, particularly Black artists, being "treated as *nothing other than* raw material."[90]

Not only is the creative work of artists of color—especially Black artists—not protected by these implementations of copyright law, but it's routinely specifically white people who benefit from their creative works. Historically, "whether in good faith or bad, white performers almost always reaped larger rewards than their black influences and songwriters."[91] These rewards are nearly always gained legally. For example, white artists covering Black artists' songs paid royalties as required, but the structure of contracts tended to mean the Black artists did not hold the songwriting or publishing rights and so did not receive those royalties, creating a situation in which only some artists benefit. *Cultural appropriation* results when culture is valued but not protected, when there is desire for the culture but never the people it comes from. People of color's creative works can be both devalued and lucratively extracted, producing "the experience of everywhere being seen but never being heard, of constantly being represented but never listened to, being treated like a historical artifact rather than a human being to be engaged in dialogue."[92] This extraction undeniably operates from appreciation, arising from seeing Black, Indigenous, and other people of color's cultural production as authentic, interesting—even exotic. As feminist theorist bell hooks describes in her famous essay "Eating the Other," while such consumers think they are respecting another culture, they're still acting out of a sense that they're entitled to it.[93] Even when cultural appropriation results from a move to see nonwhite cultures as more interesting than white culture, it's rooted in a sense that whiteness is neutral and thus privileges whiteness all over again.

It matters that cultural appropriation operates in the orbit of what historian Eric Lott calls "love and theft," combining love of Black people's culture with disrespect for Black people themselves.[94] Media industries scholar David Hesmondhalgh asks, "did the rock-and-roll acts of the late 1950s rip off black music, or was their music a creative hybrid of black and white musical styles? Did Cream and other beat groups of the 1960s exploit blues musicians when they used the blues as the basis of their hard rock sound, or were they paying a respectful tribute, which drew the attention of wider audiences to that little-known musical tradition?"[95] The answer, of course, is that it is both, but the fact that the financial benefit flows disproportionately toward the white artists cannot be disregarded. As ethnomusicologist Steven Feld argues, "musical appropriation sings a double line with one voice. It is a melody of admiration, even homage and respect. . . . Yet this voice is harmonized by a counter-melody of power, even control and domination; a fundamental source of maintaining asymmetries in ownership and commodification of musical works."[96] Engagements across musical traditions carry both valences, and it is essential to interrogate both who feels entitled to transform whose music and whose transformations are socially considered legitimate. Popular concepts of reuse, like those of authorship, are shot through with racial inequality.

Ultimately, protection of earlier artists and freedom to use for later artists must be carefully balanced. Nevertheless, the usual media industry position is that more protection is always an improvement, meaning that media industries often use copyright to prevent the kind of building on existing works that this book examines. There is a distinct benefit to artists with industry backing, as rightsholders have free rein to transform and rework their own materials; others who wish to transform existing works often must pay exorbitant license fees, risk lawsuits, or not create at all. With two similar appropriations of intellectual property, one artist can be legally protected and the other not, when the only real difference is who has better lawyers.

In a broader pattern, uses of creative works that are legal are sometimes socially unacceptable. Clyde Stubblefield, for example, who was the drummer for James Brown and came up with rhythms on his records that have been frequently sampled in hip-hop, was not credited as one of the writers of the songs and so didn't receive any royalties from either the original records or the samples. This lack of credit is perfectly legal but strikes many (including me) as wrong. By contrast, forms of transformation that are socially acceptable may not be legal. This disjuncture was particularly evident with Danger Mouse's 2004 *The Grey Album* mash-up of the Beatles' self-titled 1968 album, usually known as *The White Album*, and Jay-Z's 2003 *The Black Album*—it was both popular and critically acclaimed, but also provoked legal action from the Beatles' rightsholder, record label conglomerate EMI. This book seeks to map these spaces, between what are socially thought of as worthy kinds of new music and what is formally approved.

THIS IS HOW WE DO IT: ABOUT THIS BOOK

In order to analyze how transformative musical works are culturally understood, this book examines how mainstream press discourse talks about them. According to professional journalistic norms, press discussion is supposed to be neutral and balanced.[97] This is, of course, a fiction, because press coverage reproduces social power relations. However, given that my interest is to study social power relations, this is a benefit, not a drawback. In particular, norms of explaining "both sides" of an issue mean that a cross section of mainstream thought is available in the press, at the same time that more marginal perspectives are systematically excluded. Moreover, in addition to conveying what the journalist perceives to be a neutral account of a situation, the press helps frame public understanding of issues, thus contributing to making this the default understanding through presenting a hegemonic view as the truth. For these reasons, I use press coverage to examine social beliefs circulating widely about transformative musical works. In doing so, I specifically abstract away from particular journalists and their identities (racial, gender, or others) because, by those same professional norms, individual perspectives are supposed to be suppressed in the name of a (white and masculine) construct of universality. Moreover, an individual journalist presenting an opinion (whether they are aware of doing so or not) isn't in itself meaningful, but when there are patterns in opinions across multiple articles, by different people, in different locations and at different moments, they become suggestive of a broader hegemonic formation.

In order to capture as wide a variety of examples and circumstances as possible, I began by retrieving all instances of three key terms, "remix" "mash-up" and "cover song," in Associated Press coverage between 2009 and 2018 from online database LexisNexis, using the AP to constrain the initial number of articles to make it possible to manually read them to find transformative musical works to seed subsequent recursive searching. I first used these documents to compile a list of songs described as a remix, mash-up, or cover; albums and musical events described as including one; or artists described as making them. This set was supplemented with famous examples—like Robin Thicke's "Blurred Lines" (2013) and lawsuit against the estate of Marvin Gaye or toy company GoldieBlox's 2013 parody of the Beastie Boys' "Girls" (1987)—and examples mentioned in the literature, particularly from Tim English's *Sounds Like Teen Spirit*.[98] I then searched this list as a snowball sample, now drawing on the full LexisNexis database encompassing "more than 17,000 news, business, and legal sources," though I searched only the news sources.[99] I mined these documents for the musical objects they mentioned, then repeated this snowball sample process two more times until there were diminishing returns, as less than 1% of stories in any given search were relevant for these more obscure instances.

All articles found through these recursive searches then become the corpus of data. Articles that were from non-U.S. publications were removed during data cleaning, because they are likely to have been at least partially localized and the focus of this project is on U.S. intellectual property law and culture. To improve the relevance of the data, stories that merely mentioned that something *is* a remix, mash-up, or cover song without any descriptive or evaluative language were removed. After this data cleaning process, I reached a total of 182 transformative musical works with relevant stories.[100] Over the course of the collection process, two other categories of transformative musical work emerged from the searches: parodies and soundalike songs, bringing the total to five categories.

But what do I mean by these five categories? A cover song is a version of a song that responds to a previous recording of a song, and in particular a strong or canonical previous recording. For remixes, I follow musicologist Sheena Hyndman in defining them as "a song created using a combination of newly composed musical material and previously existing recorded sounds."[101] Mash-ups, on the other hand, are transformative musical works that combine existing songs, particularly existing recordings, and, usually, specifically have parts of more than one song. Parodies are songs that typically use the melody of an existing song as a vehicle for commentary or humor. Finally, the category "soundalike" groups a series of instances where someone notices a commonality between different songs, similar to what Burkholder describes as "paraphrasing an existing tune to form a new melody, theme, or motive."[102] In this way, the book covers a range of ways people reuse other songs in new songs, with different cultural and legal valences, to broadly trace the contours of how transformative musical works are culturally understood.

To analyze the corpus of news stories, I used a combination of Analytics-Qualified Qualitative Analysis[103] and Big Reading.[104] After sorting the examples into a subcorpus for each of the five categories (cover song, remix, mash-up, parody, soundalike song), I conducted a discourse analysis of each body of text, supported by qualitative data analysis software Dedoose. Discourse analysis is a form of close reading that attends to patterns of language use, how the transformative musical works were framed, and the underlying relations of power that shaped popular discussion. Importantly, I paid attention to power whether the journalists involved did so or not, such as noting how particular cases were racialized despite the frequent silence in the stories themselves about this system of power. In addition, I also closely read legal filings and verdicts in notable legal actions within the various categories for how these texts construct legitimacy. As a second layer of analysis, I used some computational Digital Humanities techniques. The first of these was quantitative analysis of code co-occurrence (how often two codes described the same quotation from the corpus) to examine aggregate patterns in the press data such as seeing how often a transformative musical work by a Latine artist was also discussed in positive terms or the prevalence of types of mash-up over time.[105] The second DH technique was exporting the quotations my close reading identified to data mining software Orange,[106] which enabled me to gain more aggregate insight such as word frequency in each subcorpus. These additional quantitative and computational analyses served to help contextualize the close readings. In all cases, my interest is in how musical works are made sense of once they exist. While surely these same broad cultural patterns impact the production of music to at least some degree, I begin from the moment a transformative musical work is publicly available and publicly interpreted.

The book proceeds from the least controversial transformative musical works, cover songs, to the most, soundalike songs. In the first chapter, "Judge a Song by Its Cover: Cover Songs between Transformation and Extraction," I begin with the history of covers being passed off in place of the source song as white artists covered Black artists' songs for white audiences. Then, I examine how covers are constructed as forms of nostalgia for the source rooted in respect and fidelity. I also consider the most frequent contemporary framing of covers, which sees them as creating a unique version of the source and is rooted in ideas about Romantic authorship as the expression of the self. Finally, I return to ideas of covers as free-riding on someone else's song to think about what's changed and what hasn't since the 1950s in instances when covers are used by those less famous than the source artist, particularly digitally. Ultimately, I argue, a good cover song according to contemporary standards is a new arrangement that is transformative rather than faithful, but such records nevertheless often reproduce histories of extraction of Black artists' music.

The second chapter, "Stir It Up: Remix and the Problem of Genre," first works through how remix is defined in popular discourse, finding that the question of genre permeates the discussion both in the sense that genre change is one of the key ways remixes are transformative and because there are two major genres within remix in the period this book examines that exist in relatively distinct cultural spaces. Next, I examine how and when remix is framed positively, arguing that remixes are often seen as adding value to base songs, whether through enabling industry recognition, making them valuable to more people by expanding the audience, or flatly increasing monetary value by boosting sales. As this focus on business success suggests, positive discussions of remix rarely laud their creativity and artistry. Instead, these questions show up in the negative, when remixes become the site of legal resistance, lost artistic control, and cultural appropriation. I end the chapter with a consideration of "Old Town Road" (Lil Nas X, 2018), a song whose proliferating remixes demonstrate that remix trouble has much to do with refusing the normative straight lines of the song life course.

Chapter 3, "Monstrous Mash: Mash-Ups and the Epistemology of Difference," shows that mash-ups do two seemingly contradictory things. On one hand, mash-up works by employing recognizable source texts whose meaning is made present and juxtaposed with each other through what I call the *aura function*. On the other hand, the mash-up is constructed as new and different. Combining reference and nostalgia with novelty in the same song is on one level contradictory, but on another level is aligned with the Black cultural practice of Signifyin,' known for repetition with difference. I argue that this contradiction matters a great deal; part of the greater popular discomfort with mash-up compared to cover songs and remixes is that it is more aesthetically aligned with Black cultural production than other genres are. The structural Blackness of mash-up is also tied into its negative reception, which is discursively managed through aligning mash-up with whiteness by contrast to hip-hop sampling through emphasizing labor, framing mash-up as building racial harmony by drawing on multiracial sources, and treating mash-up figuratively rather than as literal combination of songs.

In chapter 4, "Fight for Your Right to Parody: Parodies and the Cultural Politics of Kindness," I begin with two examples: an old media story of working within the system and another story steeped in Silicon Valley's ethos of asking forgiveness rather than permission. These two instances illustrate some of the foundational tensions in parody as a kind of transformative musical work. I then work through how key court cases have defined (and justified) parody, demonstrating their reliance on a notion of parody as a critical reworking. When examining which parodies are deemed good in popular discourse, by contrast, unexpected versions of songs can be seen as creative, but the content should be different, not the sound; popular assessments place significant emphasis on humor that is not present in the letter of the law; and cultural common sense doesn't use the parody/satire distinction that courts do. Moreover, diverging from the legal model of parody as critique, popular notions advocate that parodies be kind, but do so in a notably colorblind way. Ultimately, while popular discourse explicitly flags parodies' respect for the source song and legal discourse emphasizes criticism, both center parody's relationship to the source text in order to discursively manage parody's position toward the socially contested side of the transformative musical work spectrum.

The fifth chapter, "Feels like the First Time: The Politics and Poetics of Similarity in Soundalikes," explores the most contested kind of musical transformative work: the soundalike song. I find that, when examining what constitutes similarity in soundalikes, songs can be compared to specific other songs, to artists, or to whole genres. The most emphasis, however, is on melody, and there's tension between thinking of soundalikes as infringement or something more like plagiarism. Lawsuits over soundalikes—particularly, that around the 2013 Robin Thicke hit "Blurred Lines"—show that what verdicts will find infringing (intangibles like "feel") differs from what the law formally protects (what can be written in sheet music). This distinction results in extending protection in ways that make artists nervous about future production of music. Moreover, cultural commonsense around soundalikes cannot be understood without understanding power dynamics of race and gender, as verdicts are ultimately deeply shaped by who did what to whom whether they're supposed to or not. In the end, I argue, soundalike songs show how the music industry's own actions have produced outcomes it now finds threatening.

Finally, "Conclusion: Toward a Theory of Ethical Transformative Musical Works," conducts a meta-analysis of all positively and negatively assessed transformative musical works from the full data set, defining an overarching set of tensions: songs that produce emotional responses vs. those that are boring or without substance; songs that transform or even improve on their sources vs. those seen as uncreative, lazy, cash grabs, or even theft; fidelity and respect for the source artist vs. being disrespectful; and the ways cultural appropriation is decried in some instances but lauded in others. I argue for taking these beliefs seriously as the discursive construction of acceptable and unacceptable transformative musical works, but also that a broader theory of ethical transformative musical works is needed—one which only partially overlaps with contemporary popular beliefs. Finally, I articulate a normative statement of principles for transformative musical works that I contend would move forward the popular understanding of legitimate and illegitimate reuse of existing creative works.

CHAPTER 1

Judge a Song by Its Cover

Cover Songs between Transformation and Extraction

A covers album can be a tribute or a miscellany, a throwaway or a statement about what a songwriter holds dear. The production can imitate the original arrangements, the way Seal and Rod Stewart did on their recent soul collections, or apply a distinctly personal approach, as Rosanne Cash did on "The List." Meanwhile, in recording company offices, hopes arise that a familiar voice and a familiar song can add up to radio play.[1]

Cover songs might seem out of place in a book about transformative musical works. They aren't often compared to mash-ups or parodies because they are a thoroughly mainstream music industry practice. Covers don't surface in the legal conversation because there is a compulsory mechanical license to produce recordings of a composition and so they don't tend to provoke lawsuits. However, it's precisely because cover songs are so normalized that I begin the book here: they do rework their source texts, and how that happens—and how it's received—tells us a lot about popular beliefs around music, unmuddied by the controversies that make other types of transformative musical work more complex.[2]

It's important, first, to recognize that a cover isn't just any version of an existing song, but a particular kind. Musicologist Gabriel Solis argues that covers specifically come from a tradition that arose in rock music of the 1950s.[3] Multiple scholars argue that the cover song is rooted in rock music because it responds to and plays with rock's conceit that a song is an authentic expression of the singer who wrote and recorded it;[4] this ethic of expression, and the relationship to cover songs it engenders, have subsequently (if unevenly) been taken up in other popular genres. Indeed, these connections to the beliefs from Romanticism that drive hegemonic models of creativity—that the individual is the origin of art, which arises from internal genius, disconnected from any exterior influence—make covers especially interesting for this book. In particular, the covering artist responds not to a song but to a certain *recording* of a song, and specifically a strong or canonical previous recording. Sociologist Deena Weinstein traces out a history of how the practice of covering has changed even over its relatively short life span:

> Covers in the 1950s often attempted to escape their status and be taken as self standing (perfect simulation where the simulation substitutes for the reference), whereas 1960s covers paid homage to their referents. Punk covers negated the originals without attempting to obliterate them; consequently, they keep the originals in play by constituting themselves over and against them.[5]

Importantly, this attempt to substitute as a perfect simulation in 1950s covers was often specifically a recording by a white artist taking the place of a source song by a Black artist for the "mainstream," white market. This tendency changed in the 1960s with the cover as a way to show influences, and in punk, covers elbow aside a source song but don't pretend it doesn't exist, but—as I'll discuss—the racialized power dynamics of whose music is available to whom continued. This chapter follows a similar trajectory to Weinstein's timeline, examining covers that seek to displace the source, those that seek to honor it, and those that seek to do something significantly new, but disrupts this periodization, showing how all these models continue to operate in the present and are essential ways that covers function. I also add a fourth category, covers as improper songs, that both retains some characteristics of older views of covers and opens new possibilities in the digital era.

Because cover songs are so mainstream, they are the most numerous of my musical texts. This chapter examines the 99 cover song or covers album objects in my data set. Because performing music written and recorded by others is such a common practice, I excluded Christmas songs (70 objects), tribute bands (69 objects), and the re-recording of standards (seven objects), which, while deeply related practices, raise distinct enough issues that their inclusion would have made the chapter unwieldy.[6] To analyze this large body of data, I examined code co-occurrence (how often two codes described the same quotation from the corpus) to look at the distribution of positive, negative, and ambivalent reception of covers by race and gender. Additionally, given the sheer volume of data for this category, I expanded my computational analysis beyond considering word frequency in the entire body of data or even just the sentiment categories, drilling down to interrogate the most common words in each subcorpus for all codes with more than 100 quotations (12 of 55 codes).[7]

In that a cover is a re-recording of a song from someone else, the nature of the relationship to the source song tends to be a key distinguishing feature to categorize them, and this is the organizing logic of this chapter. I begin with the history of covers being passed off in place of the source song as white artists covered Black artists' songs for white audiences. Then, I examine how covers are constructed as forms of nostalgia for the source rooted in respect and fidelity. Third, I consider the most frequent contemporary framing, which sees covers as creating a unique version of the source and is rooted in ideas about Romantic authorship as the expression of the self. Finally, I return to ideas of covers as free-riding on someone else's song to think about what's changed and what hasn't since the 1950s in instances when covers are used by those less famous than the source artist, particularly digitally. Ultimately, I argue, a good cover song according to contemporary standards is a new arrangement that is transformative rather than anything like faithful, but that such records nevertheless often perpetuate histories of racial extraction.

BEEN CAUGHT STEALING: WHITENING "RACE RECORDS" AND COVERS AS MARKET SUBSTITUTION

The first, and chronologically earliest, type of cover is that which seeks to displace and substitute for the source. This practice is as old as covers themselves. When covers became popular in the 1950s, they mostly "modified the original in order to reach a wider and whiter audience."[8] These songs both responded to and leveraged the sharp segregation in the music industry, in which "mainstream" records were understood as made by white artists for white audiences and Black artists were separated on Billboard charts, by record labels, and as audiences.[9] Black artists' records were segregated into the category "race music," which, beginning in the 1920s, "came to be used by the recording industry to describe music performed by African American musicians and marketed to an African American audience"; though in 1949 the name was changed to rhythm and blues or R&B, the divide long remained sharp and sharply racialized.[10] Covering Black artists' songs thus became a way to engage with the things that were different and exciting about this music without having to engage the people it came from. The practice of whitening race records thus sits at the nexus of "nearly insupportable fascination" with Black people's cultural practices and dismissive attitudes toward Black people themselves that historian Eric Lott's study of blackface minstrelsy characterizes as "cross-racial desire."[11]

As this discussion begins to suggest, 1950s covers were marked by one-way flow into white culture, particularly from the work of Black artists. While there was nothing preventing Black artists from covering songs recorded by white artists, "there was little or no market in that direction."[12] Moreover, these white recordings were covers in particular because they "copied many features that were not present in the original notated song but had been introduced by African American composers, arrangers, and recording artists while preparing to record and recording the song," producing what legal scholar Robert Brauneis calls "mirror covers" and I call *displacement covers*.[13] That is, these songs were responses to particular recordings—and, very specifically, responses to the Black artists' innovations in those recordings. What matters here is how covers take up the specific innovations of particular artists, not general cross-racial borrowing or the re-recording of a composition, which was common in the 1940s and '50s. Displacement covers then acted as market substitutes for the source songs. Many radio stations either wouldn't play songs by Black artists at all or stopped playing source songs once there was a cover from a famous artist, which often specifically meant that a Black artist's record was only played until a white artist covered it.[14] As anthropologist Maureen Mahon notes, "Covers excluded blacks from the most lucrative aspects of the growing rock'n'roll market and laid the groundwork for the redefinition of rock'n'roll as a white cultural production."[15] Even when the production of such covers wasn't intended to shut out Black artists, it was often calculated to benefit from radio's racism. A 2015 obituary for white rock and R&B singer Frankie Ford noted that in the late 1950s he was asked "to cover songs by local black musicians whose records got limited airtime because of racial discrimination. . . . 'All the music was coming from New Orleans, yet people like Pat Boone were covering people like Little Richard and Fats

Domino and getting hits. It was a black-white thing.'"[16] Having Ford make the recordings as opposed to an outsider is an expression of recuperative city pride, but still rests on, rather than contests, racism.

The most famous of these white artists who covered Black artists' songs is of course Elvis Presley, who has often been described as fulfilling record producer Sam Phillips's possibly apocryphal wish to "find a white man who had the Negro sound and the Negro feel."[17] Most of Presley's early hits were first recorded by Black artists, from "Hound Dog" (source: Big Mama Thornton, 1952; Presley 1956) to "I Got a Woman" (source: Ray Charles, 1954; Presley 1956) to "Shake, Rattle and Roll" (source: Big Joe Turner, 1954; Presley 1956). As Mahon notes, Presley is "a tidy example of the simultaneity of miscegenation and segregation," as he "solved the problem of black people in black music" by reproducing the sound as a white man.[18] Musicologist Joanna Demers notes that some see Elvis as "the most successful example of 'blackface,'" placing him in a long tradition of white appropriation of Black people's music and culture.[19] Mahon emphasizes that "Presley could mine blackness, but he could also fall back on his whiteness when the need arose."[20] The fact that Elvis gained fame by appropriating Black people's music makes it all the more ironic that these days his estate zealously protects his intellectual property from appropriation, from his songs to the right of publicity using his image.[21]

Importantly, while common sense might suggest that displacement covers that copied characteristics of Black artists' songs and directly substituted for them are theft of the distinctive contributions of those artists, the law did not agree. At a basic level, sound recordings would not be eligible for federal copyright protection until 1972. When Supreme Records tried to argue that it was unfair competition when Decca Records copied its 1948 arrangement of "A Little Bird Told Me," a federal judge ruled that Supreme had no property rights in its arrangement.[22] The *Supreme v. Decca* decision came to be understood as asserting that "there are no property rights in a general style of performance"; a 1957 report from the U.S. Copyright Office stated that "the rights of performers and record manufacturers to control the unauthorized exploitation of a specific record," which do exist, "must be distinguished from rights to control the imitation or simulation of a style or method of performance," which don't.[23]

That this outcome was heavily racialized can be seen from the disparate way the *Supreme v. Decca* decision talks about the white artists' recording compared to the one from the Black artists: the former "is rich, against a musically colorful background. It sounds full, meaty, polished. The difference derives from the different quality of the voices of the artists, the more precise, complex and better organized orchestral background, the fuller harmonization of the responses, the clearer intonation and expression, and the more musical entrances in the Decca record."[24] Classifying the white recording as more complex and better organized invokes racist notions of inferior Black intelligence. The judge also, in his reference to clear intonation and expression, gestures toward ideas of inferior Black speech. Thus, finding the white artists' record to be of higher quality is overdetermined and says much more about the judge's culturally ingrained prejudices than it does about the song. Moreover, in an instance of what legal scholar K. J. Greene describes as the work of "innovative black composers" being "imitated so widely that it became the 'idea' and thus impossible to protect,"[25] the decision defined the changes made to the composition by the Black recording artists as "musique a faire"—on analogy with scènes à faire from film, they were classified as standard musical components, not innovations.[26] In many ways, then, these displacement covers are exactly the kind of freeloading on someone else's creative labor that opponents of transformative works and proponents of stronger copyright protection like to critique—but they are both perfectly legal and sharply racialized.

DO YOU REMEMBER WHEN WE USED TO SING? COVERS AS FIDELITY AND NOSTALGIA

Despite the roots of covers in displacement, most contemporary covers do not cannibalize their sources. Contrasting with the displacement cover, one significant theme in popular discussion is the ways covers can instead exist in a relationship of respect to the source song—particularly, a relationship of nostalgia or fidelity. This group of covers tracks with scholarly notions that covers participate in an "aesthetic standard" that emphasizes "influence and evolution."[27] Thus, covers are often judged to be good in the popular conversation when they "nail it," are "faithful," or "channel" the source artist. It undoubtedly matters that there is an underlying legal encouragement of fidelity; under the mechanical license, "the arrangement shall not change the basic melody or fundamental character of the work."[28] Valuing fidelity is why, for example, popular discussions sometimes focus on whether a particular singer's voice is well suited to the song they are covering. One article says of *American Idol* contestant Adam Lambert covering "Mad World" (Tears for Fears, 1982) that "it's a perfect song for his voice."[29] Another criticized pop singer Katy Perry's cover of "Yesterday" (the Beatles, 1965) on CBS special "The Beatles: The Night That Changed America—A Grammy Salute," saying, "It's hard to believe that anyone thought she had the right voice to handle this all-time classic. Too bad you can't 'un-hear' a song."[30]

Fidelity also appears more expansively. One article characterizes country singer LeAnn Rimes's 2011 album of songs originally recorded by men as "a beautifully-realized tribute to these classic songs-most of them at least 30 years old-recorded in the same traditional spirit in which they were first released."[31] Here, words like "tribute," "same," and "traditional" signal that continuity is what's being valued, even in an album whose conceit is gender swapping. Philosopher Kurt Mosser notes that this kind of covering is particularly common in country music; an artist seeking to place themselves in the tradition "may provide a homage-like cover, of either an extremely well-known song (e.g. Emmylou Harris's cover of Cline's 'Crazy') or a relatively obscure song which suggests a vast knowledge of the tradition."[32]

This note of nostalgia in the tendency toward approval of faithful covers also extends to valorizing other positive relationships to the past. Nostalgia is particularly strong around Postmodern Jukebox, a project that covers contemporary songs in styles of yesteryear like ragtime, doo wop, and swing; in the group's music, according to the evocative prose of one venue's press release, "the 21st century party vibe of Miley Cyrus or the minimalist angst of Radiohead is incongruously married with the crackly warmth of a vintage 78 or the plunger-muted barrelhouse howl of a forgotten Kansas City jazzman."[33] The fact that the rich imagery is reserved for the long-ago music in the juxtaposition assigns it greater value. The sense of owing something to one's musical forebears combines with the idea that covers can make the past present to produce suggestions that covers can, as discussed in the introduction with *Glee*, bring the attention of a new generation to older music. For example, singer Haley Reinhart is noted to have "introduced younger fans to songs from a previous era. The video for her hit 2015 version of the 1961 Elvis Presley chestnut 'Can't Help Falling in Love' has amassed more than 100 million views online."[34]

There is, in particular, an idea that a cover song can signal where an artist has come from—their musical ancestors. This practice first arose in the 1960s as white British artists like the Beatles and Rolling Stones used covers of Black artists' music to try to signal their own authenticity. While homage was in many ways an improvement on erasing the music's origins in 1950s covers, it was both still a way of using Black people's music to support their own careers and rooted in what popular culture scholar Francesca Royster calls "hunger for blackness as the marker of the authentic, primitive, and 'real.'"[35] Even when there is material benefit for the covered artist, it tends to be uneven. When, in 1977, the Rolling Stones covered "Mannish Boy" (1955) by Black blues musician Muddy Waters, Waters benefited. He spoke positively of the Stones, and indeed his "later recordings of the tune, and his performances of it (largely for audiences of young white people), incorporated a few Jaggerisms of vocal inflection, as well as some rock instrumental influences."[36] However, it's nevertheless true that the Stones benefited much more. This musical borrowing was not on a level playing field between artists with equal status. Even though the cover was by all appearances in good faith, as "Jagger said that he idolized Muddy Waters and wanted to record great songs associated with him to draw attention to rock's debt to blues"—suggesting the Stones sought to achieve the common boosting effect of covers—ethnomusicologist Steven Feld points out the self-importance of thinking Muddy Waters needed the Stones to validate him.[37] Moreover, this kind of reverence was uneven with respect to the Stones' music; in *ABKCO v. LaVere* (2000), ABKCO Music, who held the rights to two Stones songs that were covers of another blues legend, Robert Johnson, claimed that Johnson's songs were in the public domain and thus the covers did not warrant royalty payments to his estate.[38] These patterns of white artists identifying Black musical ancestors with no feel for the racialized power dynamics of doing so continue down to the present. In a mild form, Matt Giraud, an *American Idol* contestant who consistently sang songs by Black artists, said Michael Jackson was a major influence on him,[39] enacting the fundamental sense that Black artists are freely available for his use. This isn't to say that there shouldn't be cross-racial musical influence—aside from its inevitability, it's not inherently a problem. Rather, my argument is that when someone in a dominant position is doing the borrowing, it has to be done with awareness of the history of appropriation and theft and alongside respect and remuneration, and too often it hasn't been.

On the other hand, the call to covers as faithful and nostalgic can give rise to critiques when these criteria aren't met. In this vein, there are complaints about covers that are not "believable" or don't "do justice" to the source. For their part, artists express concern for their ability to execute covers well, as with Karen Fairchild, of country group Little Big Town, noting that "It's hard to cover things that you love and respect so much because you sure don't want to mess them up."[40] There are also stronger objections, like one article complaining that the 40th anniversary edition of Rush's *2112* album (1976/2016) includes, "for reasons that pass understanding, covers from Foo Fighters' Dave Grohl and Taylor Hawkins, Alice in Chains and Steven Wilson," suggesting that these covers are inherently unjustifiable.[41] One theme in white artists' covers of songs by Black artists in particular is that they fail to measure up. One article reports of *Idol* finalist Danny Gokey that he "tried too hard to sell up-tempo tunes by Michael Jackson," implying that he did not succeed.[42] Another noted of Phil Collins's Motown album that his "blue-eye soul is OK, but he's no Martha Reeves (of Vandellas fame) when he sings 'Heatwave' and 'Jimmy Mack.'"[43] In such ways, white artists may be free to appropriate, but that doesn't automatically make the music any good. Such discussions demonstrate a sense—which also arises around parody—that when building from someone else's song it is beneficial to be rooted in a respectful relationship to it. However, it's also clear that the racial dynamics of displacement covers must continue to be reckoned with, even as they are often elided in this conversation.

A CHANGE WOULD DO YOU GOOD:
COVERS AS TRANSFORMED VERSIONS

My third grouping of musical texts represents the center of gravity in the contemporary conversation about cover songs: those that transform their sources. This is to use transformation in the cultural rather than legal sense. Cover songs' legality relies on the mechanical license to record a composition; the concept of transformative works—which was taken up into the law by the Supreme Court in *Campbell v. Acuff-Rose* (1994) as a test for the first factor of fair use, the "purpose and character of the use," and asks whether a work is "transformative, that is, adds something new, with a further purpose or different character, altering the first with new expression, meaning, or message"[44]—does not come into play. I'm using transformative here in a more colloquial way to describe a process of change, without reference to fair use. However, I'm also arguing that scholars should think harder about the kinship between the two kinds of transformation. That is, doing something new with a song is often what is culturally valued across the different types of music this book examines, irrespective of the legal questions involved in different genres and instances. Transformativeness turns out to be a key factor in the perceived quality of cover songs.

This emphasis on transformation comes in spite of the fact that under the mechanical license, "the arrangement shall not change the basic melody or fundamental character of the work."[45] Part of the way this disconnect is managed is that legal decisions have to some extent leaned toward an expansive definition of what constitutes maintaining a song's fundamentals. Demers argues that

> courts have traditionally interpreted this clause [about the "basic melody or fundamental character"] liberally to allow for substantial disparities between an original and its arrangements. This tolerance has enabled the production of cover versions. In R&B, soul, rock 'n' roll, and folk, cover recordings have been crucibles of experimentation such that many cover songs bear no more than a passing resemblance to their originals.[46]

In fact, Mosser argues that because the most successful covers are "major interpretations," such songs tend to "function as the paradigm of the cover song in general."[47] Magnus, Magnus, and Mag Uidhir take a stronger stance, arguing that what they call a *rendition cover*, a version with partial but not total reworking, works if and only if "it departs from the canonical version in artistically interesting or virtuous ways."[48] This valorization is rooted in the fact that "rock music conceived of musical creativity in fiercely individualist terms, as matters of personal transcendence,"[49] a value system that has largely been generalized. Thus, though Michael Awkward, a scholar of African American culture, is writing about "soul covers" in particular, his insight holds more generally: covers are often "vehicles through which artists explore how they are different than other singers and who, precisely, they want and believe themselves to be." Moreover, he notes, "the most engaging and imaginative of them do not strive merely to pay tribute to and replicate beloved performances," but rather vary, including through "combative reinvention."[50] This valuation is also reflected in popular discourse, which, from a vantage after the proliferation of rockist notions of Romantic musical authorship, tends to apply these norms even retrospectively to earlier music.

At the broadest level, the value attached to transformation can be seen in the fact that some of the most frequent words in positive discussions of cover songs are "new," "original," and "unique." There is a great deal of emphasis in the discourse around cover songs on their degree and kind of transformativeness. News sources discuss a cover's "interpretation," "version," or "rendition," indicating that there are changes and that they matter to evaluating the song. More strongly, artists are praised for "making songs their own," having a distinctive "take," giving a song a "twist" or "spin," or "putting a stamp" on their covers. Covers are also treated positively when they "reimagine," "reinvent," or even "transform" the source song. Beyond a general discussion of change, particular covers are praised as "distinctive," "unique," "daring," or "clever." For example, Macy Gray's 2012 album *Covered* is lauded because its "interpretations are fearless, subversive and brave in their execution."[51]

That a positive assessment of a cover is deeply bound up in its transformativeness can also be seen from the fact that, when there's not as much change, a song often garners a tepid reception. This pattern is seen with Seal's second collection of covers, *Soul 2*, on which, one article says, "most songs are pleasant, not exciting."[52] Alternately, some articles describe such covers as "a bit blah."[53] More strongly, one story says of Phil Collins's 2010 Motown covers record *Going Back*, "The truly odd thing is that Collins has gone out of his way to make such Holland-Dozier-Holland classics as (Love Is Like a) Heatwave and Standing in the Shadows of Love sound exactly like they did in the mid '60s. To which I ask again: What's the point here?"[54] That is, Collins produces more or less an exact copy, which some popular press sources see as not worth creating. On the other hand, change for change's sake isn't necessarily well received either. One story notes that "covers albums don't get any more idiosyncratic or high concept than 'Scratch My Back.' Mr. [Peter] Gabriel self-consciously set himself limits and conditions because, he said, he finds obstacles more helpful than complete freedom."[55] Gabriel here seems to be lauding himself as an artist, but potentially comes off as trying too hard to be unique, both invoking the call to transformation and potentially not quite succeeding at it.

One key way that covers can differ from the source song is when they are created by an artist whose gender or racial identity is different than that of the source artist. In fact, such changes correlate with positive reception. Overall, interracial covers are treated positively 74% of the time, more than intraracial ones at 71%. For gender, the difference is more dramatic, with covers where the artist's gender differs from the source rated as positive 81% of the time, while intragender covers are just 69% positive. Such covers are often described as surpassing the source. In one rich example, we're told that at the Kennedy Center Honors celebration of British rock band The Who, "Soul singer Bettye LaVette punched a hole right through Pete Townshend's 'Love, Reign O'er Me,' letting all the song's emotion pour out in a way its creators never conceived."[56] Not only did this Black woman's version surpass that white man rock singer, that is, but did something he didn't even think of. Similarly, in Aretha Franklin's "Respect" (1967), the gender swap is to some extent the point, as Otis Redding's 1965 "macho strut turns into a feminist cry for recognition in Franklin's classic rendition."[57] Indeed, the Franklin cover is the paradigmatic example for what Magnus, Magnus, and Mag Uidhir call *transformative covers*: "The case of Franklin's 'Respect' illustrates how cover is a history-relative and audience-relative notion. Her version quickly became the canonical version of the song. Although a derivative work, it is much richer than the original."[58]

However, the corollary to valuing difference is that difference is frequently treated as inherently good no matter what it is, and in particular articles frequently describe interracial covers positively with no feel for the racialized power dynamics, so that in the process they tend to reproduce them. Given how central white theft of Black people's music has been in cover songs, as well as the greater volume of data in this category, I focus on white covers of Black artists here to examine how race functions as a system of power in the corpus of press data about cover songs. One journalist, after asking Roberta Flack, "Scores of artists have covered your songs. Do you have a favorite?" immediately puts in a plug that "My pick is Johnny Cash doing First Time Ever I Saw Your Face. That gets me."[59] While this example certainly shows how covers that feature racialized transformation are some of the best received, singling out the white guy as the best over everyone else who has ever covered Flack's work has a flavor of overvaluing white men—further reinforced by not letting Flack answer the question before asserting his own irrelevant opinion.

This sort of cross-racial cover is often, if unevenly, received positively. There's lots of positivity around Black artists' music in the aggregate. Covers by Black artists are described positively 81% of the time, as opposed to 74% for white artists (with an overall average of 78%). Examining intraracial and interracial covers between Black and white artists, Black intraracial covers are positive 75% of the time, compared to 69% for white ones.

Black artists covering white songs are described in positive terms 82% of the time, matching the overall average, but white artists covering the songs of Black artists are still only positive 69% of the time. As source texts, however, there's less positivity. While covers from all sources are on average treated positively 82% of the time, covers from Black sources come in the least positive, at 72% (though covers from Black and white source songs are equally described in negative ways, 10.7% and 10.8%, respectively).[60] In key ways, these patterns reflect how American culture both desires to consume Blackness and devalues it.

Genre transformation, or what philosopher Michael Rings calls "*generic resetting*: the presenting of a song in a genre different from that of the original,"[61] shows both the power of these moves and their very real limitations. For example, one story says white band Framing Hanley's arena rock cover of Black artist Lil Wayne's hip-hop song "Lollipop" "blows Weezy out of the water"[62]—suggesting he has been greatly surpassed. Similarly, in saying that "a guitar-strumming [Phillip] Phillips" of *American Idol* made songs like Stevie Wonder's "Superstition" (1972) and Usher's "Nice and Slow" (1997) "distinctively his," the article lauds the extraction of soul and R&B into coded-as-white guitar-driven folk music.[63] Given that the folk music guy is a trope often used to signify a bland or boring cover, praising Phillips in this instance is unusual, but aligned with racialized power inequalities. This instance certainly gestures toward how genre tends to be a metonym for race, which is visible at scale, with words like "rock," "country," "guitar," and "band" among the top ten most prevalent for covers by white artists and "urban" and "soul" for those by Black artists, reflecting "categories of (white) rock and (black) soul/rhythm and blues that separated black people from rock, even as black sound remained integral to it."[64] Crossing generic boundaries violates this discursive bifurcation. As *Idol* contestant Giraud points out, he was enough of an outlier for the songs he chose to sing that he was frequently compared to another white man who did much the same: "I got that a lot just based on how I looked. I think if you're a white boy in soul, you're going to get the Justin [Timberlake] thing."[65] Thus, there is a tension between positive reception of cross-racial and cross-genre covers and the boundaries created by the racialization of genre.

However, at times the issue isn't just extraction, but positioning white covers as superior almost because of their whiteness—echoing *Supreme v. Decca* and the history of duplication covers more broadly. A review of Bette

Midler's 2014 album *It's the Girls!* says that "Ms. Midler's brash, mouthy vocal persona is still capable of sounding playfully transgressive, at least by '60s standards. She injects songs like the Marvelettes' 'Too Many Fish in the Sea' with a defiant air of girl power, which in those days was synonymous with winning and worshiping a sexy bad boy."[66] To identify the way Midler's cover transforms the Marvelettes with "girl power" implies that she is more empowered than her 1960s Black women counterparts because of her own individual choices rather than structures of privilege, tying empowerment to a kind of postfeminist individualism associated with white feminism. At times, such assessments that white covers are better travel into deeply stereotypical territory. White singer-songwriter Eliza Doolittle argues that "The biggest rule of doing a cover is to make it your own"; according to one article, Doolittle certainly does so in her take on Black rapper Kanye West's "Runaway": "When Kanye sings 'Let's have a toast to the scumbags and the a—holes,' it's rough and profane. In Doolittle's hands, the same lyrics float soulfully against a light funk rhythm. It's strangely sweet and totally unexpected."[67] Praising a shift from a "rough," "profane" rap song by a Black man to a "floating," "sweet" take by a white woman feels almost too on the nose. Similarly, the story apostrophizes: "Rihanna, nobody beats you when it comes to 'S&M,' but [Mandy] Moore reigns on 'Umbrella' when the girl-next-door's cover manages to be both sexy and wholesome."[68] By identifying Moore's take as balancing "sexy and wholesome," in a way it's implied Rihanna could never manage—being more suited to raunchier fare like "S&M"—the article invokes the trope that white women are pure and Black women are promiscuous.[69]

At times, white artists' covers directly involve suppressing source songs' engagements with race and racism. One article praises white country singer Johnny Cash's cover of Bob Marley's "Redemption Song," arguing that it "embraces both mortality and spirituality" and demonstrates "goose-bump raising power";[70] however, it heaps this praise without showing any awareness that, in that Cash is not a descendant of enslaved Africans, the lyrics "Old pirates, yes, they rob I / Sold I to the merchant ships / Minutes after they took I / From the bottomless pit" are more than a little jarring coming out of his mouth. However, that unfortunate choice is easily outpaced by white British pop singer Annie Lennox singing anti-lynching protest song "Strange Fruit," the canonical version of which was sung by Billie Holiday. It would be hard to do justice to the cover under ideal circumstances, but the difficulty was compounded by Lennox's insistence on flattening the song's subject into general "civil rights." As one article notes, "to discuss a song about lynching without mentioning lynching does a historical injustice to the piece of music, and allows her to profit from her cover of the song without grappling with its history."[71] This is not to say that a white person categorically should never have covered "Strange Fruit"—after all, it was written by white Jewish composer Abel Meeropol—but it certainly struck many as troubling that Lennox was so unprepared to engage its subject matter if she was going to choose to take it on. It is perhaps a mark of the general whiteness of journalism that the controversy around this cover, though it happened in the time frame this book examines, did not appear in the main body of data about Lennox's *Nostalgia* album; instead, remembering that I had seen objections to this cover when it was released, I had to go in search of a discussion of them.

In this way, it's clear that the specific versioning of a song matters, and having an identifiably different version is often viewed positively. It's a substantial part of how cover songs are assessed, and while there's some resistance to valuing versioning as an artistic contribution in popular music, it's common elsewhere: for example, classical music fans discuss how one recording of Bach or Beethoven is better than another, even though it's the same underlying work, because the performances and performers are understood to make them meaningfully different. However, valuing creativity as doing something new and different tends to override other concerns in cross-racial covers much as it does in prioritizing transformation over the legal requirement of fidelity—a new, fresh take on a song is automatically seen as good even when it has troubling racial implications like appropriation. At the same time, in another way, there's nothing novel about these covers repeating a very old pattern of white people being appreciative of Black art but fundamentally disinterested in the people and lived experiences it comes from. However, the fact that white covers of Black source songs are the least often described positively, just 69% of the time, suggests that at least some journalists have a feel for these troubling histories.

KNOCKOFFS, TRAINING WHEELS, AND BREAKING (INTO) THE INDUSTRY: COVERS AS IMPROPER MUSIC

The B side of the Romantic ideals of creativity that lead to valuing transformation is seeing covers either as not proper songs in their own right—whether inferior copies, cheap gimmicks, mere promotion for the source—or as a space of possibility, existing outside the structures of the music industry. First, in keeping with the Romantic author notion prizing creation without influence, there's frequently a sense that covers are an inherently lesser form of music. Though many artists play and record songs they didn't write, the cover is at times treated like artistic training wheels; of one *American Idol* finalist, an article commented that "covering artists seems about her upper limit."[72] Some stories actively push away the alleged inferiority of covers by asserting that certain recordings of previously released songs aren't really covers, as in insisting that one record is "not just a covers album."[73] Covers are sometimes seen as doomed to fail artistically, as when one article cautions, "Don't mess with perfection. That maxim applies with special force to covers of Beatles tunes. Does anyone really think they're going to make them better?"[74] One frequent swipe is to describe cover songs as karaoke. This construction is particularly common in discussions of *American Idol* given its roster of amateur performers; one article says of the American Idols Live! Tour that "Yes, it is karaoke, and considering the price, a rather expensive night of karaoke. But the show doesn't aspire to be great art, and delivers on its promise of great singing and the most family-friendly show this side of the Wiggles."[75] This is a notion of covers as perhaps enjoyable but certainly not artistically worthy.

Second, covers are often seen as a way to cash in, as gimmicky, or even as free-riding on someone else's work. One story has a lengthy complaint:

> We are rapidly reaching a point where we are becoming buried in covers. During the season for "American Idol" and "The Voice," they crank out a dozen copies of old songs every week (all downloadable on iTunes). Fox's "Glee" churns out albums' worth of re-recorded songs on a regular basis. Tribute albums honoring Buddy Holly and the Muppets are fresh on the market, and that doesn't even take into account the annual onslaught of Christmas discs.[76]

Here, in addition to showing the breadth of musical texts that might be seen as covers, there is a sense that these are industrial, assembly-line products "cranked out" and "churned out" in an "onslaught"—implying quantity is the only relevant factor and excluding discussion of artistic merit. This division between artistic and market value is sometimes overt, as when one headline asked, "Cover songs: Homage or irksome marketing ploy?"[77]

Third, covers are often understood as promotion for the source song.

Singer Michael Bublé was part of one such promotional strategy when his record company invited another group, Boyce Avenue, to cover one of his songs:

> Buble [sic] introduced their version in a video released in April that links back to his original. The exposure is worth any sales lost to Boyce Avenue's cover, according to Kayla Isenberg, Warner Bros.' senior director of interactive media, who reached out to Boyce Avenue on the partnership. "The trade-off is being able to use their avenue to open up Michael and his music to this YouTube generation," she says, pointing to their 3 million subscribers and their YouTube channel's 917 million views. "We're getting massive publicity."[78]

Here, though the cover may be market-substituted for the source song sometimes, the record company decided that putting the song in front of millions of subscribers would generate benefits that outweighed costs. This kind of tactic can have substantial returns. Alongside arranging for covers, artists and their record labels may tolerate those who make them without a license in the name of promoting their products. As media studies scholar Matthias Stork argues, *Glee* saw the many videos of fans covering its performances as "additional promotional paratexts, with creative fan-producers acting as brand advocates for the show, especially for the music covers."[79] This response is on one level counterintuitive, as these were covers of *Glee*'s own covers, and the law states that arrangements "shall not be subject to protection as a derivative work under this title, except with the express consent of the copyright owner."[80] However, the show negotiated such "express consent" and secured an adaptation copyright to protect their arrangements. This copyright is what a fan cover would have violated.

This move toward thinking of covers as perhaps not great art but producing market value also encompasses the ways they are—as the musical training wheels implication discussed earlier suggests—a well-known way to break into the music industry. One artist who initially gained popularity with covers said that "many of her current followers on YouTube stumbled upon her while searching for originals. 'It doesn't feel bad that they were looking for someone else, because they didn't even know I existed. . . . They're not going to search for Kina Grannis if they've never heard of you.'"[81] In this way, capturing a search intended to find the source text—which, unlike the history of displacement covers discussed above, doesn't result in market substitution per se, though it does affect advertising dollars and data collection on the source song's YouTube presence—can benefit an as-yet unknown artist. However, covers can also limit artists. As Demers points out, on one hand, record companies often refuse to pay for licensing for more than one or two cover songs per album; on the other hand, the performer on the source song receives no royalties from a cover, but rather they flow only to those holding publishing rights, who may or may not be the same people.[82]

Moreover, as Demers notes, because "most record labels negotiate lower quarterly mechanical licenses with publishers," songwriters make less when their works are covered compared to if someone sold a copy of their composition in another format.[83] That's assuming the best-case scenario. It gets worse for the covered artist when covers act as market substitutes for their song, which is both an echo of displacement covers and a new phenomenon of digital distribution.

> Digital music stores have made knock-offs profitable in a way that wouldn't be possible with physical stores. When iTunes launched in 2001, bands like The Beatles, AC/DC, Metallica and Kid Rock refused to sell their music online, so cover artists swooped in to profit from the digital demand. Titan Music cover band Led Zepagain was one of them. Standing in the place of originals in search results, sound-alike songs made hundreds of thousands [of] dollars when consumers bought their songs. That's not illegal, says Chris Mooney, senior director of artist promotions at indie song distributor TuneCore. "A cover song does not have to be an entirely original take on a version," he says.[84]

Rather than the earlier situation where white audiences largely *wouldn't* buy Black artists' music, but would buy the same thing from a white artist, in this case audiences *can't* buy what they want, but the knockoff is still cannibalizing sales of the source track. There was an initial market failure—goods people wanted to purchase weren't available in the market. In some cases, this market failure led to so-called piracy,[85] but in others third parties filled the void by producing covers that hewed closely to the source song. As one of the participants in this industry points out in the quotation above, such practices are within the law—while covers can't change the source text too much and make use of the compulsory mechanical license, nothing in the mechanical license says they can't make an exact copy, and in fact the logic of *Supreme v. Decca* authorizes being right on top of someone else's arrangement. What's new is that these direct market substitutes rely on the ability to digitally produce and easily distribute such recordings in the very same space where consumers were seeking the source songs. They also rely on consumer confusion, so that not only the source artist but also the song purchaser often feel cheated by these versions. In the 1950s version of this practice, people didn't tend to know they were being baited and switched in the same way. The market substitution cover is perfectly legal, but hardly uncontested.

However, digital distribution of covers also opens up possibilities—it may not be proper participation in the music industry, but the discourse around these musical texts suggests that may be a benefit. As the technological landscape has shifted, alternative distribution models have appeared, as internet distribution doesn't need help from a record label.[86] As Scott Bradlee, leader of Postmodern Jukebox, argues, "this is a very good time to be an independent musician. We don't need gatekeepers. We don't need a middle man. So I never had to worry about the gatekeepers. Technology is an amazing thing for a musician. We can reach so many people"[87]—because they can distribute directly to them. News coverage also emphasizes that new platforms also serve one of the other roles of record labels in cover songs: licensing. Streaming services have systems in place for songwriting royalties, and other services such as Limelight and TuneCore handle licensing and distribution for independent artists who record covers, for a fee.[88] Through new services such as these, cover songs become a more feasible route to success.

Artists also increasingly leverage covers to move in and out of the traditional record label system. The band Boyce Avenue left the standard model, and "'Oddly enough, within three months of leaving the [record] label . . . we saw our audiences and sales double and triple in size' for their YouTube and Myspace videos; band member Daniel Manzano argued that it was 'kind of comical, actually. We didn't need a big label.'"[89] Another artist parlayed "iPhone videos of himself singing covers of songs like 'Check Yes or No,' by George Strait, a video that's been viewed 11 million times" on Facebook, into "a No. 1 debut on [the] Billboard Top Country Albums chart in December. He had the best country debut in two years in a genre where fans still primarily discover new artists through the radio. He's had three songs in the top 5 of Billboard's Country Digital Songs Sales, but he's only had one song crack the Top 40 for country airplay."[90] In such ways, artists can build significant followings, and even generate traditional success like record sales, using digital platforms.

While there are mentions of a variety of platforms in the data—music-specific ones like iTunes and Spotify and those that have broader uses, like MySpace, Facebook, and Vine—YouTube was the most important in this space during the period this book examines.[91] As one article explains, "YouTube provides musicians with a new tool to reach audiences, which has resulted in the rise of a unique community full of niche projects."[92] One term that is frequently used in these conversations is "viral," appearing in 31% of the mentions of technology. As communication scholar Limor Shifman defines it, something is viral when it is "a single cultural unit (formulated in words, image, or video) that is spread by multiple agents and is viewed by many millions."[93] This kind of rapid spread can greatly impact an artist's career, and many aspire to it. Shifman points out that "virality itself is considered to be highly persuasive: raw 'view-count' numbers inform viewers that many others have found a particular piece of content interesting."[94] That is, this is a "rich get richer" model where the popularity of a piece of content is its endorsement.

Emphasis on virality is consistent with the ways discussions of cover artists often use YouTube metrics for success rather than traditional music industry ones. Articles contend that Postmodern Jukebox are "an Internet phenomenon, scoring more than 912 million YouTube views and 3.2 million subscribers,"[95] that "their torch-song rendition of Radiohead's 'Creep' has racked up over 28 million views on YouTube, and still counting,"[96] and that their cover of Macklemore & Ryan Lewis's "Thrift Shop" "garnered more than a million views within a week of being posted."[97] These are common measurements on YouTube—aggregate channel views and subscriptions, individual video views, and speed of accumulating views—but they're quite different from the usual music industry currencies of Billboard charts or gold and platinum records.

The attention that YouTube's billion monthly users can bring is part of why it can be a vital resource for cover artists.[98] A cappella group Pentatonix, one article notes, "won NBC's 'The Sing-Off' in 2011, but it was their YouTube covers of Daft Punk, Imagine Dragons and Beyonce that saved their recording careers,"[99] letting them build enough of a following to release thirteen recordings (full-length albums and EPs) in the period this book covers. Indeed, riffing on what Carnegie Hall calls the most "well-known joke" about a destination "other than Denial—that famous river in Egypt,"[100] one article asks, "How do you get to Carnegie Hall? Practice. How do you get to the Kennedy Center? YouTube. John

Legend emcees a concert by performers who made it big thanks to the viral power of Internet video."[101] Thus, new technologies of music production and distribution have reshaped the social position and viability of cover songs as transformative musical works. The sense of covers as not proper music—as training wheels, cheap knockoffs, or mere promotion—is also joined with a sense of them as a space of musical possibility of the sort that's often seen with transformative works as a category. Here again, letting the porousness of transformation as a concept happen helps us see both what is occurring with covers and how they articulate with transformative musical works more broadly.

WITH A LITTLE HELP FROM MY FRIENDS: RACE AND GENRE TRANSFORMATION AS COVER MICROCOSM

Ultimately, transformation tends to be the deciding factor in lauding cover songs. This pattern is consistent with Romantic author ideology and its valuation of individual genius and refusal of external influence. As Solis argues, successful covers assert the authorship of the covering artist, producing "not simply a new performance of the old work, but rather a new work based on the old one—while at the same time he or she draws some measure of the original author's creativity to him or herself."[102] However, this valuation diverges from copyright law, which, as legal studies scholar Anne Barron notes, draws a sharp distinction between composition, which is seen as creative, and performance, which is not.[103] The fact that the creativity of performance is suppressed by default in legal frameworks seems to make it all the more important to insist on it in order to secure the artistic value of a cover. As new digital distribution and licensing platforms make cover songs an increasingly viable way to make music, the drive to uniqueness that's rooted in American cultural beliefs about artistry has ever more impact. Nevertheless, there is also a distinct thread of wanting to do right by those who came before, which is bound up in both ideas of musical ancestors and the legal requirement that a cover song not be significantly changed in order to benefit from the compulsory license. This is a fundamental tension.

However, transformation as a value in itself, decontextualized from questions of who covers whom, raises questions of racial equity as Black artists' music continues to be plundered by white artists—and these are some of the most praised covers of all time. In an obituary for Joe Cocker, he is lauded for his 1969 "dazzling transformation of the Beatles' 'With a Little Help from My Friends'" (1967), particularly its "gospel-styled arrangement and furious call and response between Cocker and the backup singers."[104] In particular, the distinctively transcendent component of this cover is very specifically what Mahon talks about as a frequent pattern in the 1960s and 1970s in which "the audibly black voices of African American women background vocalists provided sonic authenticity and enabled white artists to maintain a connection to the black roots of rock and roll."[105] This instance crystallizes what produces a good cover song according to contemporary standards—a new arrangement that is transformative rather than anything like faithful, that nevertheless, in its use of musical tropes from gospel, perpetuates histories of racial extraction.

CHAPTER 2

Stir It Up

Remix and the Problem of Genre

Remixing and mashing up songs is nothing new, but country is the latest genre to discover that behind a thumping techno beat sits a lucrative opportunity to breathe a second life into songs by turning them into dance tunes.[1]

As the epigraph for this chapter suggests, remix isn't new—while the above comment refers to the decades-long tradition of the dance remix, the fundamental idea that a piece of culture can (legitimately) be rearranged is older still. Even narrowing the scope specifically to popular music, musicologist Joanna Demers points to the collage-based work of Dickie Goodman in the 1950s as prefiguring what is now thought of as remix.[2] Jamaican music is also an important antecedent for remix as we know it; as Peter Manuel and Wayne Marshall note, "Jamaican DJs were voicing over records and using turntables as musical instruments at least a decade before their counterparts in the Bronx," which they identify as "an important precursor to and a direct influence on the vogue of remixes and 'mash-ups,'" as the practice of reusing riddims in Jamaican music relies on "the pleasure of hearing how different DJs will perform over the same raw material."[3] As media studies scholar Larisa Kingston Mann points out, "Jamaicans have raised the practice of adaptation and reuse to a sophisticated practice, deeply embedded in Jamaican musical tradition and owing very little to copyright conceptions of ownership and permission."[4] Demers argues that "by the 1980s, it was fashionable to remix Top 40 or rock tunes into dance versions by highlighting their rhythm breaks or adding extended instrumental sections."[5] I follow musicologist Sheena Hyndman in defining a remix more specifically as "a song created using a combination of newly composed musical material and previously existing recorded sounds,"[6] thus differentiating it from not only collage as rooted in existing sounds, but mash-up for the same reason; while, like covers, remixes respond to and rework a specific existing recording, the distinction here is that covers do not use the track itself as the raw material for subsequent creation, but remixes do. Thus, remix occupies a distinct position in terms of production—and also, as I'll show, in reception.

In this chapter, by analyzing the 33 instances of remix in the corpus, I examine how such songs are culturally legitimated or contested. I begin by working through how remix is defined in popular discourse, finding that the question of genre permeates the discussion, both in the sense that genre change is one of the key ways remixes are transformative, and because there are two major genres within remix in the period this book examines that exist in relatively distinct cultural spaces. Next, I examine how and when remix is framed positively. Remixes are often seen as adding value to base songs, whether through enabling industry recognition, making them valuable to more people by expanding the audience, or flatly increasing monetary value by boosting sales. As this focus on business success suggests, positive discussions of remix rarely laud their creativity and artistry. Instead, these questions show up in the negative, with remixes the site of legal resistance, lost artistic control, and racial extraction. I end the chapter with a consideration of "Old Town Road" (Lil Nas X, 2018), a song whose proliferating remixes demonstrate that remix trouble has much to do with refusing the normative straight lines of musical desire.

GENRE TROUBLE:
REMIX AS GENRE MIXING AND THE GENRES OF REMIX

In keeping with the fact that remixes are transformative musical works (and aligned with the broader cultural valuation—rooted in the Romantic author view of art arising from internal genius, disconnected from any exterior influence—of distance from other artists as a sign of creativity), much of the emphasis in discussions of remixes is on how they differ from the base tracks. One key shift of this type, as with covers in chapter 1, is changing the song's genre. The centrality of genre to remix is one reason genres are among the most frequent words in the data set, with "country" at #1, "dance" at #3, and "pop" at #4.

As the frequency data suggests, dance music is a key center of gravity in remix. A further discussion of remix in the context of country music from the article that provided the epigraph for this chapter shows key features of what a remix is understood to be: "producers say that blending elements together for a remix presents a different challenge. It's about adding more accelerated dance beats, drums, maybe keyboard and electronic sounds— every process is different, and sometimes it's critical to keep the original guitar track and melody to maintain the country root of the song."[7] Given that country music is traditionally associated with acoustic instruments like guitar, banjo, and fiddle, that is, the addition of "accelerated dance beats" and "electronic sounds"—often framed as the fundamental characteristics of remix—risks de-countrifying remixes and must be handled with care.

If country seems inhospitable to remix compared to pop and R&B, it's certainly not the greatest distance a song can travel to arrive at being a dance track. Seemingly anything can be dance-ified. Thus, stories discuss things like "a dance remix of the torch song" "Where the Boys Are" (Connie Francis, 1961).[8] Similarly, "The Twilight Sad tends to live up to its name, but when [punk-electronica band] Liars get their art-rocking hands on this track off The Twilight Sad's latest record, they turn the dark, funeral hymn-like song into an equally dark dance track."[9] An emphasis on such electronic additions is common in discussions of remix, for better or worse. As one article colorfully describes:

> If you listened to the radio or went to clubs in the '90s, there's a solid chance that the word remix pushes a button in your brain, cueing that familiar sound, REEEMIIIIIIIIIIIX! It's the call to shittiness. You just know an otherwise good song is about to be defiled by a bad dance beat and random record scratches. The crappy remix is painful, but it's worse when you know that remixing has awesome potential.[10]

If the quotation above about giving songs a second life suggests remixes make a song more attractive to audiences, that is, this effect is highly dependent on the execution. This category of songs then produces things like "remixer" as a job title and specific artists being known or even sought out for their remixes.

However, there is another major type of remix that adds a new artist, which I call the *featuring remix* because the usual demarcation is either "Artist 1 featuring Artist 2" or "Song Title Remix featuring Artist 2." The essential role of the term "featuring" in this type of remix becomes clear from the fact that rapper Lil Wayne "has joked that he's done so many guest spots that he's going to change his name to 'Featuring Lil Wayne.'"[11] Importantly, the featuring remix tends to also break through the genre divide—the term "crossover" is frequently mentioned in these discussions. The period this book examines included two major groups of crossover, featuring remixes. First, there were several prominent remixes of country music that added hip-hop artists, which combined with an upsurge in country dance mixes in this period to make "country" the most frequent word in the data set. One article notes that "Two of the past couple of years' biggest country hits have been full-out country-rap crossovers," pointing to "Dirt Road Anthem" (Jason Aldean featuring Ludacris, 2011) and "Cruise" (Florida Georgia Line featuring Nelly, 2013); both songs are described as "hip-hop remixes, with the original recording melded with raps and new beats," offering a definition of the genre.[12]

The other big cultural moment in remix between 2009 and 2018 was the remix of the 2017 Luis Fonsi and Daddy Yankee hit "Despacito" featuring Justin Bieber—and the follow-on Anglo/Latine crossovers it inspired. As one article explained, while the song was a big hit in the "Latin" music market, "there was a crowd the song hadn't quite won over . . . , and that was mainstream American pop fans. [Songwriter Erika] Ender said she, Fonsi and Daddy Yankee wrote an English translation of 'Despacito' in the hopes of getting an American singer to take part in a remix" in order to reach that other audience.[13] The tactic of incorporating an Anglo artist (albeit Canadian Justin Bieber) worked spectacularly, and the song tied the record for most weeks at #1 on the Hot 100 (16) that had been held by Mariah Carey and Boyz II Men's 1995 collaboration "One Sweet Day" for more than 20 years.[14]

There is in fact a fundamental bifurcation in the category "remix" between dance remixes and featuring remixes. This split is visible in the aggregate data, with "dance" the third most common word—after removing those too general (e.g., "song") and too specific (e.g., "Rihanna") to be useful for analysis; "featuring" is the sixth most frequent. This word frequency reverses the relative prevalence of the two kinds of remix: of instances with an identifiable base artist and either remixer or featured artist, 24%–30% are dance remixes and 70%–76% are "featuring" remixes.[15] Genre thus permeates discussions of remix, both in the sense that genre change is one of the key ways remixes are transformative and because there are two major genres within remix in the period this book examines that exist in relatively distinct cultural spaces. This vacillation between genre crossing at some times and sharp genre distinction at others represents a fundamental tension in remix, and the unevenness of when crossing is or isn't well received is essential to the social legitimacy of remixes.

MIX IT BABY ONE MORE TIME:
REMIX AS INCREASING RECOGNITION, AUDIENCE, AND SALES

As the huge success of Florida Georgia Line's "Cruise" with Nelly and Luis Fonsi and Daddy Yankee's "Despacito" with Justin Bieber begins to suggest, remix can expand a song's recognition, audience, and sales, and those remixes that do are generally the ones that are received positively. First, remixes are understood to garner or increase formal industry recognition for songs. Both "Cruise"[16] and "Despacito" were described as the "song of the summer" in their respective years; the latter song even gained an MTV Video Music Award nomination in that category.[17] Remixes can also expand options for recognition, as with one article assessing Sam Smith's Grammy chances in 2014: "A remix for 'Stay With Me,' featuring Grammy favorite Mary J. Blige, could compete in some R&B categories, while the remix of 'I'm Not the Only One' with A$AP Rocky could be a contender for best rap/sung collaboration."[18] Taking Smith's pop stylings and remixing them with the cooperation of artists from other genres expands their reach in terms of award eligibility because it moves those remixes into new genres.

That remixes expand the audience is something approaching conventional wisdom for industry workers. As Hyndman notes, many remixes are commissioned from professional producers by copyright holders to promote the source song.[19] At times, this idea is engaged just generally in the press coverage, as when a record executive noted that "the new track can expand the fan base."[20] By growing the audience, a remix can make a song a bigger hit. There is some dispute over the role the Bieber remix played in the success of "Despacito." On one hand, the song was #1 on the Billboard Latin chart for 27 weeks, so that "while some believe Justin Bieber helped make the song a hit when he jumped on its remix, it's quite the opposite. 'Technically, the reason why Justin Bieber discovered the song was because it was so popular already,' said Rocio Guerra, Spotify's head of Latin culture"; on the other hand, Bieber's involvement made a big difference on the mainstream Hot 100 chart, as the song went from the Top 40 to #1 after the Bieber remix and stayed there for four months.[21] This success suggests that Bieber's involvement widened interest in the song, but also points to the way music from Latine artists, however popular, has difficulty being seen as mainstream.

The idea that remixes can make songs more appealing is often applied when the base track is less popular. Sometimes this is a general discussion of remix enhancing a song's popularity, as when gospel duo Mary Mary "enlisted hit singer-songwriter Ne-Yo for a remix" of one of their tracks in order "to boost the song."[22] At other times, the boosting is explicitly about sales. For example, one industry insider felt that the songs on Kanye West's 2013 album *Yeezus*, in their default state, did not have broad enough appeal:

> [Faith] Newman, who is the senior vice president of creative and business development at music publisher Reservoir Media Management, believes "Yeezus" might not hit platinum status unless it gets a musical face-lift. "I wouldn't be surprised at all if he goes on and remixes one of those songs on his album . . . and comes up with the most amazing single and drops a bomb on people."[23]

Newman argued a remix would be necessary to extract a single from an album often described as experimental and minimalist—and in fact she was right that *Yeezus* was well short of the one million sales mark for a platinum record. At other times, the framing is about charts, as when in 2010, Peggy Lee, best known for hits from the 1940s and 1950s, saw a renaissance in popularity; among other reissues of her music, press sources note that a remix of her 1943 song "Why Don't You Do Right?" charted in several European countries, nearly 70 years after its release and eight years after Lee's death[24] or an article comments that "Jason Aldean's 'Dirt Road Anthem' got a second act on the charts with an appearance from Ludacris."[25] In such ways, remixes can, as I showed in chapter 1 with covers, give songs and artists a second life.

The academic literature on remix treats it almost exclusively as a metaphor or cultural logic—finding musical uses of the term was unexpectedly difficult. By contrast, unlike with mash up, there are not many instances in the press data of remix as a metaphor or cultural logic. Instead, the things labeled "remix" are, almost without exception, songs. However, there is a body of remixes that isn't in the orbit of the mainline music industry and can broadly be called parody or commentary remixes—but the logic of remix making a base track more interesting holds true here as well. One of the earliest examples of this type in my data is a remix of leaked audio of an on-set tirade from actor Christian Bale; "Music producer Lucian Piane who goes by the name RevoLucian online remixed the verbal freak-out into a three-minute-long hypnotic dance track titled 'Bale Out.'"[26] These sorts of responses to popular culture audio moments are relatively common, as when "amateur humorists created the Tiger Woods Voicemail Slow Jam Remix 'Name Off Your Phone,'" referencing "a request he reportedly made to one of his gal-friends" to try to avoid being caught in marital infidelity.[27] Such remixes can usefully be understood as memes. Communication scholar Limor Shifman defines memes as "(a) a group of digital items sharing common characteristics of content, form, and/or stance; (b) that were created with awareness of each other; and (c) were circulated, imitated and/or transformed via the internet by many users."[28] The above examples were each just one of a number of memetic uses of Bale and Woods in response to their respective events.

Sometimes, such remixes tend toward the overtly political. Contemporary with the Tiger Woods remix in 2010, "Remixes emerged of an upset Bill O'Reilly and of Andrew 'Don't Taze Me, Bro' Meyer," known for a viral video in which he was shot with a taser after confronting then presidential candidate John Kerry.[29] At other times, they're fully political. In 2015, "One of the most unlikely stars of Israel's election campaign is a musical artist whose popular video remixes of stump speeches have rocked YouTube, leading some of his most prominent targets to try to recruit him."[30] Usually, such remixes are acts of everyday people skewering the famous or powerful, but they have the same structure of raising interest and increasing the audience as the traditional musical kind.

In much the same way, as the above discussion of "Despacito" begins to suggest, a remix, especially for a base track in a marginalized genre, makes it more possible to expand from success on a narrower chart to succeed on the mainstream Hot 100. Of "Cruise," Florida Georgia Line member Brian Kelley said, "it's a country song, and to be played on pop radio is just not gonna happen."[31] Indeed, while "Cruise" went to #1 on the country charts, it reached only #16 on the Hot 100 until the remix with Nelly took it to #4. The success of a remix can also feed back into and shape a less mainstream base genre. This pattern is particularly visible with the fact that post-remix, "Cruise" had a record run at #1 on the country singles chart, taking hip-hop/country back to country proper.[32] While the main emphasis in the discourse of crossover remix is on the mainstreaming benefits of remix, genre change does flow both ways.

These ideas of remix as reworking a song and increasing its commercial value combine in the practice of offering remixes as a supplemental product worth paying extra for. Putting remixes on albums as bonus features—especially for re-releases that, generally, the record company needs to convince people to buy another time—is a routine practice. Michael Jackson reissue "Thriller 25" had "five remixes featuring Fergie, will.i.am, Kanye West and Akon."[33] However, there are also new versions of the remix as a sales tactic for the digital music era, such as "an iTunes Pass, which gave music fans willing to pay $18.99 access to early release singles, a new album upon its release and exclusive videos, remixes and other content."[34] The commercial value of remix, that is, is taken as a given.

As a result of this commercial value, practices of commissioning remixes have become routine in the music industry. As the record label executives that Hyndman interviewed indicated:

> the primary purpose of the remix within their business model is to promote the new releases of artists signed to their label. In promotion of these new releases, remixes are treated as disposable and interchangeable commodities that are given away for free in the sometimes vain hope that a listener who hears the remix first will be as, or more, interested in the original version that sounds markedly different.[35]

The executives' attitude highlights two things: remix is often intended to expand interest and audience, but the artists who create them are often devalued. There are some exceptions to this devaluation; of house music legend Frankie Knuckles, an article says that, though he was a veteran of the underground club scene, "In time, his style also became commercial, at least compared with other forms of '90s dance music. Mariah Carey, Bjork, U2, Luther Vandross, Lisa Stansfield, Vanessa Williams, Whitney Houston, Madonna and Annie Lennox, not to mention Michael and Janet Jackson, all commissioned remixes from the boys at Def Mix," his production company, which became "the Motown of house music."[36] That is, Frankie Knuckles and Def Mix were sought out as adding value with remixes not in general but as a particular, valuable brand. Such work is often in high demand. One DJ said that he has more requests for remixes than he can fulfill: "I kind of say, 'I will ASAP,' . . . but when exactly is that going to happen? That's the kind of spot we're in right now."[37] For this artist, there's enough demand for him as a remixer that there's a waiting list.

Others cultivate remixes without directly commissioning, such as the practice of releasing a cappella versions of hip-hop albums "to encourage remixing in clubs."[38] Remixes are now so routinized within the music industry that they have their own Grammy category: Best Remixed Recording, Non-Classical. Even unexpected, unsolicited remixes produced outside normal record industry practices can be embraced. For example, DJ Tiesto remixed "All of Me" (John Legend, 2013) as just something fun to do, and it was distributed for free as a download rather than intended to be a formal release, but "Tiesto said Legend enjoyed the remix so much that [they] made it official," and the song ended up winning a Grammy award.[39]

As the epigraph to this chapter suggests, these remixes are often—and ideally—"lucrative." As one executive flatly said, "You just doubled your profit by doing a remix."[40] Importantly, this is profit for those with financial claims on the base track but not necessarily the remixer. As Hyndman's research shows, remixers work under a variety of compensation models: work-for-hire; lump-sum payment; speculative ("spec"), "in which producers commissioned by record labels are only paid for their remix work if the record label likes the song enough to release it—many songs commissioned on spec never see the light of day—and only if the song is commercially popular"; publishing and licensing agreements, in which remixers are given partial songwriting credit and corresponding royalties and which are less common; as well as through indirect payment like live gigs.[41] The way remixers themselves often get short shrift provides an interesting contrast to the ways remixes are viewed positively as bringing success and interest to the base songs, and the distinction shows tensions between financial and artistic success. In such ways, remixes are often seen as adding value to base songs, whether through making them valuable to more people by expanding the audience, enabling industry recognition like awards, or flatly increasing monetary value by boosting sales, but importantly, all of these sources of positive reception are about commercial value and none of them are about artistic value.

DON'T COME AROUND HERE NO MORE:
LEGAL TROUBLE AND REMIX AS UNDERMINING VALUE

On the other hand, artistic value is at best an open question in remix and at worst undermined or appropriated, and the times when remixes are viewed negatively turn on this issue. First, if remixes are a way to increase sales, they can also, like covers, be seen as cheap, lazy ways to cash in. If "Dirt Road Anthem" and "Cruise" were successful remixes, with the "Cruise" remix setting a record for weeks at #1 on the country singles chart, there was also a bandwagon effect in response to this success, producing many other country tracks with added rappers that weren't deemed as good. As one article complains of "Achy Breaky 2," a 2014 remix of an early-90s country hit from Billy Ray Cyrus, "A song that became old enough to drink last year, though it always seemed pretty tipsy, 1992[']s line-dance-fever hit 'Achy Breaky Heart' has never sounded so amiable and nonirritating as it does when returning to it after suffering through the new version's shoveled-on, dubstepford-wife sound effects and its squirm-inducing shoutouts to Cyrus' daughter."[42] This description constructs remix as gimmicky, with excessive, "shoveled-on" sound effects that are mindless and identical like Stepford wives—and this remix also happens to include unfortunate references to Miley Cyrus twerking in a song from her father. Of another bandwagon hip-hop/country song from 2014, one story says that "everyone hopes the song captures the same pop party vibe that made FGL's 'Cruise' remix with Nelly a crossover hit."[43] "Despacito," too, produced a rush to capture the same success: one article commented that "in the wake of the success of Luis Fonsi's 'Despacito' remix with Justin Bieber, forced marriages are abounding."[44] Here, as with the country crossover trend, the execution of a genre-blending remix matters, with "forced" rather than apparently organic mixes less well received.

Moreover, though remixes are usually seen as adding value, that doesn't mean base track artists always welcome them. This contestation is most visible when there are legal disputes. There's a fundamental, and as yet legally unsettled, "question of what musical elements should be subject to property rights and what expression should be free for the taking (and remixing)."[45] Certainly, unlike the safety of the compulsory license for cover songs or the widely accepted fair use category of parody, remix either relies on negotiated license agreements or may have to formally litigate fair use to be legal. Questions around legality and permissions sometimes impact remix production, with one DJ noting that he had ultimately decided to remix only his own previous work on a new album, because while "I actually had a wish list that was nearing 100 songs that I wanted to mix," he was dissuaded because "with artists who are well-known, such as Seal, Justin Timberlake, there is a lot of politics that have to be waded through in order for me to get permission to remix."[46]

This tension around permission is a repeated theme. As one article notes, "Musicians are releasing entire remix albums now, inviting producers and DJs to take a crack at their songs, and of course, some producers just do it without an invite"[47]—the "invite" often looms large. One key word in these conversations about negative responses to remixes is "authorized." There were several lawsuits over remixes in the period this book examines that turned on the question of authorization. One centered on whether an Elvis Christmas remix album, made by someone Elvis Presley Enterprises had previously contracted to make other Elvis remix albums, was authorized.[48] In another incident, the lead singer of a band sued and fired his bandmates over a remix they authorized but he didn't.[49] In such ways, remixes can be stopped or never started due to legal issues.

Ideas of remix as harmful to the original song's artistic integrity may help explain such resistance—gaining financial value may matter less if it corresponds with a loss of aesthetic value. Certainly, in some instances it's easy to understand why an artist might not grant permission to remix: British eponymous band "Sade declined to release a house remix of [1993 song] 'Pearls,' perhaps because there was something a little unseemly about people dancing to a song about the Somalian civil war. Then, a bootleg of it began making the rounds to D.J.s such as Junior Vasquez and Frankie Knuckles, who turned it into one of the era's defining club tracks."[50] Similarly, one article described gospel legend Shirley Caesar as having "viral success with a remix of one of her sermon-songs" from 1988, saying that she became "a hot topic online after her song, the 9-minute 'Hold My Mule,' was re-created with a new addictive beat"[51] in 2016, but the remix was unauthorized. In fact, "Caesar said she was distressed to see people twerking and drinking" in the video remix; legal scholar Toni Lester argues that the remix violated Caesar's moral rights through damaging her image as a pastor.[52] After filing for an injunction to stop DJ Suede from selling the remix on iTunes, Caesar "endorsed a more wholesome remix" by Snoop Dogg, which was "released at Christmas to raise funds for the charities she endorses."[53] While United States law doesn't really have moral rights, or "the right of an author to have a say in how a work is used even after the economic rights to it have been transferred," such incidents make a good case for why they are sometimes a good idea.[54]

Importantly, while there are many more "featuring" remixes, when remix is discussed in general terms, press discourse defaults to dance music. This assumption can be seen in discussions equating remix with dance in the context of the Grammy awards: "EDM [Electronic Dance Music] has finally come of age in the eyes of the people who hand out the Grammys. There are now three categories for dance music, including best non-classical remixed recording."[55] A "non-classical remixed recording" could be almost anything, but it's reduced here to dance music. Because of this prioritization of dance, one of the frequent words in discussions of remix is "club," as in calling one song "club-ready"[56] or assessing another's "club appeal."[57] The slippage can also be seen in the way that, when remixes are not for such purposes, it is noteworthy. Of one artist who "records subdued, idiosyncratic electronic music that eludes easy description," a story says that "unlike most popular remixes, his are not designed to add danceability and bombast, but arranged to coax out emotional qualities that were submerged in the original recording."[58] In such ways, the primary emphasis in discussion of remix is on dance music, despite this being the less numerically prevalent sort.

The disregard of the "featuring" remix, I argue, has much to do with it being a Black-coded genre—rapping is an art form rooted in Black people's culture, and therefore unsurprisingly "featuring" remixes are much more likely to include Black artists (46.5%) than dance remixes are (28.3%). Responses to "featuring" remixes are thus often bound up in larger negative attitudes toward Black people, and, when there's a Black artist featured on a white artist's base track, perhaps even miscegenation. When will.i.am remixed "My Generation" (1965), the Who singer Pete Townshend "said he was impressed with the remix: 'It's actually very elegant, it's not gangsta,' he said of will.i.am's rap on the song."[59] As a member of Black Eyed Peas, a dance-pop and hip-hop group, will.i.am is not at all associated with gangsta rap, but collapsing any and all hip-hop into gangsta rap is a common trope that I'll also discuss in chapter 3 with mash-up. In such ways, it seems clear that "featuring" remixes are marginalized at least in part because the people featured in them are marginalized.

The racial politics of remix are at times bizarre. For example, white rapper Asher Roth released "'A Millie Remix,' a freestyle rhyme over Lil Wayne's 'A Milli' beat, criticizing rappers who boast about having millions of dollars but 'don't share, don't donate to charity.'"[60] The profound entitlement underlying Roth's belief that he was uniquely qualified to scold Black people over a cultural practice in which artists "flaunt their rise from among the ranks of the downtrodden by making public displays of their newly begotten wealth" is bad enough.[61] This entitlement is compounded by Roth's further criticism of "black rappers[,] African rappers talking about how much money they have. 'Do you realize what's going on in Africa right now?'"—a startling criticism that, in addition to flattening all Black people into "Africans," is rooted in an assumption that Black Americans somehow have a responsibility to solve the problems of the African continent that were caused by European colonization.[62]

A similar slippage between appreciating a racialized community's (economic) value as collaborators and appropriating their struggle shows up around Latine people with "Despacito." Jesus Lopez, chairman of Universal Music Latin Entertainment, said that, after the success of "Despacito," "All the Anglo artists are knocking on our door to make remixes and collaborations."[63] Such collaborations were also a political move. As one of the songwriters pointed out, the context for the song's success mattered: against the background of Donald Trump's presidency and its dehumanizing anti-Latine rhetoric, "With everything that's happening in the U.S. and the things said against Latinos, we're all singing and dancing in Spanish."[64] However, here again white folks attempt to make political points on the backs of people of color: "Bieber's manager, Scooter Braun, says his principal motivation in putting the remix together was the idea of topping the Hot 100 while Trump was in office. 'A song in Spanish is all over pop radio,' Braun said, 'in an America where young Latino Americans should feel proud of themselves and their families' native tongue.'"[65] While this resistance to the racism of the Trump administration is admirable, the idea that this white guy and his client (even if that client is Justin Bieber—the only person who got a perfect score of 100 on now-defunct social media influence monitor Klout) were inherently the most qualified to take this project on, and that it was their idea—despite what the song's writer said about seeking an Anglo artist—is concerning.[66]

Such appropriation habits are pervasive in remix. Ethnomusicologist James McNally identifies American DJ Diplo as an exemplar of "global remix," meaning "the prominent incorporation of non-Western musical elements into dance music," which "draws much of its appeal from similarly exoticized associations with global communities of color."[67] As McNally notes, Diplo extracted Brazilian music and took credit for it even though his contribution on top of the source songs was minimal, and "by declining even to cite the original artists" he presented Brazilian genre *funk carioca* as his own sound; indeed, the DJ even bragged in an interview that he could steal samples in Brazil without having to go through a legal or payment process.[68]

This notion of racial extraction and disregard of the people being extracted also shows up in humorous remix. One such remix was "'The Bed Intruder Song,' a remix of a local TV report about a botched home invasion that drew more than 120 million views on YouTube" after a young Black man, Antoine Dodson, was interviewed by the news about the fact that someone had broken into his home to harass his sister;[69] Dodson was agitated and spoke accordingly, combining both a dramatic style and African American Vernacular English in a way then perceived by white audiences as laughable. Like the Christian Bale and Tiger Woods examples discussed above, Dodson became a meme, and "Bed Intruder" demonstrates even more strongly some characteristics common to memes: "most of the men featured in these videos fail to meet prevalent expectations of masculinity either in appearance or behavior,"[70] with Bale losing emotional control, Woods begging, and Dodson framed as what communication scholar Amber Johnson calls a "homo coon, a sexualized form of the zip coon that frames black, homosexual masculinity negatively."[71] Bed Intruder also exemplifies Shifman's further point that "some people enjoy not only watching videos of others whom they perceive to be inferior, but also take pleasure in scornfully imitating them, thus publicly demonstrating their own superiority."[72] Dodson was an interesting example in this respect. Unlike the others, who were celebrities caught behaving badly, he was a regular person in a genuinely distressing situation. Making Dodson into a meme, and, like the others, the butt of the joke, has a very different power dynamic that is flattened by the circulatory habits of internet culture. In such ways, much as with difference being uncritically lauded in cover songs, the fun change of the remix flattens out the power dynamics and obscures how these patterns of who is understood as available to be remixed by whom are deeply racialized.

In such ways, it begins to be clear how it matters who's remixing whom, and for what purpose. For example, some political remixes are top-down.

The "Despacito" artists protested strongly when "Venezuelan President Nicolas Maduro premiered a remix of the song by Puerto Rican duo Luis Fonsi and Daddy Yankee Sunday, transforming the record-setting single about a slow, romantic seduction into a campaign jingle for his contested constitution rewrite."[73] Similarly, the Philadelphia Police Department posted a Facebook video, "Hotline Savesies," that one article called a "remix" of Drake's "Hotline Bling" to tell residents that they "shouldn't argue with their neighbors but instead call 911" in the face of "the illegal habit of using items like orange cones, lawn chairs and trash cans to save shoveled [parking] spots."[74] Such remixes seem more like the kind of free-riding on someone else's labor condemned in *Fisher v. Dees* (1986): "simply to reap the advantages of a well-known tune and short-cut the rigors of composing original music."[75] More importantly, they work to associate a site of (perhaps abusive) state power with a fun song that everyone enjoys, making a play to recruit consent to the remixer's exercise of power through that enjoyment. As a result, many recognize that, if remixes boost popularity or expand audiences for songs in general, they can also be used to garner popularity for one's cultural or political commentary or drum up support for a figure or organization as well. In such ways, the politics of remix can be complex—they're legally uncertain, but sometimes encouraged; they can be a site of political resistance, but also of lost artistic control; and they are often inflected by white supremacist devaluation of people of color, especially Black people.

CAN'T NOBODY TELL ME NOTHIN': "OLD TOWN ROAD" AND THE QUEERLY REPRODUCING REMIX

While, with their start in April 2019, the multiple remixes of Lil Nas X's "Old Town Road" are outside the temporal boundaries I set for this book, the song, originally released in December 2018, was such a big hit, and was so strongly propelled by the release of remix after remix, that I would be remiss not to examine it. To analyze the discourse around this song, I collected a supplemental data set from Nexis Uni (the updated version of LexisNexis) in November 2019, using the search term "'*old town road*' *remix*." With the "group duplicates" feature enabled, there were 483 results. Since I could not batch download all stories using Nexis Uni's affordances the way LexisNexis had previously permitted, I instead used the "sort by relevance" feature and paged through the stories manually, downloading those from mainstream (nonblog) U.S. sources until I had reached 100 relevant stories, which took me to story 260. "Old Town Road" crystallizes many of the larger patterns in remix discussed in this chapter: country meets hip-hop, both "featuring" and dance remixes, and uneasiness around both genre and race. However, it is also a thing unto itself, driven by memes, savvy leveraging of both traditional media infrastructures and the internet, and never taking itself too seriously.

Remixes were essential to the success of "Old Town Road." The song leveraged what one article called "a remix loophole in the Billboard chart system"—remixes are combined with the initial version in totaling sales, streaming, and airplay to determine chart position.[76] While this collapse of base track and remix(es) into a single metric for the purposes of chart position demonstrates the difficulty remix artists have in being recognized as producing valuable creative works in their own right, it nevertheless benefited Lil Nas X. The role of repeated remixes in boosting the song was widely discussed. One article argued that "these remixes absolutely helped Lil Nas X as he tried to pull off the seemingly impossible in the chart world."[77] Another story contended that, "Not only do remixes jump-start a new level of excitement for (and consumption of) a song when they're done right, but they also just allow for multiple versions of a song to feed into the same Hot 100 listing, giving the overall entry a natural advantage over songs with just one prominent version to their credit."[78] Thus, the argument is that a remix can boost numbers not only through the aforementioned "remix loophole" but also what could be described as organically—by giving audiences something new to enjoy, as I described with other remixes.

The song's official remixes all featured country singer Billy Ray Cyrus. The collaboration was in the works from the song's earliest days—Lil Nas X suggested it on Twitter the day after he released the song in December 2018, tweeting "twitter please help me get billy ray cyrus on this."[79] While at first his record label wanted a contemporary country star rather than one most popular in the 1990s, they eventually realized that "it made more sense to amplify the narrative Lil Nas X had already created online—one that caught fire in March when Billboard took 'Old Town Road' off of the Hot Country Songs chart, where it had cracked the top 20"; as one record executive noted, "it created a sense of him as an underdog, so people were rooting for him."[80] The underdog narrative arose from the song's removal from the country charts; when journalists asked why, *Billboard* said:

upon further review, it was determined that "Old Town Road" by Lil Nas X does not currently merit inclusion on *Billboard*'s country charts. When determining genres, a few factors are examined, but first and foremost is musical composition. While "Old Town Road" incorporates references to country and cowboy imagery, it does not embrace enough elements of today's country music to chart in its current version.[81]

Though "Old Town Road" was deemed not to "embrace enough elements of today's country music" to remain on the chart, the decision was deeply racialized; one article contended that:

> Billboard's decision did, however, embrace enough elements of yesterday's racism to draw everyone's attention, so in a delightful act of retaliation, Lil Nas X recruited the 57-year-old country star Billy Ray Cyrus to sing on an "Old Town Road" remix, and now a frivolous ditty about hats and horsies is prompting a broad, meaningful discussion about how racial segregation is baked into the entire idea of genre.[82]

While this was not how the collaboration came about, the idea of remix as shifting genre—and racialization—is key here. Both the reclassification and what one article termed "the song's conspicuous absence from most major country radio playlists" were "sharply criticized as unfair and even racist, prompting a debate about genre and race in Nashville."[83] Remixing the song to add a singer firmly within country music, as with other examples earlier in the chapter, also changed the genre calculation. One article framed this math as that "Cyrus hopped on a remix to add 'authenticity'— whistling and whiteness, basically."[84] That is, though, as discussed above, country-rap crossovers have been hugely popular, this one wasn't classified as country in its initial form; many suspected that it was the fact that "Old Town Road" is sung by a Black man, departing from the racial formula of "base country track from white people + Black featured artist," that pushed it out of the country category.

If the racialized-as-white space of country was inhospitable to Lil Nas X on his own, the presence of Cyrus on the song's remixes changed the genre calculation. Although the interest in Cyrus long predated the removal of "Old Town Road" from the country charts in late March 2019, the remix was actually released very shortly afterward at the beginning of April, making it look like a response. Moreover, given that the song was at #1 for only one week before the remix, but 18 weeks after, Cyrus often got the credit for its success: "Fueled by its remix featuring Billy Ray Cyrus, Lil Nas X's laconic hip-hop-meets-country track 'Old Town Road' shot to No. 1 on the Billboard Hot 100 and stayed there for 19 weeks, making it the chart's longest leader in history."[85] From this position come narratives that "The Billy Ray Cyrus–assisted remix of 'Old Town Road' was the version that spent all those weeks at No. 1, the one that will go down as one of the biggest popular songs in history, and will be played at weddings and karaoke nights for years to come."[86] This is of course not true, as the chart combined all versions, but the incorrectness of the claim serves to underscore how much the success is attributed to Cyrus. Sometimes, it's even referred to as *his* remix rather than actually masterminded by Lil Nas X, as when one article noted that "Billy Ray had earned eight [MTV Video Music Award] nominations for his remix of Lil Nas X's 'Old Town Road'"[87] and another said that "before dropping his remix, Cyrus showed love to the song."[88] In such ways, like rock'n'roll before it, the song takes part in the tradition that media studies scholar Amanda Nell Edgar identifies as "representing the white male performer as the source of black male sounds."[89] Ultimately, the genre transgression of a Black artist bringing hip-hop and country elements together in "Old Town Road" was in large part papered over in popular press discourse by giving a white man far more than his share of the credit; this move can be seen as a way to shore up the category boundaries that "Old Town Road" was showing to be arbitrary and shaky rather than firm and natural.

Yet the initial Cyrus remix was just the first of four official remixes, three featuring and one dance. One article noted that "Deploying multiple remixes of a song is not a new strategy . . . but the tactic was most effectively used by Lil Nas X as a means of perking up listeners and folding in fans of the artists hopping on the new versions. And if that blueprint can help keep an established hit at its chart peak for a few more weeks, others will embrace it moving forward."[90] That is, while other artists had used multiple remixes before—the above article references the use of this tactic with the 2016 Fat Joe and Remy Ma song "All the Way Up"—stories identified Lil Nas X's use as in a category of its own because of its greater success, creating what this one calls a "blueprint." In particular, Lil Nas X benefited from contemporary technological conditions in producing these repeated remixes. After all, "musical distribution and technology has sped up to the point of remixes being both recordable and releasable in a matter of days, if not hours."[91]

Though the popularity of "Old Town Road" was undeniably massive, the response in the press to its many remixes was, well, mixed. This response tracks, in popular discourse, the bifurcation David Gunkel describes in expert opinion between utopian views of remix as expanding musical possibility from the copyleft and dismissive views of remix as "cheap and easy" from media corporations and some artists.[92] Some found the remix boosting tactic gimmicky, as when one article said: "Nowadays, the trick to maintaining a hit song's momentum is simple: Add a new star, stir and serve."[93] This description constructs the remix as formulaic and uncreative. Another article, discussing who might next be featured on a remix, said, "I honestly think the Billy Ray Cyrus version is where the whole thing peaked, and wouldn't see myself getting too excited about any additional guests."[94] Those three more official mixes did nothing to improve on the first one, according to this story. The quantity of remixes became something of a punchline, with another article complaining that "summer 2019's chart legacy will largely be defined by its many forgettable features and a gazillion 'Old Town Road' remixes."[95] Even the artist himself seemed to acknowledge that he was taking the bit quite far, tweeting "last one i PROMISSEE" as he released the final, "Seoul Town Road" remix with K-pop star RM of BTS[96]—he also playfully engaged "on Twitter with people joking about the number of remixes, retweeting some of them."[97] As late as May 2020, Lil Nas X was having fun with the number of remixes of "Old Town Road" he had made. In response to a false claim from a Rihanna fan account that two of her songs were the only remixes ever to reach #1 on the Hot 100, he tweeted "i did not make 27 remixes to the same song to be disrespected like this."[98]

For others, the song's many remixes were beloved, or at least appreciated as weird-but-good. As one journalist described his own reactions, ascribed to a generalized "you":

> The "Achy Breaky Heart" guy absolutely crushing a guest verse on a cowboy-rap song in 2019? You had to hear it to believe it. Young Thug and Mason Ramsey getting added into the mix . . . ? It didn't make much sense, but damn if you weren't intrigued. RM sending "Old Town Road" into the K-pop universe? It had been months and months, but yup, had to play it at least once.[99]

These remixes are credited with "possibly making 'Old Town Road' not only the biggest hit in Hot 100 history, but also its most unlikely."[100] That is, the song used unexpected tactics and combined widely disparate artists and genres to produce something that perhaps shouldn't have worked—but did.

Considering the discursive construction of "Old Town Road" in its totality—seen as the song that breaks music industry rules, that refused to follow the normal trajectory of gaining popularity and then fading away, that spawned not just one offshoot but a proliferating flock, I argue that it is most productively understood as a queer text, and particularly one that highlights the contours of remix trouble. "Old Town Road" is queer because it operates on queer time, outside "temporal frames of bourgeois reproduction and family, longevity, risk/safety, and inheritance."[101] A song is supposed to go through a life cycle, but this one refused to comply with this norm. If, as queer studies scholar Kathryn Bond Stockton contends, "Perverts are 'diverts,' one could say, who extend themselves or linger," queerly refusing the call to move in lockstep from one stage to the next,[102] "Old Town Road" makes much the same move. In particular, if norms have "the goal of delivering us from unruly childhoods to orderly and predictable adulthoods,"[103] "Old Town Road" stayed resolutely unruly, disorderly, and unpredictable.

An objection might be raised that a #1 hit song seems normative, not queer. After all, if, as queer studies scholar Jack Halberstam argues, failure is queer,[104] the corollary would be that success is straight. However, queerness is a both/and logic—Lil Nas X did have success, but also left its boundaries shakier than he found them, as his success "exploit[ed] the unpredictability of ideology and its indeterminate qualities."[105] Rather than a notion of queerness standing entirely outside power (which is not possible), this is queer as "working the weakness in the norm."[106] While the huge success is in some ways normative, Lil Nas X continued to partially "stand outside of conventional understandings of success" associated with "specific forms of reproductive maturity combined with wealth accumulation,"[107] through the song's queer remix reproduction. "Old Town Road" does not "make us better people or liberate us from the culture industry," but I argue that it does "harbor covert and overt queer worlds."[108]

As communication scholar Aram Sinnreich notes, "innovative or challenging aesthetics pose a consequent threat to powerful institutions,"[109] and "Old Town Road" does just that. The traces of this queer threat show in how the song is discussed. One article commented about how "The new bumps in streaming counts, sales and overall exposure ensured that the song was never given the chance to naturally recede either from the top of the charts, or from public attention in general."[110] The key word here is "natural": through this nonnormative practice, the normative trajectory is rejected. "Old Town Road" also cultivated a queered form of desire by versioning the same thing, in defiance of consumerism's call to consume, dispose, and move on. Notably, sales are only one measure in the above comment, alongside streaming—which makes very little money for anyone involved—and general exposure; while sales are a normative kind of success, as media industries scholar Patrik Wikström notes, the other two have an increasingly fuzzy if not oblique relation to turning a profit, as "cloud-based music distribution not only promotes sales of music via other channels, it is also able to satisfy the music demand of a considerable part of the audience. Termed differently, the once strong link between exposure and sales is radically weakened."[111] While contemporary capitalism does rely on mass consumption, and often on consuming the same thing multiple times, as in albums re-released with bonus material or in new formats or for anniversaries, streaming counts and memes are fundamentally unlike purchasing and repurchasing. Thus, if, as feminist theorist Sara Ahmed argues, queering is moving slantwise,[112] "Old Town Road" is queered by its many sidesteps. After all, "Each time it courts death, it pivots,"[113] moving anywhere other than the direction it's normatively supposed to go. This movement invokes what Sinnreich talks about as recursion—in which the fixity of a linear beginning, middle, and end of musical production is disrupted,[114] but twisted to think about any given song as only ever becoming. As Nadia Ellis notes, "*queer* emphasizes practice, action, not categorical state. *Queer* shifts, it moves. It does not rest."[115]

Moreover, if there are normative parameters of acceptable genres or artists, "Old Town Road" refused these narrow objects of desire. Much like the fan-made videos splicing together TV footage and expository music that media studies scholar Julie Levin Russo discusses, its many versions "represent a queer form of reproduction that mates supposedly incompatible parts ('original' media source and 'original' creativity) to spawn hybrid offspring."[116] Even on its own terms, "Old Town Road" was composed of disparate parts, too country for hip-hop and too hip-hop for country. This pattern shows the aftereffects of the fact that both "genre" and "generation" are derived from a Latin word meaning "of or pertaining to a procreative origin."[117] Genres are supposed to be (straight) lines of inheritance, within (narrow) acceptable degrees of variation—not promiscuously anything and everything that gives pleasure. The queer boundary transgression of the initial version was intensified with the stranger and stranger bedfellows of the remixes. As one article argues, "Say what you will about the musical value of 'Seoul Town Road,' or how necessary it was to hear Young Thug's croaking flow next to the Walmart yodeling boy's wide-eyed warble; these remixes absolutely helped Lil Nas X as he tried to pull off the seemingly impossible in the chart world."[118]

Last but not least, if one or two versions of a song is the music industry standard, the reworkings of "Old Town Road" were functionally infinite. The song is an exemplar of joyful excess, of more for its own sake, not a line of inheritance but a rhizomatic proliferation. Shifman distinguishes between virals and memes, noting that "whereas the viral comprises a single cultural unit (such as a video, photo, or joke) that propagates in many copies, an Internet meme is always a collection of texts."[119] In this way, much like the case of "Leave Britney Alone" that Shifman discusses, "Old Town Road" did in fact start out as a viral, but once it began to be uncontrollably versioned, both by Lil Nas X himself and the internet at large, it became a meme. That is, if, as Shifman argues, memes are groups of digital objects with similar characteristics, created by many people, that exist in dialogue with one another,[120] then the many versions of "Old Town Road" certainly compose a meme. In the context of "Old Town Road," the fact that memes are characterized by quite a nonnormative form of reproduction, that they "reproduce by various means of repackaging or imitation," therefore takes on new meaning.[121] Not only did "Old Town Road" reproduce in a meme-like fashion, that is, but I argue that memetic reproduction is queer: slantwise and based in pleasure rather than descent.

On one hand, the song's multiremix status itself was a meme, giving rise to an MTV Video Music Awards clip before Lil Nas X's performance that was purportedly "from a distant future, in which 'Old Town Road' Remix No. 3162 was being teased," which one article describes as "priceless fun, especially when 'Old Thug' was teased as one of the guests"—as opposed to Young Thug's involvement in the third remix.[122] On the other hand, the song was also used as a base for other memes: overlaid on a clip of *Game of Thrones* character Arya Stark finding a horse amid destruction;[123] used by late night host Jimmy Fallon for an impression of presidential candidate

Bernie Sanders called "Old Town Hall";[124] producing a couple of different elementary school versions including a third grade class singing about math problems;[125] and, perhaps most absurdly, serving as the soundtrack to the trailer for action film *Rambo: Last Blood*.[126] This meme proliferation is perhaps unsurprising given that Lil Nas X, named one of "The 25 Most Influential People on the Internet" by *Time* magazine, ran a Twitter meme account before his music career took off.[127] The artist himself is steeped in meme culture, and indeed made good use of these skills by riffing on the popular summer 2019 "Area 51 Raid" meme in the video for the Mason Ramsey and Young Thug remix.[128] One article described the inclusion of "yodeling kid" Ramsey as "meme recognize meme,"[129] and indeed Lil Nas X's meme skills snowballed forward into the memetic reproduction of "Old Town Road," which snowballed into a whole world of sideways-reproducing cultural objects without clear lines of descent.

Ultimately, "Old Town Road" encapsulates many of the features of remix as a type of transformative musical work, showing both how remix succeeds and where it meets resistance. It's genre-busting, and makes some traditional gatekeepers uneasy despite its massive popularity and success by those same traditional measures. Its reception is inextricable from the racialization of the genres involved, even as it seems to gleefully defy those boundaries. This is not to say that genres are or ever have been racially pure spaces; they surely are not. Yet they are often popularly constructed as sharply racially distinguished, and this norm is violated by "Old Town Road" in particular and many remixes in general. Remixes cause trouble because they are queer in the sense of desiring across—and breaking—such genre and racial boundaries. While this desire is often recuperated into industrial sales logics, Lil Nas X shows how it can sometimes also escape into queer lines of flight. That is, "Old Town Road" was conventionally successful, but also represents something new, taking the promotional logic of the remix and the power of queer memetic reproduction to new heights.

CHAPTER 3

Monstrous Mash

Mash-Ups and the Epistemology of Difference

Imagine old, bald Pete Townshend shuffling gingerly onstage as a synth burbles up
behind him—"Let My Love Open the Door." Now imagine the rapper Pimp C already
on that stage, in a white fur suit and hat, holding up four fingers to show off his bling.
A kick line of girls in black minishorts walks it out for DJ Unk, who's rapping about a
kick line of girls, then Levon Helm appears on a drum riser to chirp out "The Weight."
Also onstage: Jay-Z, Black Sabbath, Rick Springfield, Kesha, Bruce Springsteen, Miley
Cyrus, the Ramones and Tupac and Biggie Smalls (both back from the dead) and hundreds more. . . . This is pretty much the state of affairs at a Girl Talk show these days.[1]

Mash-ups are transformative musical works that combine existing songs,
particularly existing recordings, and, usually, specifically have parts of
more than one song. They differ from remixes because they usually contain minimal new material. Music scholar David Tough traces the history
of the mash-up back to the quodlibet, which appeared in classical music as
early as the 15th century and has shown up in popular music such as "The
Other One" from the Grateful Dead (1968).[2] As defined by musicologist
J. Peter Burkholder, quodlibet is a "combination of two or more familiar
tunes, often as a joke or technical tour de force,"[3] and certainly both of
these tendencies are present with mash-ups. However, elsewhere he notes
of musical borrowing in general that "the significance of borrowed material depends in part on who or what is borrowed from,"[4] and this role of
relation to the previous work is, I argue, key to popular perceptions of
mash-ups. The fundamental distinction between the quodlibet and the
mash-up is that, like the cover song, the mash-up tends to take as its source
texts particular *recordings*, not the compositions.

Songs that would more traditionally be understood as mash-ups, particularly of the "a cappella/instrument track form," are usually identified as

starting with "Rebel without a Pause [Whipped Cream Mix]," a mash-up of Public Enemy and Herb Alpert by the Evolution Control Committee in 1994.[5] As with this example, mash-ups are often seen as having roots in hip-hop; in particular, Tough argues that mash-ups are similar to early hip-hop practices of putting rhymes over an existing musical track, like the Sugar Hill Gang building "Rappers Delight" (1980) on the base of Chic's "Good Times" (1979).[6] Mash-ups can also be seen as growing out of hip-hop in the sense that they have important overlap with some kinds of hip-hop samples—the practice of using electronically clipped pieces of existing recordings as the building blocks of new music. The sampling that is most like mash-up is what hip-hop scholar Tricia Rose describes as "a process of cultural literacy and intertextual reference. Sampled guitar and bass lines from soul and funk precursors are often recognizable or have familiar resonances."[7] That is, the specific sources used in a mash-up, as in these forms of hip-hop, are a large part of its meaning. Communication scholar Michael Serazio identifies an additional precursor of mash-up in club music practices of extending breaks and blending one song into the next.[8] Drawing from these various traditions, more widespread creation of mash-ups began in London clubs around 2000 under the names "boot-leg" or "bastard pop,"[9] and came to the United States as "mash-up" around 2002 or 2003.[10]

Over the period examined in this book, mash-up moved from being discussed primarily in terms of literal mixes of different songs to a more metaphorical life as a cultural logic of combination. In this chapter, I take a correspondingly expansive approach to mash-up, examining the 26 instances of songs, artists, and collaborations from my data set that are described using the term. On one hand, there are traditional mash-ups of the sort done with two or more existing songs. On the other hand, the term mash-up also frequently appeared in news coverage to describe other types of music: a collection of Latine/Jewish hybrid albums from the 1940s and 1950s that were reissued in the 2010s, contemporary hip-hop/classi-cal acts, and Country Music Television's (CMT) country-plus show *CMT Crossroads*. Through this promiscuous approach, considering any musical juxtaposition framed as mash-up, I examine the broad conceptual terrain of the mash-up, as well as its particular topology of value judgments.

I argue that mash-ups do two seemingly contradictory things. On one hand, mash-up works by employing recognizable source texts whose meaning is made present and juxtaposed with each other through what

I call the *aura function*. On the other hand, the mash-up is constructed as new and different. Combining reference and nostalgia with novelty in the same song is on one level contradictory, but on another level is aligned with the Black rhetorical practice of Signifyin,' known for repetition with difference. I argue that this alignment with Signifyin' matters a great deal; part of the greater popular discomfort with mash-up compared to cover songs and remixes is that it is more aesthetically aligned with Black cultural production than other genres are. The structural Blackness of mash-up is also tied into its negative reception, which is discursively managed through aligning mash-up with whiteness by contrast to hip-hop sampling through emphasizing labor, framing mash-up as building racial harmony by drawing on multiracial sources, and treating mash-up figuratively rather than as literal combination of songs.

REMEDIATION AND AURA DOWN BY THE SCRAPYARD: INVOKING THE MUSICAL PAST

In traditional mash-ups of two or more existing songs, one key feature emphasized in press coverage is the ways they are facilitated by digital technologies. Certainly, access is dramatically improved compared to analog analogues, with one artist describing the old "days where you were carrying 10 crates of records" as a more challenging time to make mash-ups.[11] Digital production definitely expands access, since, as articles point out, to sample even something originally released on vinyl there is now likely a copy online.[12] Digitization has also improved distribution—particularly, news stories emphasize, speed. Those making music no longer need to wait for the slow process of making physical discs, but can (if operating without a record deal) simply release digitally on their own timetable, as mash-up artist Girl Talk did—resulting in "a downloading frenzy that would prompt the glib MTV.com news headline 'Girl Talk Apologizes for Breaking the Internet with "All Day."'"[13]

At a more fundamental level, sampling, as the technical means by which bits of existing songs are mashed up, is a digital production technology; as Rose describes, "Samplers are computers that can digitally duplicate any existing sounds and play them back in any key or pitch, in any order, sequence and loop them endlessly."[14] The way that this practice is specifically about *existing* sounds is essential. If contemporary discourse around technology often treats technological change as advancement always replacing what came before, sampling does something different—it remediates the analog rather than displacing it. Remediation, as coined by new media scholars Jay David Bolter and Richard Grusin, refers at its most basic to "the representation of one medium in another."[15] The previous medium is essential to how the new object comes to have meaning, in much the same way as Rose describes: "rap's sample-heavy sound is digitally reproduced but cannot be digitally created. In other words, the sound of a James Brown or Parliament drum kick or bass line and the equipment that processed it then, as well as the equipment that processes it now, are all central to the way a rap records[sic] feels."[16] The specificity of the source songs—indeed, their materiality—is the reason to use a sample in mash-up as much as it was in early hip-hop; the artist is drawing on this sound (and no other).

Mash-up is in many ways exactly about carrying the old forward. The thing that was there before is overtly and intentionally present, as the mash-up's constituent parts are usually specifically recognizable in a way that they aren't always in other sample-based music.[17] DJ Z-Trip says, "I take lot from everyday pop culture, yet try my hardest to fuse that stuff with the more unknown. . . . Something recognizable with something forgotten by the masses."[18] Though there's an undercurrent here of contempt for "the masses," this statement demonstrates how using recognizable sources is a broader tenet of mash-up. As Kembrew McLeod and Peter DiCola note, one prominent artist, Girl Talk, "uses fairly long samples to create a mash-up for two or three recognizable songs at a time—as opposed to some of the hip-hop songs from the late 1980s that typically combined many more musical fragments at once, often rendering the original sources unrecognizable."[19] Mash-up, communication scholar Aram Sinnreich argues, takes the "premise that originality can be achieved, not by obscuring a song's sources, but by celebrating them," which he describes as "one aesthetic factor that sets mash-ups aside from most other forms of sample-based music"; "within the mash-up esthetic," he adds, "the only way to be original is to acknowledge one's debts to others. Furthermore, to *oppose* or *obscure* the sampling of a song is paradoxically tantamount to sullying its 'integrity.' The tacit assumption here is that the appearance of creating ex nihilo is a flat out lie, by definition."[20] This sharp break with the ideology of the Romantic author who creates from internal genius, disconnected from any external influence, is part of why mash-up is more aesthetically contested than some other forms. Mash-ups fundamentally rely on recognition of where they come from.

In fact, it's often precisely the presence or invocation of the old that is understood to make a mash-up good. Though many argue that the juxtaposition of sources is rooted in mockery or irony (and of course sometimes it is), it is frequently sincere, an attempt to engage with the past out of respect or homage as I discussed with covers and like the early days of hip-hop sampling described by Rose. Critical theorist Walter Benjamin famously argued that moving to forms of art made through processes of mechanical reproduction, like film, dissipates the authority attributed to the original, "its presence in time and space, its unique existence at the place where it happens to be"—the aura;[21] under mechanical reproduction, every copy is as good or as real or as original as every other copy, and there is no longer any sense of a "real thing" opposed to an inferior, secondary copy. Benjamin, of course, thought the decay of the aura was a good thing because it was democratizing; film could circulate to people who would never be able to go to a rarefied art museum space. Serazio picks up this concept to argue that mash-ups show there is no aura and in fact this revelation is why they are often seen as threatening—not the alleged lost sales of copyright infringement.[22] However, just because there is no single original anymore doesn't mean there is no more aura. Instead, I'd argue, what could be understood as the *aura function* is still fulfilled regardless of the particular production technologies, but simply changes forms. That is, much as philosopher Michel Foucault argues that the author of a text is less important as a specific actual human than as a concept reflecting how society constructs meaningful patterns between texts, and that the author function—the work that the concept of the author does—persists even after attempts to decenter the author as the source of meaning,[23] the aura function is about how authenticity is socially constructed, which may differ across time and over space but does not disappear as a value.

Musicologist Mark Katz gestures toward the aura function as he notes that "Authenticity is clearly a moving target. Often something is authentic to the extent that it has been replaced by something newer, less familiar, and more convenient."[24] Working his way backward, he notes:

> CDs were derided as cold, inhuman, and unattractively small—the antithesis of the LP, with its comforting tactility and oft-cited warmth of sound. Yet LPs were flimsy compared to the thicker, more substantial 78s; and to extend this further,

many listeners preferred the "warm" sound of acoustic 78s to those made by the electrical process beginning in 1925. And, of course, recording itself can be considered inauthentic compared to live music making.

Through this same process, under conditions of digital distribution the CD becomes "an object of ritual and nostalgia." In such ways, there is always an implicit "real thing" that is valued. Much like Bolter and Grusin's argument that "remediation does not destroy the aura of a work of art; instead it always refashions that aura in another media form,"[25] I contend that the concept that there is an authentic presence that can't be reproduced does important cultural work, and so therefore does not disappear with mass production, instead shifting with technological change—and continuing to shift—to describe something slightly different.

Mash-ups in particular are frequently an auratic form, where it's specifically the presence of a recognizable original—or two, or more—that creates the "wow" moment. It is the presence of these songs, and the meaning they each carry, that gives the mash-up *its* meaning. It matters that the constituent songs are identifiable. Mash-up samples are specifically long. This tendency diverges from forms of sampling where very short slices of music are used as beats or to enrich the sound. However, it *is* like what musicologist Joanna Demers describes as "conspicuous consumption" samples and critical theorist Joshua Clover calls samples as "Bling":[26] lengthy, expensive stretches of music to show off that the artist can afford to license them. As Demers describes, artists like Sean "Diddy" Combs "sampled white music as a method of displaying financial wealth."[27] In a broad sense, as legal scholar Madhavi Sunder argues, "sampling is homage: new creators use the technique to represent themselves heroically within a lineage of earlier creators and traditions."[28] In such ways, mash-up also represents a callback to the early days of sampling, in which a sample was "a challenge to know these sounds, to make connections between the lyrical and musical texts. It affirms black musical history and locates these 'past' sounds in the 'present.' More often than not, rap artists and their DJs openly revere their soul forebears."[29] This showing off and reverence and making the past present is exactly auratic, but not at all based on a unique original without copies. The auratic nature of mash-up comes through particularly clearly in one description of a mash-up as hitting "an unexpectedly moving note—a sad, wistful mash-up of UGK's 'One Day' and the John Lennon chestnut 'Imagine.' Murder, prison, drugs—'one day you here, but the next day you gone'—then those two main piano chords, C and F, as iconic as Gandhi."[30] Bracketing the racist construction of Gandhi as a symbol rather than a complex political figure, "Imagine" is "iconic," and those chords make it present in the new song. The effect is produced by being in the presence of "Imagine," through its aura. It couldn't be done any other way. Mash-up is auratic.

However, because mash-up makes the source text present, and in particular because it uses the actual bytes that make up a digital song, the literal combination of two or more songs is also the place questions of legality arise with mash-up. Though this book's analysis begins five years after the 2004 release of Danger Mouse's *The Grey Album*, questions of its legality still loom large, in part because it was so popular—it had huge numbers of downloads that would have sent a formal release shooting up the *Billboard* charts. *The Grey Album* is a high-profile instance of what music scholar Christine Boone calls a "paint palette mashup," which is "by far the rarest type, and it is the only one where recognizability of the sampled songs is not a primary consideration."[31] The Beatles tracks are chopped and flipped into unrecognizability, but, crucially, this is not to disguise them. It was important for the source to be known for the album's conceit of a mash-up of *The Black Album* and the *White Album* to get gray, so the aura function persists, if obliquely.

The Grey Album is variously described as "a mash-up that used unauthorized Beatles and Jay-Z samples,"[32] or used "uncleared Beatles samples,"[33] or "blended the Beatles White Album with Jay Z's Black Album—without acquiring rights to any of the music."[34] It's true that the samples weren't authorized—at least, not those from the Beatles; in fact, Beatles rightsholder EMI has consistently refused to license samples to anyone.[35] On the other hand, as Sunder notes, "Jay-Z had intentionally facilitated mash-ups by releasing an a cappella version of *The Black Album*."[36] That is, at the same time that lawsuits or threats thereof result from reusing some bits of music, there is active encouragement by other artists. Indeed, McLeod and DiCola argue that "the practice of releasing a capella vocals on hop-hop singles played a direct role in the emergence of the mash-up as we know it."[37] However, as they also note, there's a song on *The White Album*, "Revolution 9," that uses a multiple "found sounds," making EMI's objection at least ironic and possibly deeply cynical.[38] The questionable nature of EMI's argument doesn't stop there, as digital humanities scholar Davis Schneiderman points out; sound recordings were not protected by copyright until 1972, "making the claim that EMI 'owns' the 1968 Beatles recordings . . .—at worst—a lie in the form of a threat, and—at best—a reference to the possibility that pre-1972 state laws might offer protection to the 1968 recordings."[39]

Despite all this, it's routine to say that *The Grey Album* is illegal or unlawful—a claim made even by Danger Mouse himself. This assertion is not strictly true; even setting aside the pre-1972 question, no court made a judgment about whether *The Grey Album* qualified as fair use. Certainly, there have been cases where samples have been found to be fair use, both before *The Grey Album* (*Campbell v. Acuff-Rose*, 1994) and after (*Estate of Smith v. Graham*, 2020).[40] Particularly relevant to mash-up, *Estate of Smith v. Graham* cited *Cariou v. Prince*'s finding that "The secondary use must be permitted to conjure up at least enough of the original to fulfill its trans-formative purpose"[41] in order to extend the latter case's notion of needing to conjure the original to include sampling. Here again, making the ear-lier text present is understood to be essential to why one might sample—sometimes even by courts. Through popular beliefs about both sampling in general and mash-up in particular, then, there is repeated emphasis on making earlier songs present—deploying what I call the aura function to legitimate mash-up by emphasizing nostalgic and respectful relationships to what came before.

CH-CH-CHANGES: MASH-UP AS DIFFERENCE AND NOVELTY

However, at the same time as mash-ups are auratic invocations of the past, press discourse also includes a clear sense that what constitutes a mash-up is difference. Looking at word frequency in the corpus of mash-up data, after removing words that apply only to specific instances like "violin" and that are too general, like "music," "different" is one of the ten most frequent words. This emphasis on difference can be seen, for example, in video game *DJ Hero*, which asks players to use a turntable controller to combine songs; one article notes that "a lot of times the song choices are pretty surpris-ing ('Bustin Loose' mixed with 'Time of the Season')."[42] Similarly, "Z-Trip quickly gained popularity based on his ability to blend songs together that most wouldn't think of combining, and turning them into a new fresh sound."[43] The mark of the positively received mash-up, then, is turning dif-ference into something that works. Mash-up as a fusion of difference also carries over into more figurative mash-ups like 1940s hit "Miami Beach Rhumba," described by one story as "an improbable combination of zesty Latin dance rhythms and musical inflections born of the shtetls and ghettos of Eastern Europe."[44] Similarly, a recurring idea in discussions of the group Black Violin is that their music is notable because "for most people, classical music and hip-hop are diametrically opposed"—yet Black Violin manages to mash them up.[45] In such ways, mash-ups are understood to combine "opposed" or "improbable" sources.

Typically, the combination of difference is seen as a good thing. One article says of Danger Mouse's *The Grey Album* that the song "'What More Can I Say,' a combination of Jay-Z's song of the same name and 'While My Guitar Gently Weeps' by The Beatles[,] is fantastic. Though the two songs would usually never be mentioned in the same sentence, they fit together so naturally it's amazing no one combined them before."[46] Thus, the most positively received mash-ups reveal something previously unseen, a "natural" affinity that becomes irrefutable once exposed. In the land of figurative mash-up, there are statements like: "country singer-songwriter Sara Evans proves to be an inspired, if unlikely, musical collaborator with the veteran rock group REO Speedwagon" on *CMT Crossroads*.[47] Similarly, stories assert that Black Violin's "unique mash-up of styles works a lot better than you'd think."[48] In such ways, positive responses to mash-ups fairly consistently rest on them being "unlikely" yet "working better than you'd think."

Such examples show that the mash-up is culturally understood as a form in which difference usually comes together in the end—and indeed "together" is the fifth most used word in the data. Often, these discussions involve spatial metaphors of worlds joined and gaps transcended. The late DJ AM "jumped across various genres and eras to combine songs from artists as different as Jay-Z and Journey."[49] Taylor Swift and Def Leppard's installment of *Crossroads* was described as an event in which "two divergent musical worlds collide."[50] Sometimes the metaphor of bringing together difference tends more toward craftsmanship: artists blend, fuse, mix, and meld things together. What comes of a mash-up is often something new or unique. Z-Trip can "breed new music that feels as much cutting edge as nostalgia driven."[51] Thus, a positively received mash-up is a new thing that in some instances transcends its constituent parts.

In particular, the difference that matters in mash-up is often about genre; five of the top ten words in the data set are names of genres (hip at

#1 and hop at #2, classical at #4, rock at #9, and pop at #10). Some mash-ups are directly described as "genre-busting,"[52] "genre-blending,"[53] or "genre-blurring."[54] As Katz argues, "a large portion of the mash-ups circulating in cyberspace engage in the 'genre clash' approach."[55] However, even when it's not directly named, the standard formulation of mash-up's difference hinges on genre. Stories may list two or more genres that an artist engages, as with Dee Jay Silver's "style of music, which blends together country, hip-hop, rock and house into one rhythmic sound."[56] Alternately, the illustrative songs or artists to show a mash-up maker's combinatory range may be from different genres, as in "an unlikely pairing of Soulja Boy, the hip-hop idol, with the avant-garde electronica of Aphex Twin."[57]

This combination of disparate sources is part of why mash-up is routinely described as requiring specialized knowledge. As Z-Trip argues, "It takes a broad love of music to be a good DJ."[58] Even in *DJ Hero*, where the song combinations are preselected, stories assert that it "isn't for everyone. It just doesn't have the accessibility of 'Guitar Hero'"[59]—which seems to imply that educated taste is required. Mash-up is also understood as needing talent, producing moments where stories discuss mash-up artists' "raw talent"[60] or even "uncanny talent."[61] For their part, Black Violin are sometimes described as "virtuosos,"[62] and member Kev Marcus contributes to this narrative of musical genius when he describes a moment of realization:

> There was a song on the radio by Busta Rhymes called "Gimme Some More" and it had this eerie violin line in it. So I learned the violin line by myself at home and I programmed my phone to play that when it rang. I didn't think anything of it and I was in orchestra class and my phone rang and then the whole class was like, "How did you get that 'Gimme Some More' on your phone?" I showed my friends how I did it, and I showed them the notes and the violins learned the notes. Then me and Wil, we could play the middle part, and we were just kinda playing the viola line in the middle, and then we taught the cellos the low part. . . . And we walked in wearing tuxedos and the whole orchestra's playing Busta Rhymes' "Gimme Some More" and all the other orchestras were jealous. To me, that was sort of the moment of genius where we were like, "Oh. When you take the violin and you do hip-hop or pop things with it, people really lose their minds." It was really something we thought was super easy for us. Because we grew up hip-hop and we studied classical, so for us blending it together was super duper easy. We don't even think anything of it. But it was really us recog-

nizing that other people really liked it and taking that recognition and turning it into a career.[63]

The casualness with which he describes what are actually pretty impressive musical abilities to hear a song on the radio and be able to teach all the parts to their high school orchestra, and the length at which the article describes it, reinforces the sense of mash-up artists as talented.

There is, moreover, a sense that those who create mash-ups are innovative. A story lauds Black Violin's "winning ingenuity and spirit of inventiveness."[64] Even a journalist who otherwise is unimpressed with mashups admits that "Danger Mouse cleverly put a Vulcan mind-meld on the Beatles' 'White Album' and Jay-Z's 'The Black Album.'"[65] Importantly, creating mash-ups is understood to require a combination of skill and musical knowledge. As one article argues, "The key to a great DJ is one who is able to negotiate a significant skill set with a great ear for music."[66] Similarly, another story notes that Black Violin "demonstrate their technical expertise and clever musical savvy to showstopping degrees."[67] These descriptions identifying mash-up artists as having unique talent can be seen as a way of smuggling the Romantic author back in to what is otherwise a very different kind of creativity. This pattern both demonstrates the tenacity of Romantic authorship as a value and begins to suggest that the transgression of mash-up is perceived as needing to be managed, which I'll discuss in more depth later in the chapter.

SOURCES AND SIGNIFYING: MASH-UP'S STRUCTURAL BLACKNESS

If mash-up combines disparate sources, it matters particularly much that what's considered disparate tends to operate on a Black/white binary. Quote-unquote "rap" (rarely hip-hop) is the most common anchor point for statements emphasizing how varied the sources of mash-up are. Rap is juxtaposed with classical, 80s new wave, metal, folk, punk, and country— all genres typically racialized as white despite having more diverse histories. Less often, the anchor is instead the similarly racialized genre R&B, juxtaposed with psychedelic rock, pop, and classical—as in "Bach and Beyoncé."[68] This racialization has a number of consequences.

First, with white mash-up artists, combining differently racialized sources often recapitulates histories of racial theft. As discussed in earlier chapters, there is a history of white artists picking up aspects of Black artists' music, whether directly covering songs or building from musical expression originated by Black people, and often doing so without crediting those source artists, let alone compensating them. Often, when white folks like rock musicians Rolling Stones or Eric Clapton copy blues sounds or electronica artist Moby samples blues recordings, it's seen as "homage," and the aura function is key here. White artists incorporating music from Black artists with respect and acknowledgment, in which they know the origin and make an effort to ensure their audience does too—maintaining the aura function—is ethically very different from either obscuring or even just failing to highlight origins, shifting from reference/reverence to theft and treating these artists as raw material. Mash-up has the potential to commit this white theft of Black people's music all over again with hip-hop as the building block rather than blues. One article notes without awareness that mash-up artist Girl Talk "loves hip-hop the way the Stones loved the blues,"[69] and is unintentionally accurate given the parallel thefts—he does love it in precisely the same way, through treating it as a musical parts emporium that he can use to assert his own artistry. For Girl Talk—far more so than the Stones, who did make efforts to name and honor these influences, if unevenly— Black people's music is raw material for the taking; however much love is involved, it's rooted in the unequal power relation that makes Black people's cultural products available for white use. However, deracination does not mean that cultural products are deracialized, and in fact their racialization is a significant portion of their value.

In "Eating the Other," feminist theorist bell hooks describes such practices as "a consumer cannibalism that not only displaces the Other but denies the significance of that Other's history through a process of decontextualization."[70] Eating the Other is a desire to consume the culture but without the people it came from or the historical context that gave rise to it. As Jack Hamilton notes in his analysis of race in the development of rock music, white rock artists often "held black music on a mystified pedestal, viewing it as raw, powerful, and important but at the same time denying it as presently viable."[71] This is love that relies on distance from the people creating the culture through imagining its creation as long ago and far away. As media industries scholar David Hesmondhalgh points out, this practice becomes even easier with technologically enabled techniques like sampling, where the music of the Other can be appropriated without even the formerly required step of encountering the musicians in person.[72] The same digitization that increases access and lets more people make music also increases access to music made by Black people and lets white people appropriate it ever more easily.

Importantly, these appropriated bits of culture are not just generally partial and made to carry the weight of standing in for the entirety of the culture from which they originate—which would be bad enough—but also deeply stereotypical. With regard to music, Hesmondhalgh refers to these decontextualized bites as "aural stereotypes."[73] Because the term "stereotype" is associated with derogatory representations, they are often mis-recognized when they are apparently rooted in appreciation or desire for the culture in question, but these practices of desire for Black people's music frequently err in assuming that it is freely available for white people to consume in a decontextualized, eating the Other way. Through the insatiable hunger of whiteness, a cultural landscape emerges in which "histories and experience once seen only as worthy of disdain can be looked upon with awe."[74] However, this awe is not therefore necessarily an improvement, as "when race and ethnicity become commodified as resources of pleasure, the culture of specific groups, as well as the bodies of individuals, can be seen as constituting an alternative playground where members of domi-nating races, genders, sexual practices affirm their power-over in intimate relations with the Other,"[75] reducing entire populations to how they please white people.

Moreover, the Black/white binary provides opportunities for anti-Black sentiment to attach to mash-up. In press discussion of mash-up, hip-hop is associated with borderline-negative traits such as "attitude"[76] and "brashness."[77] In a typical, though particularly colorful, example, one story notes that "What keeps [the mash-up] from being cloying is the hip-hop—hip-hop's violent imagery, its phallic boasting, its mad embrace of sex and death."[78] In this description, all hip-hop—not just the particular song mashed here—is constructed as inherently about violence and death, raising the specter of Blackness as intrinsically violent by collapsing the distinction between gangsta rap and all other genres. It also produces a wobble between sex and violence using the trope of Black men's genitals as a threat. Such examples make clear how samples as recognizable, decon-textualized slices can approach caricature of Black people.[79] In particular, this use of hip-hop shows what legal scholar K. J. Greene describes as "the imposition of vicious dignitary harm to blacks as a group through negative cultural stereotyping."[80] Moreover, examining form rather than content, features characteristic of the African Diaspora's musical traditions are criticized—such as critique of Black Violin for its music "landing loudly on beats two and four."[81]

As part of the larger formation producing this anti-Black sentiment, proximity to whiteness in mash-up is valued. In one such example, Black Violin is described as having "an urban sensibility that also displays some Old World instrumental acumen,"[82] ascribing value through proximity to Europeanness in the musical equivalent of calling them "articulate." Similarly, while *The Grey Album* "may be unexpected and unusual, old news to some and completely illegal, it is an exceptional example of what hip-hop today should be"[83]—apparently, what hip-hop should be is intertwined with the Beatles, one of the whitest bands ever. This valuation of whiteness thus works in tandem with the devaluation of Blackness to circumscribe acceptable mash-ups.

It is in this context that accusations of mash-up as unoriginal copying take on new meaning. A perceived lack of musical creativity often underlies criticism of mash-up, as in: "(Are you beginning to notice a trend with these leech-the-Beatles projects?) Beatallica features the predictable choking-Rottweiler vocals and Beavis-and-Butt-headian guitars."[84] To critics, mash-up artists are not only "leeches" but not even musically interesting because they are "predictable." Similarly, one article was not impressed with what it termed Black Violin's "monotonous brew."[85] These mash-ups are the same, and not in a good way. At times, mash-ups are seen as not doing anything more than creating versions of what already exists, a claim apparent even beyond hip-hop based mash-ups. Of "Miami Beach Rhumba," one commentator says "It's basically a klezmer riff."[86] Another describes a key figure in Jewish-Latine fusion music as having "specialized in Latinizing standards,"[87] positioning his changes as more garnish than recipe. Similarly, Black Violin is described as producing "a hip-hop adaptation of Bach's 'Brandenburg' Concerto No. 3"[88] and having "composed a version of Vivaldi's 'Spring' for the HBO show 'Ballers.'"[89] Adaptations and versions are not the stuff of musical genius that arises in other discussions of mash-up, or indeed even in other discussions of these same artists. Perhaps most damning are the comments that treat mash-up as conceptually repetitive. One article directly declares mash-up unoriginal, saying, "It's not the most original conceit: blending rappers with the Beatles."[90] Similarly, some "wonder if the formula of mashing rappers over pop and indie-rock tracks is wearing thin."[91] Mash-up is allegedly formulaic. Hence, one story contended, "This mash-up shtick has gotten out of hand."[92] Mash-up is a shtick; it's a gimmick; it's not substantive, this argument says.

This combination of mash-up as tending to exist on a Black/white binary, as invoking negative stereotypes about Black people, and as unoriginal moves it into the formation legal scholar Anjali Vats describes as "copyright thuggery," a trope that "weaponize[s] familiar racial scripts of Black men as dangerous, deviant criminals" in a copyright context.[93] As Vats describes, copyright thuggery has been attached to sampling from early in its history; "an early copyright-infringement case involving sampling, Grand Upright Music, showed the tendency of courts to presume criminality and bad intent on the part of Black artists, in a way that they rarely did when considering white infringers."[94] The case, over Biz Markie's sample of Gilbert O'Sullivan's "Alone Again (Naturally)" (1972) in his "Alone Again" (1991), established a notion that using pieces of existing music taken directly from recordings is fundamentally illegitimate; in "a now infamous appeal to the seventh Commandment,"[95] the judge's ruling declared, "Thou shalt not steal."[96] Moreover, as Vats notes, the verdict included "unprecedented recommendations of criminal prosecution in addition to customary civil penalties."[97] Similarly, a 2005 court case, *Bridgeport v. Dimension Films*, "infamously declared, 'Get a license or do not sample'" in response to an N.W.A. song.[98] This decision said that any sampling, no matter how small, was infringing, not fair use. In such ways, the roots of sampling in the Black musical form of hip-hop combine with the broader cultural criminalization of Black people to construct sampling as always and inevitably theft, by the transitive property.

If mash-up's tendency to engage with hip-hop imports negative beliefs about sampling as copyright thuggery, sampling also positions the form of the mash-up as more culturally Black than other types of transformative musical works. That is, race doesn't just shape the constituent parts of mash-up but the form itself. This cultural Blackness of mash-up is why the exceptions to the Black/white binary come from figurative mash-ups— things like the Latine/Jewish albums and *CMT Crossroads*. Mash-ups that are literally combining songs tend toward combining music from white and Black artists. In this way, the content and the form are both more aligned with Black cultural practices than other transformative musical works are. As literary scholar Henry Louis Gates notes in the introduction to the 2014 edition of his classic *The Signifying Monkey*, "jazz . . . is based on the art of riffing, on repetition and revision, the very definition of signifying on the tradition"; that is, jazz's formal properties of repetition with difference are an instance of the African American cultural practice of Signifying, and "through 'sampling' . . . , hip-hop took signifying to a new and electrifyingly original level."[99] As Gates explains, Signifying "depends for its effects on troping, it is often characterized by pastiche, and, most crucially, it turns on repetition of formal structures and their differences."[100] Repetition with difference is what sampling in the hip-hop tradition enables, and becomes part of mash-up as well through its use of sampling—indeed, repetition with difference is precisely the discursive space the mash-up inhabits. Mash-up is not, itself, Signifying, but it structurally resembles it enough to pick up some of its cultural connotations, especially when it already relies heavily on both sampling and Black artists' music. In such ways, then, negative reception of mash-up cannot be understood without taking seriously the ways both its form and content draw on Black people's cultural practices—Signifying and hip-hop—in such a way that racist beliefs stick to mash-up.

MANAGING MASH-UP:
FIGURATIVE MASH-UPS, LABOR, AND THE MELTING POT

It is in this context that it matters particularly much that mash-up is a recontextualization of hip-hop turntable practices, done largely by white artists, that often combines music across racial lines. Mash-up has properties that derive from Black people's cultural forms, and I argue that the distinctive features of the discourse of mash-up are about managing the dissonance of largely white mash-up artists using Black people's sounds and a Black cultural form. This management happens in three ways: moving away from literal mash-up, emphasizing labor, and employing melting pot logics.

The first management strategy is expanding the concept of mash-up beyond hip-hop and its links to Signifying. In press coverage overall, 67% of the mentions were about figurative mash-ups, compared to 33% for the literal mixing of different songs. Indeed, the extent to which "mash-up" refers to either or both of these forms shifted over the period examined here. Early on, a majority of the instances are literal mash-ups (between

56% and 62% of instances in 2009, 2010, and 2011); in 2014–2018, by contrast, the instances are 82%–100% figurative each year, with 2012–2013 as a transitional period. The temporal distribution also suggests moving away from mash-ups as a music trend combining two or more distinct songs at the same time that the framework that combining different things, particularly in music, is a "mash-up" became routine in culture.[101]

In looking at figurative mash-ups, it is clear that they keep only some parts of what mash-ups are overall: mash-ups that do not literally combine two or more songs do still combine different genres. I push the boundaries of the term here in response to one or more articles explicitly calling such musical combinations "mash-ups," which was how I identified these instances. In this vein, there is a discussion of "the Yiddish or Jewish mambo, a mash-up of Jewish folk songs, Yiddish tunes and klezmer melodies with the Latin rhythms that took American ballrooms by storm in the 1940s and '50s."[102] However, the term also circulates beyond musical contexts. This usage gives us a discussion of "movie, literary, TV and music mash-ups like movie Shaun of the Dead and Girl Talk music remixes that blend genres."[103] In this story, from the transitional period when figurative uses of mash-up began to predominate, mash-up is used for any genre blurring. In the clearest example of how mash-up took on a life of its own, scientists are described as having "achieved something unprecedented in the history of DNA. Going beyond remixing the DNA music, they mashed it up with an alien beat. It was the genetic equivalent of Danger Mouse's 'Grey Album.'"[104] By this point, mash-up exists fully as a cultural logic, available to use metaphorically to explain less familiar things. In such ways, figurative mash-ups demonstrate the construction that mixing different sources, especially in music, is "mash-up," disarticulating it from hip-hop and Signifying.

The second way of managing mash-up is getting it out from under copyright thuggery by emphasizing labor. That is, as Vats explains, "racial scripts" assert that "Black people lack the creativity, work ethic, and intelligence to imagine in a manner consistent with copyright law,"[105] but I find that this stereotype is evaded through framing mash-up as work. The idea of sampling as lazy is overdetermined; in addition to racist scripts about Black creators, Rose points out that, "Prior to rap music's redefinition of the role samplers play in musical creativity, samplers were used almost exclusively as time- and moneysaving devices for producers, engineers, and composers."[106] That is, sampling *was* a shortcut and not a creative choice—until it wasn't. This idea that drawing on previous work is lazy recurs repeatedly over time; the Ninth Circuit ruled in *Fisher v. Dees* (1986) that musical reuse is not fair use if "the composers' purpose was simply to reap the advantages of a well-known tune and short-cut the rigors of composing original music."[107] While it's unlikely this is a source known to any of the journalists writing about mash-up, the underlying logic that it is only legitimate to leverage someone else's work if you do work of your own is a clear thread in the discourse around mash-up. As a simple example, a news story about *DJ Hero* emphasizes that "you are actively blending two songs together to create something new";[108] the weight of that "actively" is that the game won't mash the songs up for you, so you better work.

Sometimes discussion of mash-up goes further to frame it as labor-intensive. In one article, Girl Talk (Gregg Gillis) was quoted as saying: "The process I use for making music is pretty meticulous. I work for eight hours on this small bite that maybe will be used nowhere or maybe a 30-second moment on an album somewhere."[109] That he would put in so much work for 30 seconds—and, implicitly, *per* 30 seconds—frames Girl Talk as hard-working. Such labor is a consistent trope about Gillis in particular, an instance of which in a description of one of his live shows is worth quoting at length:

> Eight or 10 loops were going on his laptop's screen all at once, all of them on mute until he clicked them on—sampled melodies, a cappella raps, amorphous sounds, "pace keepers" (breaths, pants, "heys," "yos"). Unless, like Gillis, you somehow have all of this memorized, you won't know until you click on a loop where it will be in its cycle—beginning, middle or end. He had to account for the lag time between when he clicked the mouse and when the sound actually cut in. If he missed even slightly with a loop of rap, for example, the loop might be 64 beats long—which could be almost a minute of music—and for that minute all his rhythms would be misaligned. Triggering samples requires dexterity; three in a row is a feat. He could just let his laptop do the work, and 99 percent of his audience would never hear the difference. Gillis says he would hear the difference.[110]

This description highlights the complexity, expertise, and work ethic that goes into mash-up. Girl Talk explicitly insists on doing the more labor-intensive thing because of his own standards. This story goes on to detail how Gillis wears "a sweatband" to perform, and "wrapped athletic bandages carefully around both of his feet: for the next 70 minutes on stage, he would dance so hard that he would be sick to his stomach afterward, like a marathon runner," again emphasizing that this music-making is hard work. As historian David Roediger has argued, the historical invention of whiteness came out of a move to "displace anxieties within the white population onto blacks." Particularly, slurs used against whites perceived as lazy became ways of stereotyping people of African descent. This construction allowed the lack of work ethic these insults implied to be constructed as a Black trait, a constitutive Other to a whiteness correspondingly defined as hardworking.[111] The discourse of mash-up thus substitutes the hardworking white artist for the lazy Black sampler. A key part of discursively framing mash-up as legitimate and worthy is therefore explaining the level of labor involved. These questions of labor can then map onto longstanding stereotypes.

The third way of managing mash-up in popular discourse, particularly when the divergent musical sources come from artists with different racial or cultural identities, is to invoke American melting pot logics that say racism can be solved by different groups coming together—logics which elide the structural domination that produces race as a meaningful category in the first place. This is to say that close attention to the racial structures of mash-up shows that the trope of "transcending difference into something new" rests on a suppression of racial power dynamics. The seams start to show when people protest a little too much about how there are no seams. This structure includes explicit invocations—and refusals—of racial and ethnic difference. Black Violin's Kev Marcus explicitly says "It doesn't matter if you're black, white, purple or green. You can be 5 or 95."[112] While deploying the classic colorblind tactic of invoking fictitious races to elide real racial dynamics is surely a savvy and even necessary branding strategy for Black Violin, it still plucks a discordant note in the "combining things works so well" song. The desire to suppress race as a site of conflict may be prudent, and it's not at all hard to see why Black Violin might, mere weeks after Donald Trump's inauguration as president, say that "The platform of music is universal for bringing people together. It's even more so important now,"[113] but it still acts to suppress how difference actually culturally works. Such optimistic takes are common, with the curator of an exhibit "exploring American Jewish life in the post–World War II suburban boom through vintage recordings" arguing that *Bagels and Bongos* "tells us the boundaries between communities were porous, and traditions were mixed and matched and borrowed."[114] Ultimately, the narrative is that "the cultural ravine is rarely as wide as it looks,"[115] kumbaya.

Through expanding mash-up beyond Black cultural practices of hip-hop and sampling, emphasizing constructed-as-white labor, and treating race as a source of pleasurable difference rather than a system of oppression, mash-up is articulated to whiteness. But didn't I just say it was Blacker than other transformative musical works? Mash-up is both more closely aligned with Black cultural practices than other transformative musical works are and less aligned with them than hip-hop is. As Sinnreich argues, "mash-ups tend to follow a more traditional European structural logic, while hip-hop and turntablism tend to follow a more traditional Afro-diasporic structural logic. In a word, mash-ups are coded as 'white,' while hip-hop is coded as 'black,'" and indeed "today's mash-up and techno musicians are overwhelmingly white."[116] Danger Mouse, as a Black DJ, is of course an important exception, but by the 2009–2018 period, mash-up's racialization had shifted. Its proximity to whiteness can be seen in praise for a Girl Talk concert, where the story says he "managed to turn a computerized performance into something that must feel almost exactly like playing rock 'n' roll in the ordinary way."[117] That is, a guy with a boatload of samples, many of them from hip-hop, gets mapped onto the white-coded genre of rock, not any kind of sample-based music, recapitulating the racialization of mash-up as white.[118]

This whitening of mash-up thus helps explain why mash-ups, which at least echo, if not originate in, hip-hop practices and which use the same digital technology to recontextualize existing pieces of music in new songs as hip-hop samples—and, indeed, are texts in which the recombination is often the only change made, unlike common transformational practices in hip-hop—have not been subject to the same legal scrutiny. For the most part, there haven't been lawsuits over them. Of course, for creators without deep-pocketed record labels behind them, legality tends to be decided de facto as a retreat in the face of a cease-and-desist letter rather than through winning a lawsuit. Thus, Beastie Boys/Beatles mash-up *Ill Submarine* was "pulled down, reportedly after threats from the Recording Industry Association of America."[119] And of course, EMI hit Danger Mouse with a cease and desist that succeeded in stopping his own distribution—though not channels such as the guerrilla action Grey Tuesday:

Hundreds of Web sites had announced that they would post the album on "Grey Tuesday," February 24, 2004, as a gesture of protest against a copyright system that fails to acknowledge the importance of mixing and sampling to musical creation. The [cease and desist] letters demanded not only that The Grey Album not be distributed but that recipients identify "any third parties" who had supplied them with copies, provide an accounting of "all units of the Grey Album that have been distributed via your website," and "make payment to Capitol in an amount to be discussed." Danger Mouse himself, Brian Burton, had agreed to Capitol's demands, and so did some recipients of the threatening letters. But DownhillBattle.org, coordinator of Grey Tuesday, reported that "for 24 hours, over 170 sites made the album available in protest, defying legal threats."[120]

In addition to this mass disobedience in support of *The Grey Album*, media studies scholar Steve Collins points out that the fact that there are so many mash-ups in general shows that the cultural sense of what's acceptable exceeds the letter of the law.[121] *The Grey Album*, obviously, is a glaring one of the exceptions to tolerance of mash-ups, but Grey Tuesday exactly demonstrates Collins's point that there are extralegal norms of fair use.

As *The Grey Album* example suggests, legal action is unevenly distributed. For Girl Talk, though multiple websites posted lists of every sample on one of his albums, he "has never been sued. No one has ever asked him to stop doing what he's doing"; in fact, "One of the acts he samples on [one of his albums], the Toadies, proudly put a link to Girl Talk on their home page."[122] This outcome is a sharp contrast to techniques used by some hip-hop producers to prevent lawsuits by disguising their samples through taking very short sections, rearranging parts, or other electronic transformations. This incident suggests, again, how mash-up is culturally whiter than hip-hop sampling and manages to evade the association with copyright thuggery that has led to lawsuits in hip-hop. While McLeod and DiCola argue that the best-case scenario for mash-ups is to be an ignored noncommercial musical form,[123] mash-ups may not persist as a rebellion but may be absorbed into the industry. Some mash-ups, like 2004 Jay-Z/Linkin Park project *Collision Course* and 2007 album *Mashed*, are even official media industry products. I contend that this pattern has everything to do with how mash-up is recuperated into whiteness and its cultural Blackness is managed. Much as historian Eric Lott argues about blackface minstrelsy, mash-up demonstrates that popular discourse is "far from unenthusiastic about black cultural practices or, conversely, untroubled by them."[124] Sampling as the auratic invocation of a source, but a repetition with difference, is desirable; its associations with copyright thuggery and hip-hop and sampling are not. These associations then need to be managed.

A WHOLE NEW WORLD: MASH-UP'S PROMISE OF TRANSCENDENCE

In the end, managing the discomfort around mash-up works; despite occasional detractors and by dint of some heroic racial repression, mash-up is culturally understood as an almost utopian form. Discussions of mash-up with clear value judgments range from majority positive to overwhelmingly so; 68% of figurative mash-up instances were treated positively (18% negative, 14% ambivalent), and 88% of literal mash-ups were treated positively (9% negative, 3% ambivalent). However partial the positive assessment may be, it does rest on specific pillars: mash-up is seen as good because it is seen as transformative, revolutionary, and creating something new that transcends its consistent parts, and indeed "new" is the seventh most common word in the corpus, thus indicating how mash-up's positive position is enabled by normative framings that create ties to Romantic authorship. Mash-up, news stories argue, is able to "impress music fans who have heard it all before."[125] This capacity comes because it's new—these are new songs[126] and new sounds[127] created out of old music. Thus, the executive director of one local performing arts center lauds Black Violin for "reimagining pieces" of music.[128] "Reimagine" is joined by a constellation of related terms: reinvent, rework, and perhaps most important from the legal perspective, transform. One discussion of a Beatles/Beastie Boys mash-up uses several of them, telling us that the artist "doesn't merely match key and pitch, but massively reworks both the original Beatles tracks and the Beastie Boys' verbal delivery," which, the article argues, "proves how well-suited the Beatles' music is for co-opting and transforming" and demonstrates "John, Paul, MCA, George, King Ad Rock, Mike D and Ringo to be an utterly convincing supergroup."[129] Another cluster of transcendent discourse centers around the idea of mash-up as "groundbreaking."[130] In this orbit is the intense response of one DJ to the artist who first inspired him: "This guy was amazing. I literally say that day changed my life."[131] Once you encounter mash-up at its best, that is, your world will never be the same.

Another major utopian theme is that in mash-up two and two make five, or even more. A mash-up isn't just its constituent parts, but different, and particularly greater. Thus, there is discussion of "a musical form all its own: the Yiddish or Jewish mambo."[132] Similarly, "Black Violin is neither hip-hop nor classical: it's both."[133] Thus, mash-ups at their best aren't simply "Latine + Jewish" or "hip-hop + classical," but their own thing, both things at once and then some. This idea that mash-up constitutes a new concept comes through as well in one club owner's recounting of the history of the form; once his club had introduced "the West Coast style of hip-hop mixed with rock 'n' roll . . . , every other venue bit that formula. And now all the venues today still use that formula."[134] That is, while mash-up may be routine now, this is the result of the change it has wrought in music. Though in this particular case he clearly wants to glorify his own club, a broader idea comes through that this is a distinct form that has produced a new musical landscape. Through stories like these, it's clear that sometimes a mash-up reaches the level of a "masterpiece"[135] that's greater than the sum of its parts.[136] As one story put it, "If they do this right, it's almost like an M. C. Escher painting: Do the steps go up or down? They fit together magically."[137] Indeed, sometimes mash-up is held up not as the new of now but the coming "future."[138]

While there is much to critique in papering over hard questions in mash-up with utopian rhetoric, mash-ups can in fact be a site of resistance to power. As one article notes, "In America we were taught that Yiddish died out in the '40s and the '50s. . . . But there was still a record-buying market for pop classics translated into Yiddish."[139] Here, mash-ups—of pop with Yiddish—help preserve cultural identity under the pressure to assimilate. Mash-ups can also be a site of interethnic solidarity: "Latins and Jews have 'an affinity' for each other with the whole idea of 'a shtetl/ghetto culture.'"[140] The shared experience of marginalization, that is, generated these mash-ups. Another article puts a finer point on the role of dominant whiteness as what's being resisted through orientation to other marginalized groups: "It wasn't just about becoming a suburban white American. It was also about learning to dance mambo and maybe speak a little Spanish."[141] This cross-cultural engagement is like what postcolonial theorist Homi Bhabha calls hybridity in a colonial context, "a problematic of colonial representation and individuation that reverses the effects of the colonialist disavowal, so that other 'denied' knowledges enter upon the dominant discourse and estrange the basis of its authority—its rules of recognition."[142] Through these forms of mash-up where whiteness is not a pole, the dominance and authority of whiteness is contested. In the end, while mash-up has a great deal of internal variety—literal and figurative, more and less creative, overtly or subtly racialized—the overall arc of its narrative is toward something new and better.

CHAPTER 4

Fight for Your Right to Parody

Parodies and the Cultural Politics of Kindness

His brand of parody is generally considered legally safe under the First Amendment's free speech protections and "fair use" interpretations of U.S. copyright law, but Yankovic still prefers to work with the permission of the artists whose songs he tweaks. That's meant that he has skipped Paul McCartney, Prince and Eminem, all of whom declined to give permission when he approached them with parody ideas.[1]

As the epigraph begins to suggest, parody songs are profoundly shaped by a tension between the law and popular perceptions about what is acceptable. Occupying this space is one key way parody differs from other kinds of transformative musical work. In this chapter I focus specifically on popular music parody, which music scholar Sharon Hochhauser traces to 1959:

> most often credited with starting this trend is Tom Lehrer's "The Elements," in which the periodic table is sung to the tune of Gilbert and Sullivan's "I Am the Very Model of a Modern Major General." The form found further support in Frank Jacob's 1970 book *Sing Along with Mad Magazine*, which contained such songs as "Blue Cross," in which the lyrics to Irving Berlin's "Blue Skies" are modified to poke fun at the health insurance industry.[2]

I examine the 11 instances of parody in my data set to understand how legal questions shape popular understandings of parody, in conversation with social beliefs about what makes a parody good. Overall, I find that the difference between the law and popular perceptions is perhaps wider with parody than anywhere else, and that popular acceptability, uniquely among the genres this book examines, includes additional requirements the law does not consider.

Here, I begin with two examples—an old media story of working within the system, and a story steeped in Silicon Valley's ethos of asking forgiveness rather than permission—that illustrate some of the foundational tensions in parody as a kind of transformative musical work. I then work through how key court cases have defined—and justified—parody, demonstrating their reliance on a notion of parody as a critical reworking. When examining which parodies are deemed good in popular discourse, by contrast, I find that unexpected versions of songs can be classified as creative, but the content should be different, not the sound; that there is a significant emphasis on humor not present in the letter of the law; and that popular assessments don't draw the parody/satire distinction courts do, but, diverging from the legal model of parody as critique, do care about a distinctively colorblind notion of kindness. Ultimately, while popular discourse explicitly flags parodies' respect for the source song and legal discourse emphasizes criticism, both center parody's relationship to the source text to discursively manage its position toward the socially contested side of the transformative musical work spectrum.

POLITELY REQUESTING PERMISSION: "WEIRD AL" YANKOVIC AND THE PROFESSIONAL PARODIST

The most famous musical parodist of the past half century, or maybe ever, is "Weird Al" Yankovic. Since the late 1970s—his first hit was "My Bologna," a parody of The Knack's "My Sharona," in 1979—when his music was broadcast on *The Dr. Demento Show*, a nationally syndicated radio show devoted to novelty records, Yankovic has made a successful career of parodying other people's songs. This position as a traditional media industry success profoundly shapes his parodies, from getting permission to situating himself in traditional models of music production and distribution even as digital distribution has become more prevalent.

Both the press and Yankovic himself assert the legal legitimacy of his songs in varying ways. At times, the framing is that his work is legal because of freedom of speech, as in: "Under our freedom of speech, I don't really need permission to do these parodies, but out of respect for the artists, I won't do one without permission."[3] However, free speech and copyright aren't exactly related. While legal scholar Wendy Gordon argues that intellectual property law should include free speech protection, she acknowledges that judges in intellectual property cases haven't tended to do so.[4] That is, while copyright law perhaps *should*—logically or morally—consider freedom of speech, there is no legal requirement to, and in practice it tends not to. Generally, the pressure valve on copyright is not the First Amendment, but fair use, and at other times, Yankovic references this justification instead, with one article noting that "he suspects his parodies would be protected under fair-use rules."[5] As I'll show, Yankovic is likely right in his interpretation of the law. Interestingly, despite proclamations that he has a right to parody (however it happens to be justified), typically the immediate next statement is, as in the above examples, that Yankovic gets permission anyway. Thus, the usual framing plays it both ways—Yankovic gets credit for his respect for other artists and their wishes even as he insists he has no legal need to do so.

However, in one high-profile incident during the period this book examines, Yankovic departed significantly from his typical approach, saying, "I did it anyway, and she saw it and loved it, so I got her blessing."[6] The song was Yankovic's 2011 "Perform This Way" parody of Lady Gaga's "Born This Way" (2011), and a fuller account tells the story somewhat differently: Yankovic first sent in a "short description of the song's conceit" for approval, only to need to quickly write and submit the full lyrics, only to be told he needed to send the "finished track."[7] In this version, recording his parody without permission was not ignoring a refusal, but part of the process of trying to get approval. However, when the song was then rejected, Yankovic didn't meekly accept it the way he is sometimes portrayed as responding to denials, either. Instead, the story goes, he took to the internet to complain, and only after this complaint gained traction (in part because "Yankovic's Twitter and YouTube fans yelled about the perceived snub across the cyber-universe") was the request approved, allegedly because initially Gaga's "management refused permission" and she "had never even been told he wanted to cover her song."[8] The shifting explanations—from only recording with permission to doing it anyway, from ignoring a refusal to routing around obstinate gatekeepers to get to the true approval behind them—produce different understandings of Yankovic. What's consistent across them is a sense of him as an underdog, at the mercy of more powerful media figures. However, the "Gaga Saga," as his complaining blog post called it,[9] did somewhat tarnish his "nice guy" image. Thus, as one story notes, "Mr. Yankovic seemed somewhat chagrined by this incident one month later and said any causticity in his blog post came from fear that his work on 'Perform This Way' would be wasted."[10]

This story of struggles to get permission contrasts interestingly with an incident 15 years earlier. In 1996, rapper Coolio was famously "not OK with" Yankovic's "Amish Paradise" parody of his song "Gangsta's Paradise," famously made without permission.[11] While Yankovic insisted that the conflict with Coolio was "the result of a major miscommunication," as an executive from Yankovic's label had "bumped into Coolio at a party and reported back that the rapper was OK with the idea" when he wasn't, the fact is that the song wasn't then withdrawn, which a practice of not doing parodies without permission would suggest it should have been. Here again, much like the Gaga example, Yankovic was not quite as nice as his reputation: he "sent him a humble letter of apology" but also said "I think he'll eventually be fine," expecting Coolio to get over it.[12] Nevertheless, as these two instances already begin to suggest, the question of niceness is key to popular perceptions of parodies.

Of course, regardless of how he positions himself, Yankovic's permission-seeking is quite practical. It is, as one article notes, "partly to avoid lawsuits and partly to work out royalty arrangements. (Mr. Yankovic said the original artists retain their publishing rights on his parodies, while he splits songwriting credit with them.)"[13] That is, while Yankovic has a good chance of winning a copyright lawsuit with a fair use defense, it would be prohibitively expensive to litigate a suit every single time he writes a song. Instead, it's easier to work with the source artist. Otherwise, without a fair use declaration, a parody would be a(n infringing) derivative work and not copyrightable in its own right. In that Yankovic makes parodies for a living, and did so under a traditional record contract for most of his career, there's little chance he would release music without such a license. These negotiated agreements therefore protect his parodies not as freedom of expression, but as a business venture.

Moreover, artists are often happy to be parodied. First, like cover songs and remixes, parodies can drive interest in the source, producing a benefit to the parodied artist. Second, they're often thought of as a mark of success—being famous enough to parody means you've arrived. Certainly, this is a common story about 1992 parody "Smells Like Nirvana": "as legend has it, frontman Kurt Cobain didn't actually realize he'd 'made it' until Yankovic lovingly satirized their biggest hit."[14] The sentiment was echoed more recently by the manager of rapper T.I., parodied by Yankovic in 2008: "This dude did Michael Jackson, and now he's asking to do you? ... For sure, it was definitely a validation and a certification you have a real hit."[15] Moreover, the compatibility with the industry is increased by the fact that, "while Yankovic sometimes aims his sights directly at an artist . . . , a majority of his parodies play with the song structure, rhyme scheme, and singing style of the original artist while covering a different comedic premise."[16] That lack of artist mockery, as I'll show, is also an important factor in parody acceptability.

This friendly stance toward the people he parodies corresponds to Yankovic's participation in the mainstream music industry. Unlike many other parodists, he has released full albums of songs, complete with promotional cycles and music videos. However, by the point this book examines, his strategies were shifting. For Yankovic's 2014 *Mandatory Fun* album, "he launched a full-scale assault online, debuting a new music video for a song from the album every day leading up to its release on popular comedy sites like 'Nerdist' and 'Funny or Die.' It worked: the videos racked up a combined 20 million views during the week, and 'Mandatory Fun' sold 104,000 copies during its first week."[17] Another story put the emphasis a bit differently: "Rather than releasing a single to radio, Yankovich [*sic*] bombarded the Internet with one video a day for eight straight days and allowed social media to handle the rest."[18] If the first description positions Yankovic as a planning mastermind (and while both rely on curiously militaristic metaphors), the second story's invocation of letting social media handle the promotion gestures toward seeing such platforms and their users as places to extract what I have elsewhere called "promotional labor."[19] In this way, rather than using the old, expensive promotional apparatus, music can spread person to person. Yankovic specifically uses the term viral: "I thought that because of people's short attention span on the internet, the best way to do that would be to do a world premiere video every single day because it seemed like the cycle of a viral video is roughly 24 hours."[20] Though media scholars Henry Jenkins, Sam Ford, and Joshua Green are deeply, and rightly, critical of the idea of virality because it frames people as being passively infected and ignores the role of human agency in sharing culture,[21] the obfuscating work that "virality" does as a concept is often exactly the point—it produces a notion of automatic promotion and distribution without human intervention, actively hiding the (exploited) labor involved.

Yankovic turns out to have been right about the power of internet video, and the strategy resulted in his first #1 album, which was also "the first comedy album to hit number one since Allan Sherman's 'My Son the Nut,' did it in 1963."[22] Thus, not only did the strategy produce results, but better results than any other time in Yankovic's career—or anybody else's in more than half a century. Moreover, this increased success came at a more challenging time:

> To some, the news that this is Weird Al's first No. 1 album may come as a surprise. He has sold over 12 million records in the US, and has definitely been more of a culturally relevant name at other stages in his career. His most fertile ground was arguably in the 80s and 90s, when a few megastars dominated the pop culture landscape and songs on the radio were well-known by a wider group of Americans.[23]

Without that shared cultural landscape, Yankovic's job is much harder than it used to be, making *Mandatory Fun*'s success all the more impressive. Importantly, despite departing from traditional promotion, Yankovic sought (and achieved) mainstream music industry success, which is central to his work.

This music industry insider position means Yankovic's approach to changing technology is quite different than, say, the cover artists discussed in chapter 1. Indeed, he frames YouTube as a threat. In one article, he complained:

> It is getting a little bit harder in terms of the parodies, because there are so many people doing parodies now on YouTube and various other places that it's difficult to come up with an original idea, or a unique idea. . . . I mean, I don't think I'll be the first person, or certainly not the only person, to ever do a parody of any given song, and it's just difficult to not be perceived as dated when my parodies come out now, because everything is so immediate.[24]

Part of this complaint is about the traditional release schedule that one article called "downright glacial."[25] But there's also a hint of frustration at the sheer volume of competition enabled by internet distribution. Social media in general is constructed as threatening in these sources, with Yankovic saying: "I got dragged onto social media almost against my will just because it started out with me trying to fight against the people that were basically committing identity theft. . . . There were people originally on MySpace and later on Facebook and Twitter that were claiming to be me, which obviously upset me."[26]

While this theme of the internet as threatening might seem that it should be chalked up to the generation gap or baby boomers' fear of technology, I'd argue that it is more significantly shaped by Yankovic's status as not only the most famous parodist but financially unique: comedy radio host Dr. Demento pointed out that "In terms of someone who's consistently making money at it, Al is pretty much it."[27] This position thus conditions his conservatism toward these alternative forms of distribution. Overall, then, the single most important characteristic of Yankovic's work is how he operates within the mainstream music industry—perhaps at odds with those who refuse his parody requests, but generally in compliance with, and leveraging, the legal and industrial systems at play in order to legitimate his parodies.

GOLDIEBLOX AND THE THREE BEASTIES, OR MOVE FAST AND VIOLATE COPYRIGHT

Toy company GoldieBlox, by contrast, were less widely beloved parodists. In 2013, they released a video advertisement that reworked the Beastie Boys' classic 1986 song "Girls." In it, three girls reject narrow gendered toy options, instead engineering a Rube Goldberg machine out of typically feminine toys, "set to alternative lyrics that, unlike the original message of the song, promote girls as intelligent and capable":[28] "Girls to build a spaceship / Girls to code the new app / Girls to grow up knowing / That they can engineer that." That is, unlike many of Yankovic's parodies, GoldieBlox performed the kind of criticism of the source song usually attributed to parody, flipping the script from "Girls, to do the dishes / Girls, to clean up my room / Girls, to do the laundry" to support girls in STEM. As the company's founder claimed, "We wanted to take a song we weren't too proud of, and transform it into a powerful anthem for girls."[29] Thus, the company's official position was that it had "created its parody video specifically to comment on the Beastie Boys song, and to further the company's goal to break down gender stereotypes and to encourage young girls to engage in activities that challenge their intellect, particularly in the fields of science, technology, engineering and math."[30] This stance was in line with their broader brand identity as a company that makes engineering toys targeted to girls.

This much, everyone agrees on. But when the legal trouble around the song started, there was not a shared sense of what was happening. To their defenders, particularly those focusing on the message of the song and video, GoldieBlox were pro-girl transformative creators. The company's founder claimed that the "video was made with the best of intentions."[31] Similar to Yankovic, GoldieBlox both insisted on their right to parody and framed themselves as friendly toward, or at least considerate of, the parodied artists: their lawyer said that "although the video has been taken down and we would prefer an amicable resolution, we strongly believe that the parody constitutes fair use."[32] They were willing to play nice, that is, but not without continuing to assert the legitimacy of the parody. Once legal action was in motion, the company's founder published an open letter, which one article characterized as "GoldieBlox says it just wants to go back to business as usual":[33] "We don't want to spend our time fighting legal battles. We want to inspire the next generation. We want to be good role models. And we want to be your friends."[34] The letter also said that:

> we were completely unaware that the late, great Adam Yauch had requested in his will that the Beastie Boys songs never be used in advertising. Although we believe our parody video falls under fair use, we would like to respect his wishes and yours. Since actions speak louder than words, we have already removed the song from our video. In addition, we are ready to stop the lawsuit as long as this means we will no longer be under threat from your legal team.

This statement does several things. First, it frames the video's removal as both respect for Yauch's wishes and a goodwill gesture, while continuing to assert the right to parody. It also somewhat misrepresents the legal situation, framing themselves as "under threat" from Beastie lawyers while glossing over the fact that GoldieBlox filed a preemptive suit. Ultimately, the feminist message inclined many people to support the video (and GoldieBlox), even under the shadow of copyright infringement, interpreting the company as the underdog who only sued to protect themselves from beastly Beasties and their lawyers.

Others saw things differently. As one story notes, though many loved the video, GoldieBlox "seemed to lose some of that love when news of the lawsuit came out. Some have called the company 'entitled.' Did the company react too quickly? Or is it reacting to the criticism that's being hurled at it?"[35] Despite the attempt by GoldieBlox's PR team to deemphasize the preemptive lawsuit, that is, some found the aggressive legal stance off-putting, undermining the goodwill the company had garnered through the parody's message. Additionally, the Beastie Boys published their own open letter, arguing that: "As creative as it is, make no mistake, your video is an advertisement that is designed to sell a product, and long ago, we made a conscious decision not to permit our music and/or name to be used in product ads. . . . When we tried to simply ask how and why our song 'Girls' had been used in your ad without our permission, YOU sued US."[36] Here, the Beastie Boys walk a similar line as GoldieBlox themselves—they express appreciation in order to temper the fact that they reject the parody because it is an advertisement. The implication is that, had someone simply parodied the song without embedding it in an ad, the band would have had no objection. The response also highlights that the Beastie Boys did not initiate the legal fight. Instead, GoldieBlox filed a complaint for declaratory judgment to have the song deemed non-infringing (as Robin Thicke had done with "Blurred Lines" earlier that year, which I'll discuss in chapter 5). Thus, it mattered that, as one expert interviewed in a news story noted, "They may be commenting on the misogynistic lyrics of the Beastie Boys, but in doing that, clearly their motive is to sell their own toys."[37]

Indeed, there was a broader question about the parody's intent: were GoldieBlox cynical opportunists trading on the familiarity of "Girls" or hoping for attention-generating controversy, or were they sincerely communicating a message with the cognitive dissonance of the new lyrics against the sexist original? As one article pointed out, "Given the speed with which the GoldieBlox complaint appeared, indeed, it's reasonable to assume that they had it in their back pocket all along, ready to whip out the minute anybody from the Beastie Boys, or their record label, so much as inquired about what was going on."[38] The perception that they were trigger-happy on the lawsuit—whether planned from the beginning or just a quick reaction, makes GoldieBlox seem much more opportunistic and the "just pro-girl" reading harder to sustain. As one article framed the situation, "GoldieBlox neither sought nor received permission to create these videos: it never licensed the music it used from the artists who wrote it. That wouldn't be the Silicon Valley way. First you make your own rules—and then, if anybody tries to slap you down, you don't apologize, you fight."[39] GoldieBlox, this interpretation says, is more like Uber or Airbnb—flouting laws that it finds inconvenient using its venture capital–backed deep pockets—than it is like Weird Al's earnest reputation.[40] Certainly, this argument that "GoldieBlox's conduct has been intentional and will-ful" was also made by lawyers for the Beasties: "GoldieBlox has engaged in the systematic infringement of intellectual property from numerous popular music groups, including Beastie Boys . . . Queen, Daft Punk," and more.[41] This accusation that GoldieBlox are serial infringers underscores how important the context of a parody is for its reception.

Another important factor in interpreting the GoldieBlox dustup is how one understands the Beasties. As one article framed the situation, "Over a music career of more than 25 years, the Beastie Boys evolved from a goofy rap trio to a conscientious band with more nuanced positions on politics and art"; this statement then puts them in a different position in relation to "a company that feels just as strongly about its own socially aware messag-ing," assuming that's what GoldieBlox sincerely is.[42] The Beastie Boys who in the 1990s organized the Tibetan Freedom Concerts,[43] spoke out against anti-Muslim bias,[44] and advocated for an end to sexual violence against women at concerts[45] are a quite different opposing force than the lyrics of "Girls" alone would suggest. As one story puts it, "the Beastie Boys them-selves long-ago eschewed the sort of beer-swilling sexism of their debut album, and became advocates for women amidst a general hip-hop climate of misogyny."[46]

The Beasties' own feminist inclinations were on display in their open letter: "Like many of the millions of people who have seen your toy com-mercial 'GoldieBlox, Rube Goldberg & the Beastie Boys,' we were very impressed by the creativity and the message behind your ad. We strongly support empowering young girls, breaking down gender stereotypes and igniting a passion for technology and engineering," they said, before going on to object to their music being used in an advertisement.[47] In this context, the argument from the Beasties' countersuit that "Beastie Boys Parties have suffered and will continue to suffer injury" and "are entitled to recover from GoldieBlox . . . the gains, profits, and advantages GoldieBlox has obtained as a result of the wrongful conduct" seems much more legitimate.[48]

On the other hand, forbidding the use of their music was a bit ironic given the Beasties' own extensive history of building on other artists' music through sampling. In fact, 1989 Beastie Boys album *Paul's Boutique* has so many samples that Kembrew McLeod and Peter DiCola estimate that, were they all licensed using standard terms, "The Beastie Boys would lose an estimated $7.87 per copy sold," because they would have had to license "more royalties and more publishing than the amount that they would receive" from each sale.[49] However, McLeod and DiCola note that, "despite the fact that the group is known for sampling and even though the Beastie Boys themselves have had to scrap tracks because of uncleared samples (AC/DC and the Beatles have both denied them permission), the group sees no contradiction in the way they police their own work."[50] This willingness to appropriate from others thus exists in tension with refusing to allow appropriation from their own songs—though the advertisement function of the GoldieBlox parody certainly differentiates the two forms of reuse.

In the end, GoldieBlox backed down, agreeing to a settlement requiring: "(a) the issuance of an apology by GoldieBlox, which will be posted on GoldieBlox's website, and (b) a payment by GoldieBlox, based on a percentage of its revenues, to one or more charities selected by Beastie Boys that support science, technology, engineering and mathematics education for girls."[51] Overall, this incident shows that the social meaning of a transformative musical work depends less on things like "the purpose and character of the use, including whether such use is of a commercial nature or is for nonprofit educational purposes; the nature of the copyrighted work; the amount and substantiality of the portion used in relation to the copyrighted work as a whole; and the effect of the use upon the potential market for or value of the copyrighted work"[52]—the enumerated criteria of fair use—than on popular assessments of who's doing what to whom. To know what to make of the GoldieBlox song, that is, it mattered whether they were earnest supporters of girls or cynical Silicon Valley opportunists. It mattered whether the song was a critique of a sexist record or an attempt at free-riding on a well-known tune. And it mattered whether the Beastie Boys were sexists or conscientious artists.

The uncertainty about the song's nature is also reflected in shifting terminology about it. The song is usually framed as "parody" (50 instances), but some also refer to it as a "spoof" (18 instances) or "satire" (one instance). These terms are similar, but not interchangeable. The *Oxford English Dictionary* defines parody as "modelled on and imitating another work, esp. a composition in which the characteristic style and themes of a particular author or genre are satirized by being applied to inappropriate or unlikely subjects, or are otherwise exaggerated for comic effect."[53] The emphasis is on imitation of a source text with a comedic twist. By contrast, a spoof "satirizes a particular genre," not an individual work.[54] A satire "uses humour, irony, exaggeration, or ridicule to expose and criticize prevailing immorality or foolishness, esp. as a form of social or political commentary."[55] GoldieBlox argued they had made a parody, because, as I'll show next, that tends to be the better legal argument, but the song is probably better classified as a satire criticizing gender constructs, despite this term being least used in popular discourse around the song. Nevertheless, the shifting terminology underscores how the song produced such wildly divergent responses: people's interpretation depended on what was happening, which wasn't clear. Ultimately, the moral of GoldieBlox and the three Beasties is that parody is both a defense against claims of copyright infringement under the fair use umbrella and a cultural/political vehicle for meaning—and the two may have little to do with each other, complicating questions of legitimacy.

THE FAIREST OF USE? LEGAL APPROACHES TO PARODY

By contrast to these forms of contestation in popular discourse, in legal conversations, parody is often treated as one of the paradigmatic examples—if not *the* paradigmatic example—of transformative work. Parody has routinely been included in illustrative lists of types of transformative work ever since judge Pierre Leval initially formulated the concept, saying: "Transformative uses may include criticizing the quoted work, exposing the character of the original author, proving a fact, or summarizing an idea argued in the original in order to defend or rebut it. They may also include parody, symbolism, aesthetic declarations, and innumerable other uses."[56] Leval's model was later cited by the U.S. Supreme Court in taking up the idea of the "transformative work" into the law in *Campbell v. Acuff-Rose* (1994), a case about a 2 Live Crew's (1989) "Pretty Woman" parody of Roy Orbison's (1964) "Oh, Pretty Woman" that cemented the link of transformative reuse and parody. In *Campbell*, the Court said, "parody has an obvious claim to transformative value."[57] The connection of parody and transformation has repeatedly been identified by courts, with the Ninth Circuit later adding that "a parody's aim is, by nature, to transform an earlier work."[58] More specifically, the Second Circuit had previously contended that "parody and satire are valued forms of criticism, encouraged because this sort of criticism itself fosters the creativity protected by the copyright law."[59] That is, not only does parody often not violate copyright, but in fact supports its goals. Certainly, seeing parody as particularly exemplary of transformative works, and therefore particularly likely to be fair use, is a pattern that holds at scale. Legal scholar Neil Weinstock Netanel analyzed court cases from 1995–2010 that engaged the concept of "transformative use" and concluded that a fair use determination was statistically significantly more likely when courts found the use of intellectual property was "for purposes of parody, criticizing the author, biography, history, general social and political criticism, litigation, or intermediate copying."[60]

This robust connection of parody to fair use happens despite the fact that parody is not one of the enumerated examples of fair use in Section 107 of the U.S. Copyright Code, which legislatively established fair use in 1976—"for purposes such as criticism, comment, news reporting, teaching (including multiple copies for classroom use), scholarship, or research";[61] however, criticism *is* one of the examples, and parody is tightly connected with criticism in the legal conversation. In fact, parody is linked to both of the common meanings of criticism, as a synonym for analysis and as a synonym for disapproval, which are often conflated. At times, the former meaning comes to the fore, as in: "Parody is regarded as a form of social and literary criticism, having a socially significant value as free speech under the First Amendment."[62] However, elsewhere critique is differentiated from general commentary: "A parody is a work that seeks to comment upon or criticize another work by appropriating elements of the original."[63] This slippage of parody and the disapproving kind of criticism may be due in part to the fact that, as Gordon notes, critical speech is particularly important to protect, as "a paradigm instance of when we do *not* want a speaker to obtain a copyright owner's permission is when the speaker's use will be critical of the copyrighted work."[64] Additionally, being critical, or mocking, helps ensure that the new work is using the source text for a different "purpose and character" than the source, one of the essential markers of a fair use.[65] However, one unintended consequence of this conflation is that, as legal scholar Rebecca Tushnet points out, it becomes challenging to argue for fair use without a negative stance toward the source text.[66]

One reason for the assumption that parody's criticism is disapproval is that legally, parody is protected specifically as commentary on the source text. In *Campbell*, the Supreme Court explicitly linked parody to commenting on the source song: "While we might not assign a high rank to the parodic element here, we think it fair to say that 2 Live Crew's song reasonably could be perceived as commenting on the original or criticizing it, to some degree. . . . [Its] words can be taken as a comment on the naivete of the original of an earlier day."[67] As noted in *Rogers v. Koons*, "the copied work must be, at least in part, an object of the parody, otherwise there would be no need to conjure up the original work."[68] This is the distinction between parody and satire, in which "Parody needs to mimic an original to make its point, and so has some claim to use the creation of its victim's (or collective victims') imagination, whereas satire can stand on its own two feet and so requires justification for the very act of borrowing."[69] Satire, as comment on something else entirely, does not have this additional likelihood of its reuse of a text being fair use. Thus, if the source text is definitionally the object of commentary in a parody, it's easy to see how, with the addition of a model of critique as disapproval, this view slides into seeing the source text as the target of attack.

One important kind of commentary or criticism is the idea of parody as talking back to a cultural object, particularly an influential one. This construction was established early on in *Elsmere v. NBC* (1980) as an especially important feature of parody: "Just as imitation may be the sincerest form of flattery, parody is an acknowledgment of the importance of the thing parodied."[70] Power differentials are often important to this understanding of how parody critiques. Of Alice Randall's 2001 novel *The Wind Done Gone*, a parody of Margaret Mitchell's 1936 novel *Gone with the Wind*, the Second Circuit found that: "Randall's work flips GWTW's traditional race roles, portrays powerful whites as stupid or feckless, and generally sets out to demystify GWTW and strip the romanticism from Mitchell's specific account of this period of our history,"[71] and these aspects were essential to finding the novel to be a parody and fair use. This instance really is critique as disapproval. As Gordon argues, "Randall's novel seeks to undermine and parody Margaret Mitchell's *Gone with the Wind* through use of Mitchell's own characters. Randall in a recent interview made clear that *Gone with the Wind* had injured her, and many other African-Americans."[72] It is through parody, that is, that cultural institutions as powerful as *Gone with the Wind* can be turned back upon themselves—and, in this instance, their harmful racial politics can be contested. In such ways, as legal scholar Madhavi Sunder notes, "individuals express themselves through critique, comment, or parody of cultural authorities, all the while seeking to represent themselves within a culture that had previously overlooked, or even worse, oppressed them."[73]

However, at the same time as there is emphasis on being critical as negative and disapproving, there is a recurring slippage in another direction, to the commonsense notion of parody as funny. In *Campbell*, the Court said, "Parody's humor, or in any event its comment, necessarily springs from recognizable allusion to its object through distorted imitation. Its art lies in the tension between a known original and its parodic twin."[74] This comment's framing begins with the popular understanding of parody as humorous, and then corrects to the actually protected category of commentary. Later, the opinion makes a stronger argument for humor by saying that "It is this joinder of reference and ridicule that marks off the author's choice of parody from the other types of comment and criticism that traditionally have had a claim to fair use protection as transformative works."[75] Here, ridicule is declared essential to the category of parody. In the earlier case *Elsmere v. NBC*, there was a similar default to assuming humor in parodies as part of making an unrelated argument (about the amount and substantiality of use): "a parody frequently needs to be more than a fleeting evocation of an original in order to make its humorous point."[76]

This seeming contradiction of negativity and humor can perhaps be explained by the way the courts make sense of the fourth factor of fair use, "effect of the use upon the potential market for or value of the copyrighted work."[77] While common sense might assume that examining the effect on the market suggests commercial reuses of someone else's creative work are presumptively unfair, the market factor is actually parsed more finely. In *Campbell*, the Court said that "as to parody pure and simple, it is more likely that the new work will not affect the market for the original in a way cognizable under this factor, that is, by acting as a substitute for it."[78] In this way, the Court noted that what copyright prohibits is the creation of market substitutes. Parodies are therefore framed as outside of the market that is legally protected, as neither funny parodies nor critical ones compete in the same market as the source text. On one hand, as legal scholar Lydia Pallas Loren notes, creators aren't likely to produce or license work critical of their own works,[79] and a rightsholder could not reasonably expect to control such a market of derivative works.[80] On the other hand, while there are derivative markets rightsholders do control, parodies don't participate in them: in *Campbell*, the Court found "no evidence that a potential rap market was harmed in any way by 2 Live Crew's parody, rap version."[81] Moreover, if parody suppresses demand for a product, that is not sufficient to prove market harm either: "when a lethal parody, like a scathing theater review, kills demand for the original, it does not produce a harm cognizable under the Copyright Act."[82] Making fun of something and thus changing popular opinion for the negative is not the same as serving as a market substitute. Overall, then, parodies are, while not presumptively legal, well-positioned in copyright law to be found fair use, particularly as criticism of their source texts, suggesting a high degree of legal legitimacy tied to a negative relationship to the source.

TICKLING FUNNY BONES AND DOING RIGHT BY SOURCE ARTISTS: DEFINING GOOD PARODIES

However, analysis of press discourse shows that, in the popular conversation, social assessments of parody often diverge significantly from—and take precedence over—legal ones. Accordingly, it's important to ask: What is it that makes a parody "good" in popular discourse? One key aspect of positively received parodies is fidelity to the original. Late night host Jimmy Fallon's musical parodies in particular are often positively described as "dead-on"[83] or that he is "transforming into"[84] the parodied artists, or even with statements like: "We still think that was the real Neil Young on stage with Bruce Springsteen."[85] The exactitude of Fallon's re-creations is routinely emphasized in positive commentary. Related to this praise, commentators approve of how Fallon "plays it straight (the key ingredient why these music parodies work so well),"[86] signaling the kind of earnestness also valued about Yankovic. On the other hand, lack of fidelity makes a bad parody, as when one of Yankovic's songs, "which sounds more like Linkin Park than it does intended target Imagine Dragons," is dubbed "the worst" of that particular album.[87] Similarly, musical skill is important, as when one article says of Yankovic that "people generally walk away from his live shows impressed with not only the humor, but the high level of musicianship."[88] Parodies, that is, should not only do the source song correctly, but with skill.

However, this drive to sameness contrasts with a tendency to value parodies that are unexpected. Thus, parodies described in positive terms are also often, perhaps counterintuitively, characterized using words like "bizarre."[89] Often, a parody—like a mash-up—is enjoyable because it's unlikely: "Where else are you going to hear [Neil] Young (or a believable facsimile) singing the immortal line, 'Smell you later,'" one story asks of

Fallon as Young singing the *Fresh Prince of Bel Air* theme song.[90] There's also a sense that unexpectedness is where creativity or cleverness come in, as in terming Fallon's parodies "Brilliant. Absurd. Zany. Stupid. Good-natured. And very, very likable"[91] or calling Yankovic's album "quite smart."[92] Fidelity and creative change are in tension with parody similarly to cover songs, but here the balance point is clearer: unexpected versions of songs can be creative, but it should be the content that differs. The sound should remain the same. As communication scholar Matthew McKeague notes, "One tactic Yankovic uses is increasing the tempo of a song he is parodying and changing the key, if necessary, to fit within his vocal range or in an attempt to make the song sound funnier overall. Otherwise, the music is intended to sound as close to the original as possible."[93] The exception to this pattern is when parodies are intentionally bad, as in "A hilariously horrible rendition of 4 Non Blondes' 'What's Up.'"[94]

While, strictly speaking, the law does not require parody to be funny, humor is nevertheless often invoked in the popular conversation, much as this supposedly irrelevant factor crops up in legal discussions themselves. At times parody and comedy are treated as interchangeable, as in a discussion of one artist: "Sometimes called the Weird Al Yankovic of country music, Georgia native [Cledus T.] Judd is known for his parodies of popular country music songs as well as original comic tunes."[95] This statement implies that the parodies and the originals are both subsets of the category "comic tunes." Similarly, a positive description of another parody says that "the song is very funny and captured the intensity of the moment."[96] Thus, being funny is an assumed part of a parody, particularly a good one.

Despite how central parodying specific songs is to fair use, this connection does not often appear in the press data. Instead, much of the conversation is about using songs to parody their source *artists*. Thus, one story says of Yankovic that "the accordion-wielding, ultra-prolific satire champ has mercilessly subjected every major pop artist of the last 25 years to his incorrigible, hilarious lyrical rewrites."[97] The target is the artist, which muddies the definition of parody. Similarly, beyond a specific artist, Yankovic is described as having "gone to great lengths to make sure pop music takes itself a little less seriously" with his parodies.[98] This statement operates at a broader level, but is still framed as musical commentary on music and so reasonably close to the formal definition of parody. However, using a song to comment on society in a satire, targeting something other than its source, is (as noted above) not a strong argument for fair use, and some, if not many, parodies—especially Yankovic's—fall into this category, as with "'Mission Statement,' which satirizes ornate and ultimately hollow corporate speak."[99] However, as I have already shown, the legal categories and distinctions are often not reflected in popular discourse; parody and satire tend to be treated interchangeably, as are targeting the song, the artist, or society.

This is not to say that the target doesn't matter in the popular conversation. Indeed, a frequent question in assessing parody's legitimacy is whether it is kind or meanspirited. The phrase "at the expense of" tends to carry much of the weight in these conversations, though it is not used consistently. Sometimes, it is used to insist on a parody's good nature, as in one story's report that, "As for mocking the stars, Yankovic sees it more as a flattering 'having fun at their expense. It's all in good fun.'"[100] Here the argument is that it's just "fun," not mockery. At other times, the phrase signals something to avoid, as when one article's praise notes that "Fallon is not goofing on the artist and the laughs are not at the expense of the artist."[101] Despite the apparent contradiction, the point is the same: mocking the artist is frowned upon. This value judgment stands in opposition to the legal position, which is unconcerned with the parody target's feelings, which musicologist David Sanjek describes in the context of *Campbell v. Acuff-Rose* as "no writer wants a parody or some 'version' thereof to dismiss her or his efforts, yet whatever discomfort that person might feel is not sufficient grounds for infringement."[102]

However, it's only partially true that Fallon doesn't make fun of the artists he parodies. Certainly, he is not making fun of Neil Young, Bob Dylan, David Bowie, or even often-mocked Michael McDonald when he faithfully imitates their distinctive styles. Nevertheless, Fallon's parodies engage with more than one artist, singing a song from one artist in the immediately recognizable style of another. Such songs resemble what Hochhauser calls the *reflexive parody*, in which the humor comes from "covers of popular songs performed in a seemingly incongruous style and presented through a third-party fictional character."[103] In particular, many of the source songs in Fallon's parodies that receive press coverage are both on the frivolous side and originally sung by Black artists—Will Smith's corny *Fresh Prince of Bel Air* theme song, his daughter Willow's "Whip My Hair," or "Pants on the Ground" from the *American Idol* audition of "Atlanta civil rights veteran 'General' Larry Platt."[104] Part of the humor of these parodies is putting a goofy song into the mouth of a more respected musician, as when "Fallon (as Young) transforms Willow Smith's pleasant pop trifle into a hippie protest song, with a totally game Springsteen growling, 'You got to whip your hair' and adding a 'Badlands'-inspired 'whoa, whoa, whoa' refrain to the chorus."[105] It's funny because Springsteen and Young would never sing something so banal. They're not the butt of the joke, but then-ten-year-old Willow Smith may well be. This incident then strikes a discordant note in the otherwise consistent pattern of valuing parody as kind.

This juxtaposition gives these parodies a flavor of minstrel show; while there's no blackface, the idea of Black people as inherently unserious and indeed laughable persists as an undertone. As historian Eric Lott notes in his foundational history of blackface minstrelsy, "minstrel performers often attempted to express through ridicule the real interest in black cultural practices they nonetheless betrayed—minstrelsy's mixed erotic economy in celebration and exploitation," or "love and theft."[106] Enjoying these songs and finding them fun can therefore coexist easily alongside mocking them and their artists. This pattern then casts the 1996 Weird Al-Coolio incident in another light; much like emphasizing the silliness of Will or Willow Smith, Yankovic parodying Coolio's famous sticking up braids on his album cover, and doing so with the title *Bad Hair Day*, similarly treats Black people's practices as laughable. Moreover, evacuating "Gangsta's Paradise" of its racially specific description of the struggle with gang violence has an additional valence. There's nothing funny about what Coolio is describing, which treating anything and everything as fair game for parody elides. As humor scholar Raúl Pérez notes in his study of racist humor, comedians and joke books "have been increasingly marketed as 'equal opportunity offenders' who target 'everyone' since the civil rights era, which has allowed humorists to circumvent accusations of racism while making use of racist discourse."[107] While superficially, Fallon and Yankovic make fun of "everybody equally," the origins of such justifications in excusing racist humor and their performances' echo of minstrel mockery hollows out the kindness that is seen as characteristic of their public personas.

In fact, it suggests a model of kindness as colorblindness, in which politeness matters more than justice. These parodies are certainly not meanspirited, but by glossing over racial power dynamics, they reproduce them; as sociologist Eduardo Bonilla-Silva points out, arguments that race does not matter are part of colorblind racism, as "the elimination of race from above without changing the material conditions that makes [sic] race a socially real category would just add another layer of defense to white supremacy."[108] Acting as if race is not a system of power doesn't make it true, and Fallon's and Yankovic's nice guy images don't mean they're not white men mocking songs by Black people. Overall, when examining parodies deemed good, unexpected versions of songs can be seen as creative, but the content should be different, not the sound; there is significant emphasis on humor; and popular assessments don't draw the parody/satire distinction the courts tend to, but do care about a colorblind notion of kindness that elides the racial dynamics of mockery.

CONCLUSION

Ultimately, what's distinctive about parody as a kind of transformative musical work is the discursive emphasis on the relationship to the source song. For these songs, popular discussions stress not only fidelity, but respect or even kindness, from Jimmy Fallon's Neil Young impression to GoldieBlox professing their love of the Beastie Boys. This focus on being nice diverges significantly from the law's tendency to construct parody as criticism. Parody is thus the place where the legal and popular constructions of acceptability are most polarized. However, in both of these models, the works' transformativeness is at the forefront, whether because they are framed as a commentary on the source song or because they are notably funny. These constructions can be understood as ways of managing parody's departure from the ideal of the Romantic author—there is no denying a parody draws heavily on an existing text, so framing *how* it draws on that text is evidently key to its legitimacy. The relationship to the source text as a means of social acceptability is, as legal scholar Anjali Vats argues, a trap: in cases like *Campbell* and *Suntrust*, the Court created "a rule of parody that functionally ghettoized Black creatorship instead of marking it as original in its own right. Put differently, the rules of copyright infringement remained prefigured in a manner that privileged particularly white and Euro-American norms of 'originality' with little space for fair use, at the expense of people of color."[109] By reinforcing a notion of a clear distinction of an original and a parody, other forms of reworking, such as those arising from African Diaspora practices like Signifying,[110] are delegitimized. Although popular discussions draw rather different distinctions about "good parody," they share this relational model of approval.

Feels like the First Time

The Politics and Poetics of Similarity in Soundalikes

It comes right down to knowing the difference between being inspired and stealing. Why would I want to, or have to, steal from anybody to make my music? Inspiration can be subliminal. As a songwriter, you're obviously trying to create a brand-new feeling that comes from your heart. But you can't help but be inspired by all of the greatness that came before you. In popular music, you know, there's only so many chords being used. On the Internet, there's this thing where this band plays the same four chords, and they do 75 hit songs with the same four chords in the exact same pattern. That just shows you some of the limitations in popular music.

—ROBIN THICKE[1]

Recent years have seen several controversies over songs perceived as sounding like other songs. Unlike the other kinds of transformative musical works discussed in this book, the "soundalike song" isn't a category in the law, in routine music industry practice, or even in everyday speech, but I construct it here because it usefully groups a series of instances where someone notices a commonality between different songs.[2] The soundalike is thus similar to what musicologist J. Peter Burkholder describes as "paraphrasing an existing tune to form a new melody, theme, or motive."[3] Creating the "soundalike" category enables us to recognize common structures at work in such instances: while some of these songs result in copyright infringement lawsuits, others are discussed in terms of plagiarism, and still others are waved off as coincidental, all of them raise questions about the distinction between influence and copying, the role of artistic intent, and the limits of the law.

Here, I explore the 13 instances in my data set of the most contested kind of musical transformative work: the soundalike song. I find that, when examining what constitutes similarity in soundalikes, songs can be compared to specific other songs, to artists, or to whole genres, but the most emphasis is on melody, and there's tension between thinking of soundalikes as infringement or something more like plagiarism. Lawsuits over soundalikes, and in particular that around 2013 Robin Thicke hit "Blurred Lines," show that what legal decisions might find infringing—intangibles like "feel"—differs from what the law formally protects—what can be written in sheet music; this disconnect results in extending protection in ways that make artists nervous about future production of music. Moreover, cultural commonsense around soundalikes can't be understood without considering power dynamics of race and gender, as both popular perceptions and verdicts are ultimately deeply shaped by who did what to whom, whether they're supposed to or not. Ultimately, I argue, soundalike songs show how the music industry's own actions have produced outcomes it now finds threatening.

THE SOUND OF SIMILARITY: SOUNDALIKE SONGS, GOOD AND BAD

What, then, is a soundalike song? In the press coverage, specific musical aspects of songs I'm calling soundalikes are only sometimes mentioned, but when they are, the most frequently mentioned site of similarity to source songs is melody/ies (6.59% of quotations), which is joined by "chord" (4.4%), note/s (4.4%), riff/s (3.3%), and "licks" (1.1%) in a grouping relating to commonalities of specific notes in a particular arrangement (19.78% overall). Other terms relating to musical composition are the "pace," "cadence," or "rhythm" (1.1% of quotations each; 3.3% in total). There are also less-tangible forms of similarity in "vibe" (1.1% of quotations) or "feel" (5.49%), and even quite generic terms like "elements" (4.4%) or just sound/s (6.59%). In a typical instance, Robin Thicke argued of Sam Smith's "Stay with Me" (2014) compared to Tom Petty's "I Won't Back Down" (1989) that it was "the same notes, on the same timing, in the same rhythm. The two songs are exactly the same."[4] Similarly, one article discussing several soundalike songs contends that, "Before Radiohead was at the forefront of edgy and experimental alternative rock, the band was known for writing mopey songs, like 'Creep.' Many noticed that the [Radiohead] single borrowed chord progressions and melodies from the Hollies' 'The Air That I Breathe.'"[5] Those arguing for similarity typically aren't trained musicologists; some of them are professional musicians being interviewed (or testifying in court cases), but most are journalists, and many are not even music journalists. Thus, these judgments usefully speak to quotidian understandings of similarity in music—what's most recognizable is melodic similarity, and other kinds of comparison get fuzzy in a hurry.

Alongside these differing ways songs are seen as resembling each other, there are different understandings of what it means, normatively, for songs to be similar. Some positive assessments argue that the music industry "has always made room for pastiche, homage and creative cannibalization of the musical past," putting soundalike songs into that tradition.[6] As this example begins to suggest, there are different relationships of soundalikes to previous music. When two specific songs are seen as similar, one common framing is that the second artist is "inspired" (10.99% of quotations, in various forms of "inspire"). This is the framing Thicke uses, defensively, when asked about "Blurred Lines" and its resemblance to Marvin Gaye's 1977 song "Got to Give It Up" (which sparked a lawsuit I'll discuss later): "I know the difference between inspiration and theft. I'm constantly inspired, but I would never steal. And neither would [song cowriter] Pharrell."[7] Songs are also described as "erected in the image of"[8] or "an homage to"[9] their forebears. These examples demonstrate how such songs can be seen as transformative musical works that incorporate, but also build from, what came before.

Some songs are described as sounding like another artist rather than a specific song. Country singer Jason Aldean, one story commented, "sounded like a collision between classic rock and contemporary country" in concert, noting in particular that "there were echoes of classic rock: Bon Jovi on 'Relentless,' Tom Petty on 'Wide Open' and AC/DC on 'She's Country.'"[10] These framings move away from some of the one-to-one song correspondences that tend to generate lawsuits, instead operating more like lines of musical descent. Of an earlier Robin Thicke album, one article says:

Mr. Thicke, 34, wears his classic-soul literacy like a merit badge, offering loose, untroubled emulations of Marvin Gaye ("I Don't Know How It Feels to Be U"); Otis Redding ("Angel on Each Arm"); Stevie Wonder ("Lovely Lady"); and even Prince, in vintage slow-jam mode ("Mission"). The allusions have as much to do with background color as with the timbre and style of the vocals.[11]

This kind of soundalike is emulation, allusion, or style—and seen as deserving at least merit-badge respect. A similar kind of soundalike resembles a genre. The period this book examines included a revival of 1970s-type sounds, leading to comparing contemporary pop songs to genres from that era. Thus, of 2013 Daft Punk hit "Get Lucky," one article notes that it "reinforces a recent Top 40 trend of hit songs that mine the sounds of 1970s disco and R&B, among them Justin Timberlake's 'Suit & Tie' and Robin Thicke's 'Blurred Lines.'"[12] Similarly, another story put Mark Ronson's 2015 hit "Uptown Funk" in the context of "the current retro-'70s funk-soul trend, forged by songs from Justin Timberlake's 'Suit & Tie' to a host of singles shaped by Pharrell."[13] In such instances, the soundalike participates in what Burkholder calls "stylistic allusion, alluding not to a specific work but to a general style or type of music."[14]

In soundalike songs that reference artists or genres, there is a consistent generation and status gap—the earlier music is nearly always framed as "classic." Accordingly, in positive interpretations, sounding like such earlier music gets framed as respect or appreciation for important work from the past. It could be seen as a cynical ploy for Thicke to say that he credited Barry White on a post-lawsuit song because "I wanted to make sure I would never be in a difficult situation with one of my idols ever again,"[15] but his statement nevertheless participates in this discursive practice of overtly respecting musical forebears. This framing lets newer songs be constructed as descending from revered musical ancestors, which is sometimes reinforced by the language used. One article described a 2014 documentary about funk music as:

> a long-overdue tribute to a musical seed that continues to grow, flowering most recently in Daft Punk's Get Lucky, produced by none other than [legendary funk and disco artist and producer] Nile Rodgers. "Funk never died, it's just evolved," [journalist-turned-filmmaker Nelson] George says. "It's not the mainstream music in America, but it informs most of our music. I'd argue that (Robin Thicke's) Blurred Lines is a distillation of funk."[16]

Here there are three different metaphors—a seed flowering, evolution, and distillation—and two of them are thoroughly organic and point to drawing on musical ancestors in ways framed as distinctly natural.

Soundalikes can also be defined by contrast to their nearest musical neighbors, samples and interpolations. Confusion between the soundalike and the sample came into play in relation to the "Blurred Lines" lawsuit, which initially also involved an argument about whether it infringed Funkadelic song "Sexy Ways" (1974); George Clinton took to Twitter to say there was "No sample of #Funkadelic's 'Sexy Ways' in @RobinThicke's 'Blurred Lines,'" adding that "We support @RobinThicke @Pharrell!"[17] The soundalike is collapsed into the sample even though the lawsuit was not about the use of the actual digital bits of previous recordings as samples, but rather the alleged replication of sounds. The long history of sampling disputes over Clinton's music, with suits brought by "sample troll" Bridgeport Music,[18] who holds the rights to much of his catalog, may be part of why the two are conflated here, but it also speaks to a more general kinship between these categories.

Soundalikes also, and perhaps more closely, resemble interpolations. In interpolation, artists record their own version of a musical composition so that they can entirely bypass (notoriously difficult and expensive) sample licensing; interpolations implicate only the copyright in the composition, not that of the sound recording. As legal scholar Robert Brauneis has pointed out in his analysis of "mirror covers"—which similarly reproduce sounds and engage only with the copyright on the composition—"Whether other elements, such as a singer's timing that anticipates or lags the beat, or the timbre of the singer's voice, or the choice of instrumentation, would also count as part of the musical work, is still open to question."[19] These aspects are frequently where the similarity of the soundalike comes into play, particularly alongside melodic similarity that may or may not exactly replicate a previous song. As Brauneis notes, legally, "the latitude to imitate [a song] through independent fixation is limited by what features of it count as parts of the musical work,"[20] and aspects of the track's "feel" generally don't. Since soundalikes are played by new musicians and produce a recording that resembles the previous one, they are very much like interpolations—except there's rarely the same intent to circumvent the copyright on the earlier song's master recording.

Nevertheless, soundalikes are at times treated as a subset of interpolations or samples. For example, when Smith's "Stay with Me" was nominated for a Grammy award, the Recording Academy clarified that the writers of "I Won't Back Down," who had been granted cowriter status to avoid a lawsuit, were not considered Grammy nominees but "would be given certificates to honor their participation in the work, just as any other writers of sampled or interpolated work."[21] This instance underscores the fact that the music business doesn't have a category for songs that end up sounding like other songs not by directly copying digital bits (samples) or replaying a section to avoid needing to copy those digital bits (interpolations), but by inspiration or happenstance.

Other understandings of soundalikes are much less positive. One constellation of terms for songs described negatively revolves around theft (9.89% of quotations, in total), with terms like rip off (4.4% of quotations), steal (3.3%), lift (1.1%), and pilfer (1.1%), as when Led Zeppelin was accused of having "ripped off a riff used in 'Stairway to Heaven.'"[22] The less accusatory version speaks of borrowing (5.49% of quotations), though sometimes the discussion is specifically about "unfair" borrowing. A second cluster of discourse frames soundalike songs in terms of copying (4.4% of quotations), which often means specifically *lesser* copies: the version, redo, or knockoff (1.1% each, for a total of 3.3% of quotations). In this vein, one story argues that "the Strokes all but Xeroxed the beginning of 'American Girl' [Tom Petty, 1976] for their breakthrough hit, 'Last Nite'" (2001).[23] In a milder version of this critique, there are ideas like having too much of an earlier song, sounding too close, or owing a debt (3.3% of all quotations).

Like positive-to-neutral discussions of soundalike songs, negative responses also construct them as drawing on earlier and more respected artists. In one particularly colorful example, an article compares "Uptown Funk" unfavorably to its contemporaries: "none of those songs milked the past as cynically as this. 'Uptown Funk' makes 'Blurred Lines' seem like a work of stunning originality.[*sic*] It isn't even a song. It's a vamp, in a style patented, and made deep, by James Brown."[24] This is an accusation of using the past excessively and insincerely; in particular, the allegedly inappropriate similarity is not just stylistic but a copy of the format, with a bonus metaphorical use of intellectual property terminology to describe styles highly associated with particular artists as "patented" by them. Using the frame of originality as this story does is recurring (5.49% of quotations), whether referring to its alleged absence in the second song or its presence in the first.

Further, there is slippage in soundalike songs between copyright infringement and plagiarism (3.3% of quotations). One article comments that, "While many of these plagiarism cases are very much malarkey (Does anyone really believe Tame Impala stole an obscure song from Argentina for 'Feels Like We Only Go Backwards'?), some actually have merit."[25] "Credit" (9.89% of quotations) is a key term in distinguishing appropriate from inappropriate musical similarity, as when one story notes that "On Tuesday, a federal jury in Los Angeles concluded that Robin Thicke and Pharrell Williams, the performer and primary songwriter-producer of the 2013 pop hit 'Blurred Lines,' committed copyright infringement by using elements of the 1977 Marvin Gaye song 'Got to Give It Up' in their composition without proper credit."[26]

Even when the term "plagiarism" is not directly used, that is, the idea that reuse of someone's work must be credited imports norms around plagiarism into a copyright context where, strictly speaking, they don't belong. This slippage reflects what legal scholar Rebecca Tushnet calls "the pervasive confusion of nonlawyers between copyright infringement and plagiarism."[27] Rather than credit itself, what actually matters in these incidents are the royalties that come with being recognized as a writer of a song, yet this concept appears less often than the "credit"-and-"plagiarism" cluster, with 5.49% of quotations mentioning royalties and 2.2% having compound mentions explicitly linking credit with royalties or payment. The idea that reuse relates to reproduction comes into play here as well; as McLeod and DiCola note, "the word plagiarism is derived from the Latin term for 'kidnapping,' which adds an interesting dimension to the parent-child authorial metaphor."[28] "Plagiarism" thus names impermissible travel of musical offspring. Ultimately, when examining what constitutes similarity in a soundalike, the most emphasis is on melody, but within this construction, songs can be compared to specific other songs, artists, or whole genres, and there's tension between thinking of soundalikes as theft or something more like plagiarism. The greater popular fuzziness around definitions of soundalikes compared to other transformative musical works is part of why interpretation of their legitimacy varies so widely—because there isn't a social category for them, the meaning is often in the eye of the beholder.

BLURRED CRIMES:
SOUNDALIKES BETWEEN LAW AND POPULAR PERCEPTION

Though infringement is, as discussed in the previous section, often collapsed into plagiarism, there are also instances where infringement is very much the framing—particularly, in lawsuits. In the period this book examines, two major cases generated a lot of press coverage. First, in August 2013, Robin Thicke, Pharrell Williams, who performs under the mononym Pharrell, and Clifford Harris Jr., better known as T.I., preemptively sued the estate of Marvin Gaye to try to have their song "Blurred Lines" declared not infringing of Gaye's "Got to Give It Up," claiming the Gaye estate had threatened a copyright infringement lawsuit. Second, in May 2014, the estate of the band Spirit's founder, Randy Wolfe, claimed that Led Zeppelin's "Stairway to Heaven" (1971) violated the copyright of "Taurus" (1968). In the overall data, 7.69% of quotations mention infringement, such as one article commenting of "Blurred Lines" that "'Got to Give It Up' was a clear inspiration for it, but were Mr. Thicke and his songwriting partners merely inspired by Gaye, or did they infringe on the copyright of the earlier song?"[29]

Press discussion is much more extensive for the "Blurred Lines" case, whether because it ran its course from filing to the Ninth Circuit's verdict on the appeal in the period this book covers or because it was a hot contemporary song; as a result, it will be my focus in this section with some selected examples from other cases.[30] The earliest published discussion of the song's similarity to Gaye's work came in response to a question about "the origin story behind your new single 'Blurred Lines.'" Thicke (now infamously) said, "Pharrell and I were in the studio and I told him that one of my favorite songs of all time was Marvin Gaye's 'Got to Give It Up.' I was like, 'Damn, we should make something like that, something with that groove.'"[31] Though Thicke later recanted this statement as part of strategically disclaiming any responsibility for the song, the dispute that followed fundamentally centered on what it meant to resemble a "groove." Ultimately, a federal jury decided it meant copyright infringement, awarding a judgment of $7.3 million.[32] The ensuing controversy over the verdict illuminates how similarity and acceptability are interpreted in soundalikes.

One thing the "Blurred Lines" lawsuit demonstrated was that the musical elements that U.S. law says are subject to copyright and the factors people use to assess similarity are poorly aligned. Legal scholars Kal Raustiala and Christopher Jon Sprigman argued in *Slate* that "the problem—and the reason the verdict in Blurred Lines is such a disaster—is that the jury appears to have been swayed by things that were not supposed to matter."[33] Strictly speaking, legal scholar Tim Wu noted in the *New Yorker*, "The question is not whether Pharrell borrowed from Gaye," because clearly he did, "but whether Gaye owned the thing that was borrowed," which Wu contends he did not.[34] In one of the more detailed comparisons of the two songs, one story ran through many of the soundalike criteria discussed earlier: "Yes, 'Blurred Lines' approximates the rhythm and timbre of 'Got to Give It Up,'" but, the article asks, "is that theft? Listen. Both songs have cowbell-ish percussion that plunkity-plunks at a similar tempo, but the patterns are different. Both songs have rich, teasing basslines, but the notes and rhythms of each are dissimilar."[35] The consensus from these commentators, then, is that, while there are definitely elements of the songs that are similar, the similarities are not of a sort that are managed by copyright.

This question of what is protected is the crux of the matter. Given the distinction the law makes between a composition copyright and a master recording copyright—and since soundalikes don't sample the recording—only the composition matters. Accordingly, what's legally protected is a subset of the popular criteria for similarity—just the melody and cadence, things that can be written in sheet music. This is also one reason it mattered that, during the "Taurus" case, Led Zeppelin guitarist Jimmy Page testified that he couldn't see similarities in the sheet music. Whether Page could actually interpret the music or not, the argument that the allegedly stolen elements can't be picked out in the sheet music was savvy, disclaiming both Page's knowledge of the previous song and the compositional identifiability of the alleged copying.[36]

If the only aspect of a song that can ever be relevant in a lawsuit over a soundalike is the composition, then the only thing that is protected about a song is which notes are played, in what cadence, not any of the more intangible or non-notatable aspects of the "feel" apparent in the recorded version. As Demers argues about cover songs, rightsholders "can prevent others only from imitating its melody and lyrics. Every other musical aspect specified in the piece can be copied by someone else, meaning that things like dynamics, timbre, articulation, and rhythm bear the legal status of ideas rather than expressions"[37]—and U.S. copyright protects expressions, not ideas. One article critiqued this legal principle and its application in the "Blurred Lines" case: "Owing to the specifics of copyright law, the jury was instructed to base its decision on the sheet music, a fact that reflects how inadequate copyright law is when it comes to contemporary songwriting and production practices."[38]

If, in positive discussions of soundalike songs, the framing is about intergenerational influence and respect, backlash to the "Blurred Lines" decision makes that relation antagonistic, framing newer artists as harmed by the more established. Indeed, the story that critiqued the lack of recognition for contemporary songwriters above goes on to frame Williams as the underdog whose work is not respected due to "bias": "Relying on the sheet music exposes a generational bias, too—implicit in the premise of the case is that Mr. Gaye's version of songwriting is somehow more serious than what Mr. Williams does, since it is the one that the law is designed to protect."[39] Of course, the law doesn't actually care about the process of songwriting the way this comment implies—whether a song is written and then played, or written at all, is irrelevant—rather, the issue is that only what *can* be written is protected, which protects Williams as much (or, crucially, as little) as Gaye.

Ultimately, the argument of those objecting to the "Blurred Lines" verdict is that "what the 'Blurred Lines' team copied is either not original or not relevant"[40]—but I disagree. By the letter of the law, no: rhythm, background noise, falsetto, funky bass, cowbell, or any of the other elements are not relevant, either because they're not original to Gaye, not copyrightable as part of a composition, or both. But these elements are relevant to how people understand music, including jurors and—as discussed in chapter 1 with *Supreme v. Decca*—judges.[41] Similarly, when one story critiques the "Blurred Lines" verdict because it shows that "copyright law may be of less use to modern songwriters and producers using cutting-edge methods" whose work doesn't correspond neatly to the legal contours of composition,[42] I'd actually argue that it demonstrates the opposite: those making legal decisions, at least the jurors in the Gaye/Thicke case, agree with this article about what deserves protection. The capital-L Platonic Ideal of the Law says one thing, but non-notatable aspects of a song's "feel" are clearly relevant to listeners, including jurors and judges, which makes these aspects carry legal weight whether they are supposed to or not. What the law says is not how people experience music, and neither is it how people hear similarity.

Indeed, I would argue that, while none of the individual elements are unique to Gaye, the combination of them is what makes "Got to Give It Up"—and also what makes "Blurred Lines." That's not something existing law can account for, but it is experientially true, which has to be taken seriously if for no other reason than that it affects verdicts. One article warns of the effect of the "Blurred Lines" precedent on "a creator like DJ Mustard, whose bailiwick is everything but the notes. Like him, whole generations of songwriters may remain vulnerable, their innovations implicitly less valuable because no one's figured out how to adequately write them down,"[43] but I'd say it's quite likely that DJ Mustard's intangibles would be protected just as much as Marvin Gaye's were, because it wasn't the sheet music that was relevant to the jury in the "Blurred Lines" case, even though it was supposed to be. Thus, the answer to Brauneis's rhetorical question—"How much of what is added to a previously notated song while making a sound recording of it counts as a copyright-protected musical work?"[44]—would seem, at least in this case, to be much or even all of it.

One of the major arguments against the "Blurred Lines" verdict is the potential for chilling effects on future music. In an interview four months after the decision, Thicke says: "if the verdict holds up, I believe that it will have a ripple effect on the arts and the industry in general. . . . I sure hope [the appeal] comes out a different way for Pharrell and me, and also for the future of creativity."[45] Of course, it's expected for someone appealing a verdict to hope it is overturned, and not surprising for that person to warn of dire consequences of the precedent, but concerns about the future of creativity and ripple effects across the arts were also shared by others. Indeed, in August 2016 a number of artists, including "members of Train, Linkin Park, Earth, Wind & Fire, the Black Crowes, Fall Out Boy, Tool and Tears for Fears as well as Rivers Cuomo of Weezer, John Oates of Hall & Oates, R. Kelly, Hans Zimmer, Jennifer Hudson, Jean Baptiste, Evan Bogart and Brian Burton (Danger Mouse)" filed an amicus brief in the "Blurred Lines" appeal to highlight the risk of the decision to benign influence or inspiration.[46] As Raustiala and Sprigman note, some worried the verdict "may end up cutting off a vital wellspring of creativity in music—that of making great new songs that pay homage to older classics."[47] This is, in essence, an argument that the "Blurred Lines" verdict makes people afraid that previously acceptable kinds of inspiration are now actionable infringement. Certainly, Burkholder has shown that various types of musical reuse are routine in the history of Western music; he delineates typologies that include "modeling a work on an existing one, assuming its structure, incorporating a small portion of its melodic material, or depending upon it as a model in some other way," "paraphrasing an existing tune to form a new melody, theme, countertheme, or principal motive," and "stylistic allusion, alluding not to a specific work but to a general style or type of music," all of which echo in the soundalike.[48] If these have historically been entirely reasonable ways to build from existing music, but now are considered copyright infringement, one can see why artists might be worried.

Thus, the verdict was framed as harming future music. As Raustiala and Sprigman contend, while basic fairness might dictate that Gaye's estate be compensated for his inspiration to "Blurred Lines,"

> Basic fairness is not the goal of our copyright system. The reason we have copyright—the reason we protect songs, books, and other creative works for the life of the author plus 70 more years—is to adequately incentivize artists to produce new creative works. Copyright, at bottom, is about ensuring the flow and growth of culture. We encourage new creations by making sure creators know they stand to reap the benefits.[49]

The assertion here is that the "Blurred Lines" decision harms not just Thicke, nor even other artists, but culture itself. This line of argument rests on the fact that the purpose of copyright in the U.S. Constitution is "To promote the Progress of Science and useful Arts, by securing for limited Times to Authors and Inventors the exclusive Right to their respective Writings and Discoveries."[50] The idea is that, because there is a state interest in promoting knowledge and art, the state grants short-term monopolies on otherwise uncontrollable expression to provide an incentive to create. From this perspective, newer artists who are inspired by existing copyrighted music lose their incentive to create if it will just generate a lawsuit anyway, resulting in fewer new works for the public that copyright law is supposed to serve.

However, the incentive model has not really motivated copyright for approximately half a century. Instead, the understanding is that creators are owed something—nearly indefinitely—for having created. This logic is most visible in the tying of copyright to the life of the author. From 1790 to 1976, copyright terms were a fixed length. This system operates under a logic of "make a thing and benefit, but then make something else to benefit again." Even a copyright term for the life of the author would potentially encourage—or at least enable—people to create new things for the rest of their lives. By contrast, extending copyright past the life of the author, as started with the Copyright Act of 1976 (life of the author plus 50 years) and continued with the Sonny Bono Copyright Term Extension Act of 1998 (life plus 70) shows that a framework of "what authors deserve" was, by that point, the norm. This logic is even more clearly visible in setting up separate, longer standards for corporate authors (120 years after creation or 95 years after publication), which ensures nothing more or less than that corporations get paid for the intellectual property they own. Some may find this system reasonable because what artists deserve is important, but it's not about encouraging creativity. It may continue to have that effect, but the basic orientation has changed.

In this new orientation toward ensuring people get paid for intellectual property they own, the casualty is culture, because old creativity becomes permanently locked down, never available to inspire new creation. As Raustiala and Sprigman argue, "the jury's verdict casts a huge shadow over musical creativity and takes what should be familiar elements of a genre, available to all, and privatizes them."[51] While I'm cautious about declaring bits of culture "available to all"—particularly things created by marginalized populations,[52] as I'll discuss further in the next section—privatization is definitely the name of the game. Ensuring the rightsholder gets paid is about safeguarding private property. It is not about serving the public through creativity, and therefore it is not what U.S. copyright law, in its inception, was for. It is therefore important to recognize that this is a beast of the music industry's (and other media industries') own making—in pushing for ever-expanding copyright to line their pockets with revenues, the music industry contributed to a notion of permanent control of creativity that is now coming home to roost. This is the context in which lawsuits over soundalikes, and in particular that around "Blurred Lines," show that what a legal decision might declare infringing—intangibles like "feel"—is often different from what the law formally protects, namely, what can be written in sheet music; this disconnect results in extending protection in ways that make some artists nervous about future production of music.

WHOSE FUNKY MUSIC, WHITE BOY?
RACE AND GENDER CONTESTATION IN SOUNDALIKES

The fact that people hear similarity between songs differently than the law defines it is one major factor in how soundalike songs are interpreted. However, people's sense of how things should work also comes into play with respect to the racial and gender politics of soundalikes—regardless of the law's ostensible silence on race and gender when it comes to copyright. This is to say that when examining popular sensemaking around soundalikes, who did what to whom matters a great deal.

One of the key issues in the "Blurred Lines" case—and looking back at earlier instances of soundalikes of Otis Redding, Stevie Wonder, etc., from Thicke—is that he has been "accused of appropriating black music."[53] Thicke is part of what anthropologist Maureen Mahon describes as a group of "white performers whose success was a result of their ability to mine African American traditions in a way that appealed to white audiences."[54] Scholars frequently talk about this mining of sound in terms of appropriation.[55] Cultural appropriation, as feminist theorist bell hooks explains, is a form of "consumption wherein whatever difference the Other inhabits is eradicated, via exchange, by a consumer cannibalism that not only displaces the Other but denies the significance of that Other's history through a process of decontextualization."[56] That is, a white person consumes the culture of the Other precisely for its "exotic" difference, but removes from the equation both the people the cultural object comes from and the reality of their experience that produced the culture in the first place. As Mahon explains, while "borrowing and mixing are normal aspects of musical development," a "dialectic of miscegenation and segregation surrounds the appropriation of black music by whites," as "white appropriation of black sound and style was devastating to many of the music's originators,"[57] because the financial and recognition benefits went to the white appropriators, not the originators. It isn't that there should never be cross-racial or cross-cultural musical influence—indeed, it would be impossible to prevent it—but historically it has tended to be appropriative in the context of music (as in so many others). Similarly, hip-hop scholar Tricia Rose points out that "Although the terms dilution and theft do not capture the complexity of cultural incorporation and syncretism, this interpretation has more than a grain of truth in it."[58] This is not borrowing and mixing on equitable terms.

These appropriative practices also have legal consequences. Musicologist Matthew Morrison notes that "Black performance practices, or the intellectual performance property of black people, have a history of being absorbed into popular entertainment, making them ineligible for copyright and available in the public domain."[59] Legal scholar K. J. Greene makes a similar point, saying, "Black musical production has been so foundational to American music that the work of Black innovators becomes a mere 'idea' not subject to copyright protection."[60] This pattern of absorption and imitation is thus appropriative not just in a general, cultural sense, but specifically in terms of intellectual property and its financial rewards. Greene makes an even stronger assertion, saying, "the fleecing of Black artists was the basis of the success of the American music industry."[61]

Though historically, cultural appropriation has been mainstream and uncontroversial, there is a growing awareness of its ethical problems. The long history of white people stealing Black people's music with impunity, from Elvis to the Rolling Stones to—in the words of *The Simpsons*—"Jimmy Page, one of the greatest thieves of American Black music to ever walk the Earth,"[62] is now increasingly seen as troubling, and this history hung over the "Blurred Lines" case. Awareness of the problems of cultural appropriation has also impacted subsequent cases like the lawsuit of Black rapper Flame against white pop singer Katy Perry, described as "a kind of culture-borrowing tax" for her foray into trap music.[63] Growing negative attitudes toward cultural appropriation therefore had much to do with the fact that the legal strategy in the "Blurred Lines" case was to put a lot of emphasis on Williams—a Black man—as the sole writer of the song. As one reporter noted when asking Thicke about it, "you testified that you were intoxicated at the time of those press interviews and that you misrepresented both the extent of your role in writing the song and the influence of 'Got to Give It Up' on the song."[64] This would ordinarily be a strange legal approach, as it undermines the credibility of the lead plaintiff in the lawsuit—but it makes a great deal of sense as an attempt to distance the song from that history of white people stealing Black music.

While much of the white appropriation of Black artists' music, especially early on, were the cover songs discussed in chapter 1, there was also more amorphous copying of sounds, and this copying is what contemporary soundalike songs often replicate. That is, rock music copying the sounds of the blues can be seen as, if not quite the origin of the soundalike song, a particularly well-known example of systemic, intentional production of soundalike songs, in ways that were at the very least unconcerned with exploitation of the source artists and genre. Morrison uses the term "Blacksound" to describe the ways "white (and other nonblack) people freely express themselves through the consumption and performance of commodified black aesthetics without carrying the burden of being black under white supremacist structures."[65] This is, precisely, cultural appropriation: valuing the culture and discarding the people and their experiences. Mahon argues that rock music "is rooted in black music traditions, drawing heavily on the musical and vocal inflections, linguistic choices, and body movements that characterize African American performance",[66] these roots also impact the soul and funk precursors picked up by songs like Thicke's. This sonic borrowing had even produced previous soundalike lawsuits, as "the black women's vocal sound that propelled girl group music was so ingrained in the mind of former Beatle George Harrison that he replicated it too faithfully on his 1970 release 'My Sweet Lord'; the writers of 'He's So Fine,' a hit for the Chiffons in 1963, successfully pressed their claim that he had plagiarized their song."[67]

The "Blurred Lines" verdict was thus often seen as reparative of that history of appropriation. In a basic sense, it was reparative in a way evocative of K. J. Greene's argument in favor of extending thinking about reparations beyond slavery or Jim Crow, the contexts where they are typically raised, to the theft of Black people's intellectual property; Greene argues that Black artists should be systematically compensated for the thefts embedded in record contracts, the negative impacts of low literacy on copyright registration, and lack of moral rights for sound recordings.[68] One article explicitly describes a popular perception of the verdict as a correction of past wrongs: "An entire generation of American bluesmen died before sniffing the monthly private helicopter fuel budget of the rock-and-rollers who ran off with their sound. Others have settled out of court. And that's one reason why a cheer went up on social media after Tuesday's verdict was announced. This time, the young cads didn't get away with it."[69] This history also had everything to do with why the "Blurred Lines" verdict "felt right" to people. Similar to the question of shifting the meaning of copyright discussed above, if past music industry practices hadn't been so egregious, the "Blurred Lines" infringement verdict may never have happened. As Rose notes in her discussion of hip-hop sampling, cases based on something other than the musical composition are more likely to produce reparative results: "many black artists do not have publishing rights to their songs, which means that sound recording use, the least legally protected area, is the most likely territory for older recording artists to make claims."[70] Thus, the combination of which rights are held and what similarities tend to count for listeners makes an outcome like that of "Blurred Lines" more likely.

Moreover, "Blurred Lines" was something of a perfect storm, as it also had public perception problems with respect to gender. Certainly, the song first came to my attention through the feminist critique of it as a rape culture anthem, in which Thicke sings that, although the "good girl" does not appear to be interested, he knows she wants it.[71] As legal scholar Anjali Vats describes, "at a moment in which (white) feminists were vocally protesting rape culture, Thicke became an easy target, because of his unsavory politics. His white masculinity and erratic antics made him both a saleable artist and a compelling villain, particularly with Motown legend Gaye on the other side."[72] The song's misogyny was overt enough that it did not take a feminist scholar to see it, with one article describing it as having "some bonehead, aggressively sexist lyrics."[73] Moreover, the unrated version of the video, which featured nude models, was banned from YouTube.[74] Indeed, such critiques were widespread enough that when VH1 held an #askthicke Twitter event, the hashtag was hijacked to critique the misogyny of "Blurred Lines."[75] Overall, there was a critical mass of contempt for the song's gender politics. Thus, Wu says, "many find the song's lyrics and its music video morally objectionable, and it does not help that Mr. Thicke, with his aviators and swaggering demeanor," is an unappealing figure; to add that the song is stolen, Wu notes, "completes the 'jackass' narrative nicely."[76]

In a broad sense, then, who and what was valued was essential to making sense of "Blurred Lines." The "jackass narrative" and swagger, while legally irrelevant, turned out to be quite relevant in practice. The Gaye estate's lawyers certainly knew it. Wu notes that, "taking advantage of the fact that Gaye is considerably more popular and respected than Thicke, [they] made a dispute between two groups of wealthy people seem like a battle between good and evil. Rather than focussing on what Gaye's estate actually owned, the trial became a referendum on Thicke's character. As for that, the verdict was already clear."[77] This, of course, is not how the law is supposed to work, but it is often how the law actually does work.[78] In a dispute between a person or category that one likes more and a person or category that one likes less, interpretation favors the liked. Therefore, when nasty Thicke was bested by beloved Gaye, "there was far more Schadenfreude than sorrow," in Wu's phrase.[79] According to the letter of the law, of course, these factors aren't supposed to matter. Nevertheless, they do, and they always have—they've just usually benefited white people.

However, there is more than one Black artist involved in "Blurred Lines," complicating an easy reading of the verdict as restitution for white theft, which is why Vats calls it only a "seemingly racially reparative outcome."[80] On one hand, the song does represent and replicate decades of theft from Black artists through cover songs, shady contracts, and sonic pillaging. On the other hand, Williams's involvement means it collides with practices of reference and reverence between Black artists. As Rose describes in the sampling context, such musical reuse "is about paying homage, an invocation of another's voice to help you say what you want to say."[81] To think only about what's lost or gained by Gaye's estate is to miss this role of intragroup homage. This framing also displaces the fault for previous theft by white record executives and artists onto Williams. As Rose notes with hip-hop, "these cries of thievery against rappers are suspect given that they have been used to obscure the most serious and profound thefts against black artists"; that is, focusing on sampling misses that "the primary theft against the musical forebear took place in the record company offices long before many rappers finished grade school."[82] The theft in the original contracts is the "serious and profound" one priming the desire for a reparative outcome, not the reuse in sampling or as homage, yet the latter is what tends to be more heavily policed due to what Vats calls the perception of "copyright thuggery," or the ways "racial scripts about Black people as dangerous criminals with an innate desire to steal, because they had no work ethic or sense or imagination . . . , spilled over into copyright law, where judges presented Black artists as per se criminals instead of resourceful individuals who produced creative music."[83]

As Vats describes, the "Blurred Lines" case created a tension "between embracing nostalgia and reparation for Gaye, who was arguably a better creator than Pharrell but certainly no better a feminist than Thicke, or a commitment to the musical innovation of hip hop and an interpretation of the public domain that had historically disenfranchised Black artists."[84] This wasn't a simple instance of Thicke as a white thief of Black artists' music that was unfairly treated as part of the public domain, but one that also touched on whether referential Black art forms like hip-hop were legitimate. Here again, who was doing the reusing matters—an interpretation that identifies Williams as the sole author, as Vats does, looks different than seeing the emphasis on his authorship as strategically disclaiming Thicke as a coauthor. Similarly, a nostalgic reverence for Gaye encourages ignoring his misogyny even as Thicke's is emphasized. Ultimately, Vats argues, "Blurred Lines" "was a so-called 'hard case' because it pitted people of color against one another in a manner that required the erasure of one or more forms of systematic discrimination while also refusing to take a critical look at the persistent problems of racial capitalism."[85] That is, the case called to either provide reparations to Gaye's estate or legitimate Williams's referential reuse, eliding the ways both were disadvantaged by the white supremacy structured into the music industry. In all of these ways, then, it is impossible to understand how people make social sense of soundalikes without race and gender; as is clear from the "Blurred Lines" case, verdicts are ultimately deeply shaped by understandings around who did what to whom in terms of cultural appropriation and desires for restitution for harms.

CONCLUSION: AGGRESSIVE MANEUVERS COMING HOME TO ROOST

Ultimately, one of the things that soundalike songs show particularly clearly is how the music industry's own actions have produced outcomes it now finds threatening. By being part of the broader media industry push for ever-expanding copyright that would let them control the revenue of songs for ever-longer periods, they contributed to the notion of permanent control of creativity that is now causing soundalikes to be treated as theft. Through indiscriminate musical appropriation in previous eras, they primed a desire for a counterweight to take back what had been stolen. Last but not least, I'd argue, the music industry's avaricious approach to popular forms of musical reuse—from sampling to filesharing to using music in online home video—has laid the groundwork for the proliferation of soundalike lawsuits currently making their way through the courts. In this section, I turn to a pair of early 2020 articles handwringing about the effects of lawsuits over such songs on the future of music and explore both the ways the current legal landscape is understood and the ways it is the result of the industry's own practices.

The fundamental argument of these articles bemoaning lawsuits over soundalikes is that such suits frighten the industry. Indeed, one article is even called "How Music Copyright Lawsuits Are Scaring Away New Hits."[86] The story goes on to put a finer point on it, saying that "Most of the world knows Robin Thicke, Pharrell Williams, and T.I.'s 'Blurred Lines' as a half-forgotten hit song from 2013. The music industry remembers it as its worst nightmare."[87] While this is of course a rhetorical flourish, the idea of losing copyright control as the industry's worst nightmare is indicative of how its priorities are popularly understood. The second article contends that "a new trend pulling more pop stars into courtrooms is a dangerous one"[88]—again identifying this as a significant risk. One result of this fearful situation, as the first article describes, is a rise in taking out errors and omissions insurance, commonly used by producers of documentaries to guard against defamation lawsuits, whether on individual songs or a broader swath of an artist's catalogue.

A significant aspect of why lawsuits for soundalikes are troubling, according to these articles, is that reuse of previous works is a routine part of creativity. The second article insists that "Originality is a con: Pop music history is the history of near overlap. Ideas rarely emerge in complete isolation. In studios around the world, performers, producers and songwriters are all trying to innovate just one step beyond where music currently is, working from the same component parts."[89] Similarly, a forensic musicologist interviewed in the first article contends that "There are no virgin births in music. Music comes out of other music"[90]—thus invoking the musical offspring metaphor again. This argument has been made both by music scholars and legal ones. Burkholder points out that "If we examined all music that borrowed in some way from its predecessors, we would be examining all music."[91] Legal scholar James Boyle asks, "given that we all learn from and build on the past, do we have a right to carve out our own incremental innovations and protect them by intellectual property rights?"[92] However, note the difference: Boyle is critical of expansive claims of control over the first work, whereas the press articles are advocating for a more general right to exist for second comers. These are two fundamentally different orientations toward how musical reuse should work. In particular, the second press article is concerned about the ways that rejection of borrowing "forecloses on the possibility that there is some value in copying, or duplicative ideas. It also suggests that all copying is alike" as well as "fails to make a distinction between theft and echo, or worse, presumes that all echo is theft."[93] This argument leaves intact the near-total control the music industry has posited, arguing instead for something like a carveout.

Similarly, these articles critique the idea that the features of songs that generate such lawsuits can be owned at all. As the first article notes, "While copyright laws used to protect only lyrics and melodies . . . , the 'Blurred Lines' case raised the stakes by suggesting that the far more abstract qualities of rhythm, tempo, and even the general feel of a song are also eligible for protection—and thus that a song can be sued for feeling like an earlier one."[94] In much the same way, the second article argues, "in almost all of these cases, the scope of the alleged infringement is so minor, so generic, that it suggests that a basic element of composition is up for an ownership grab."[95] This expansiveness is indeed absurd, but it has also been standard practice for quite some time. Boyle argued in 2003 that expanding intellectual property rights should be understood as "a second enclosure movement," in which "things that were formerly thought of as either common property or uncommodifiable are being covered with new, or newly extended, property rights."[96] Twenty years later, those property rights to the commons are almost fully entrenched.

Indeed, the irony of contemporary hand-wringing over the harms of illegitimately expansive property claims is that critical legal studies scholars have been warning of these consequences since the mid-1990s. Boyle warned in 1997 (before the Sonny Bono Copyright Term Extension Act made copyright terms 20 years longer or the Digital Millennium Copyright Act [DMCA] made it possible to lock a public domain work behind digital encryption and opened the door to rampant—and, until *Lenz v. Universal* [2015], unaccountable[97]—internet takedown demands by rightsholders) about the logic that "leads us to have *too many* intellectual property rights, to confer them on the *wrong people*, and dramatically to undervalue the interests of both the *sources of* and the *audiences for* the information we commodify."[98] That is, expansive rights for one creator freeze an incremental addition to culture as fully created by that one individual in a way that is ultimately arbitrary; such freezing harms those this creator built from as well as those who may want to continue building. This is to say that "every potential increase of protection . . . also raises the cost of, or reduces access to, the raw material from which you might have built those products,"[99] which is exactly what the music industry is now concerned about in the wake of the "Blurred Lines" verdict. Ultimately, as Boyle notes, such expansion of rights "clearly has the potential to harm innovation as well as to support it."[100]

Given this rejection of the legitimacy of claims to ownership, these articles construct soundalike lawsuits as cynical ploys for cash. The second article calls those who file them "copyright trolls," bent on "turning inevitable influence into ungenerous and often highly frivolous litigation."[101] "Copyright troll" is a term usually used for "an entity whose business revolves around the systematic legal enforcement of copyrights in which it has acquired a limited ownership interest,"[102] like Bridgeport suing on the basis of their shady ownership of George Clinton's catalog. Copyright trolls (like the patent trolls of which they're a snowclone)[103] are usually seen as suing in search of money just because they can, not because something they created has actually been appropriated. This is perhaps somewhat true when the estate of a deceased artist like Marvin Gaye or Randy Wolfe of Spirit takes legal action, but it frames more obscure artists seeking to recover from the more powerful as equally suspect. The first article notes that "Plaintiffs in copycat cases are largely targeting megahit songs because they've seen where the money is, and the increasing frequency of those court battles in headlines is causing an avalanche effect of further infringement lawsuits."[104] This statement, too, invokes the idea that plaintiffs haven't really been harmed: people see that such suits are a way to get money, and therefore they proliferate. Thus, the common position is that these suits are only about extracting money from successful people.

These stories also touch on the role of the jury members' understandings as a source of trouble in soundalike cases. The second article seeks to dismiss quotidian intuitions, saying "Juries filled with non-music experts are ill-suited to make decisions."[105] However, juries are non-experts in all legal cases. That's the point of a jury. The forensic musicologist consulted in the first article takes a more even-handed approach, noting that "because cases are decided by 'the average listener, who is not an educated musicologist or musician . . . [record] labels are very afraid.'"[106] Such commentary shows that there is starting to be a recognition that how everyday people understand music needs to be taken much more seriously.

The second article notes with some concern that, in place of "the idea that there is a determinable origin point where a sonic idea was born," a song is now "an asset, and a perpetual one at that."[107] However, this is precisely the shift that the music industry cheered on when it benefited them. They also worked to inculcate music as total property as a norm in the minds of everyday people, suing file-sharers for huge sums to make an example of them and scare others into behaving, and making a habit of aggressive cease and desist and DMCA takedown notices for any and all uses of music on the internet—from parodies to unlicensed covers to transformative uses. Music industry practices thus contributed significantly to a world in which many believe that any use of someone else's music is presumptively illegal. They therefore should not be surprised when juries made up of people steeped in such norms view a lot of kinds of musical influence as theft that were formerly considered acceptable.

Ultimately, what soundalikes show perhaps better than any other kind of transformative musical work is that analysis should pay attention to what everyday people believe is important. The "Blurred Lines" case operated at an interesting intersection, between (a) a strict copyright interpretation that said the song was in the clear and (b) a series of approaches that wanted Thicke to be punished—whether informed by the history of white theft of Black people's music, distaste for the gender and sexuality ideologies of "Blurred Lines" itself, or an expansionist, industry-cultivated notion of copyright—and in the end this incident showed two key features of how law tends to work. First, social beliefs about creativity, originality, and worthiness impact decisions about whether works are infringing or transformative. Second, when thinking about reuse, assessing whether it's legitimate often reflects the power dynamics of the work—as the "Blurred Lines" jury apparently did, considering who did what to whom. In the conclusion, I propose that analysis take seriously such everyday intuitions not as misapplications of the law, but as a normative statement of principles that would advance thinking about legitimate and illegitimate reuse of existing creative works.

Conclusion

Toward a Theory of Ethical Transformative Musical Works

I began this book asking what the discourse around transformative musical works can show about how creativity is socially understood, how concepts of creativity and reuse are racialized, how quotidian beliefs about creativity and legitimacy in transformative musical works compare to what the law protects, and the stakes of assessing musical reuse the way popular discourse currently does. I end by articulating the overarching set of popular beliefs uncovered through the individual chapters' analyses of cover songs, remixes, mash-ups, parodies, and soundalike songs. I argue for taking these beliefs seriously as the discursive construction of acceptable and unacceptable transformative musical works, but also that a broader theory of ethical transformative musical works is needed—one which only partially overlaps with contemporary popular beliefs. I begin this concluding chapter with a metaanalysis of the general trends in positively and negatively received transformative musical works. Next, I examine how the actual law is not the same as how the law is used as a tool in lawsuits is not the same as how the law plays out when interpreted by judges and juries. Finally, I articulate a normative statement of principles for transformative musical works that I contend would advance understanding of legitimate and illegitimate reuse of existing creative works.

WHOLE LOTTA TRANSFORMATIVE MUSICAL WORKS: OVERALL POPULAR APPROVAL AND DISAPPROVAL

To understand the broader patterns in the reasons transformative musical works are viewed positively or negatively, this section conducts a metaanalysis. To do so, I first created two aggregate data sets, one of all quotations that reflected a positive stance across all types of transformative musical work and one of all quotations that were negative. These were analyzed for word frequency to identify commonalities and differences. Overall, there are 4.94 times as many positive quotations as negative, and looking at the 20 most frequent words in each grouping, many are on both lists in corresponding numbers—roughly five times as many uses in the positive data set as the negative one. The places this pattern does not hold—when a word is more positive or negative than expected, and words that appear on only one list—are therefore interesting and revelatory. Second, I grouped the characteristics of positively and negatively received transformative musical works that emerged from the qualitative analysis into themes. Combining these two forms of analysis reveals multiple tensions across the types of transformative musical work: songs that produce emotional responses vs. those that are boring or without substance; songs that transform or even improve on sources vs. those seen as uncreative, lazy, cash grabs, or even theft; fidelity and respect for the source artist vs. being disrespectful; and how cross-racial musical reuse is decried in some instances but lauded in others.

One theme that, perhaps unsurprisingly, shows up only with positive assessments is high musical skill. However, this value takes different forms in different types of transformative musical work. There is particular emphasis on vocal power in cover songs that does not appear elsewhere, for example. In mash-up, by contrast, the musical knowledge needed to select and skillfully combine source songs stands out as valued. Good musicianship is also emphasized with parody, in part because precision in reproducing the music of a source song is fundamental to making it a vehicle for parodic content. In at least this one way, then, there is a clearly shared (if more or less expected) value system across popular discourse around transformative musical works.

Moving away from more narrowly defined musicianship, disagreements about valued and devalued characteristics quickly arise. Songs, especially cover songs, that evoke emotion are viewed positively. So too are cover songs and remixes that are intense, exciting, or danceable—"fun" is in the top 20 words only for positively rated songs. Negatively received songs, by contrast, may be boring or repetitive. Specifically, they're often seen as empty—remixes and covers in particular are often negatively described when perceived as style without substance, gimmicky, or overproduced.

Transformative musical works thus need to strike a balance—they need to be interesting and enjoyable, but not *only* interesting and enjoyable, as they must also comply with notions of artistic works as carrying meaning; this valuation aligns with Romantic author ideas of art as self-expression, as opposed to treating these songs as pure commercial entertainment.

The third theme shows that the degree of transformativeness is key to popular reception of transformative musical works. "Rendition" and "version" are among the top 20 words for both positive and negative commentary, but are disproportionately associated with positive comments (rendition, 46% more frequently positive than the baseline; version, 27% more positive). This valuation is consistent with the ways notions of change and difference are associated with a positive reception in cover songs and mash-ups. In much the same way, novelty, originality, and unexpectedness are positively valued characteristics of covers, mash-ups, and parodies. Corresponding to this valuation of difference is the negative valuation of formulaic, assembly-line production of transformative musical works that arises with some cover songs and "jump on the bandwagon" remixes— songs may be seen as bad if there's not enough difference. This formation is also why negatively assessed transformative musical works are often those seen as not substantively different or as unoriginal, which is particularly apparent around mash-ups and soundalike songs. However, difference for the sake of difference, if it is not successfully harmonized or seems forced, is also viewed negatively—songs are bad if there's too much difference, or the wrong kind. Here again, a balance is required, but a belief in the value of originality persists even in musical works that are clearly reworking other works.

This question of whether and how the transformative musical work differs from the source song has additional impacts. Frequent ideas of covers as free-riding on other people's songs, remixes as lazy ways to make money, and parodies as trying to gain attention at someone else's expense all critique a perceived lack of effort. Viewed this way, the positive valuation of laborious production of mash-ups, seemingly an outlier, can be understood as part of a larger formation in which legitimate transformation requires adding labor—in talking about reworking, that is, the operative word is "work." This valuation echoes in popular perception the ruling in *Fisher v. Dees* (1986), which condemned free-riding on someone else's labor "simply to reap the advantages of a well-known tune and short-cut the rigors of composing original music" in the case of a parody song.[1] If, drawing on John Locke's theories of property, "property rights in one's body and its labor entail property rights in the products of that labor," a theory commonly picked up into copyright,[2] it is no wonder the "sweat of the brow" doctrine should get mapped onto the sweaty, visibly laboring body of someone like Girl Talk. Such labor can at times result in transcending the source, as in covers perceived as better than the source and mash-ups seen as more than the sum of their parts. This occasional transcendence exists in tension with seeing covers and mash-ups in particular as inherently lesser forms of music, highlighting that *how* the transformative musical work is done matters quite a lot. "Copyright" is among the top 20 words only for negative commentary, suggesting that the idea of cashing in without doing labor lends itself to seeing reuse of existing works as copying or even infringement, which arises particularly acutely with soundalike songs. In such ways, it's clear that making changes, and particularly doing the labor of making changes, is what—when successful—wards off accusations of copying and theft in transformative musical works.

The fourth theme apparent across multiple types of transformative musical work is the importance of the artist making a transformative musical work having respect for the source song or artist. There's a clear belief that cover songs and parodies that are in some sense faithful to the source text are good, for example, and correspondingly that those that don't do justice to the source are bad. This valuation would seem to be in tension with the value of transformativeness discussed above, but makes more sense in the context of norms of respect for musical forebears. Thus, there are arguments that cover songs owe something to the source text and should do right by it, that parodies should be respectful or even kind, and that soundalikes often emerge from inspiration or homage rooted in respect and appreciation. Respect is also the discursive formation that supports both the aura function in mash-ups, in which value comes from making the source present, and critique of insincerity in using existing songs in soundalikes. In this vein, there's a consistent sense that good transformative musical works support what they transform, with covers, remixes, and parodies in particular often driving interest in the source song, thus giving rise to commissioning remixes and covers. This norm of respect for source texts and artists articulates with the requirement that transformative musical works put in labor to change the source song—in taking existing music as raw material, producing something new from it must be done thoughtfully and well. However, as I've discussed, this is often a colorblind notion of kindness and respect that elides the racial dynamics of who has the power to borrow from whom.

As this role of colorblindness begins to suggest, the picture of positive and negative assessment is fuzziest when it comes to the role of race as a system of power shaping transformative musical works. On one hand, sometimes white extraction of Black people's music is viewed negatively, as seen from white covers of Black artists' songs being the least often described positively and often seen as failing to measure up to the source text. There is, correspondingly, an interest in reparative responses to cultural appropriation, particularly visible in popular approval of Robin Thicke facing consequences for appropriating from Marvin Gaye with "Blurred Lines." However, popular discourse reinforces racial extraction at least as often. Interracial cover songs may be negatively viewed in the aggregate, but they're sometimes praised—and in particularly inappropriate instances like Johnny Cash singing about himself as a slave while covering "Redemption Song" or Annie Lennox completely evacuating lynching from "Strange Fruit." Uneven positive treatment is also visible in the fact that "country" and "guitar" are among the top 20 words only for the positive data set, indicating disproportionate positive use of words more associated with white artists in contemporary music. The word remix, on the other hand, is disproportionately negative (28% less positive than the baseline)—and remixes, as both a form of transformative musical work emerging out of turntable arts and often featuring rappers, are more associated with Black artists than many of the other genres. The interplay between condemning and supporting appropriation shows also in the fact that "funk" appears in the top 20 most frequent words only for the negative data set. This pattern is likely because it catches the short end of both of the trends—on one hand, as anthropologist Maureen Mahon points out, funk is a Black genre, and is often the category ascribed to music that, were it played by white men, would be called rock;[3] on the other hand, in the period this book examines, funk was also a site of negatively valued cultural appropriation. In such ways, though use of raw material must be respectful and add something, this norm is, as most things are, unevenly available based on the race of the reusing and reused party. As I'll show at the end of this chapter, it is essential to account for this dynamic in a normative theory of transformative musical works.

LAW AND EVERYTHING AFTER:
THE LETTER AND SPIRIT OF THE LAW, AND WHAT REALLY HAPPENS

Of course, popular notions of creativity must inevitably confront the ostensibly fixed reality of the law. As legal scholar Cheryl Harris notes, the usual assumption is that "neutrality means the existing distribution, which is natural," but in fact this distribution is a reflection of power relations.[4] The law is, as Critical Race Theory and Critical Race IP scholars have shown, not the monolithic and objective thing it pretends to be—in fact, the letter of the law differs from how the law is used as a tool in lawsuits differs from the law as interpreted by judges and juries. The formal legal status of transformative musical works is uneven. Cover songs are thoroughly legal, provided that they comply with the terms of the compulsory mechanical license to produce recordings of a composition. Nothing else has that level of security, but parody comes closest, often treated as one of the paradigmatic examples—if not *the* paradigmatic example—of transformative work; parodies are routinely included in illustrative lists of types of transformative work, including when the U.S. Supreme Court took up the concept of "transformative work" into the law in *Campbell v. Acuff-Rose* (1994)—a case about a parodic song. On the other end of the spectrum, mash-up is shadowed by the notion that using music taken directly from recordings is fundamentally illegitimate, a common assumption since *Grand Upright v. Warner Brothers* in 1991 despite the fact that there have been cases where samples have been found to be fair use.[5]

However, within this broad sense of legal or illegal the details are more complex. Given that a cover song, legally speaking, is simply making a recording of someone else's composition, the idea that a specific performance of a song has its own creativity can't be accounted for in the law, which is reinforced by the compulsory license's requirement that a cover song not be significantly changed. This same composition-over-performance model shows up in soundalikes, in which the only thing that is formally protected about a song is which notes are played, in what order and cadence, and not intangible or non-notatable aspects of the "feel" apparent in the recorded version. In this way, covers and soundalikes often participate in the long tradition of not protecting "features that were not present in the original notated song but had been introduced by African-American composers, arrangers, and recording artists while preparing to record and recording the song."[6] As this history begins to suggest, copyright law doesn't protect everything one might think it does (or should). For example, while copyright perhaps *should*—logically or morally—consider freedom of speech, the law doesn't require such protection, and in practice it tends not to do so. Copyright doesn't even protect what it was designed to, having morphed from its constitutional mandate of serving the public through providing incentives for creativity to ensuring the rightsholder gets paid as an end in itself.

Moreover, what the law formally protects is not necessarily what people use it for. That is, people file lawsuits or send cease and desist letters as a tool to exercise control over music they hold the rights to—whether their claims are legally legitimate or not. Remixes and soundalike songs were targeted for multiple legal actions in the period this book examines, despite diverging from each other with respect to the letter of the law; parody and mash-up had fewer legal interventions, but still some. Analysis of popular discourse shows a frequent sense that lawsuits or cease and desist letters can stop mash-ups and remixes or even make it so that they aren't attempted for fear of legal action.[7] Moreover, while many transformative musical works have potential claims to be fair use—even strong ones—the resources required to actually litigate fair use mean it's often more a theoretical point than a material possibility, emphasizing another way lawsuits serve as tools to suppress transformative musical works rather than adjudicating legality itself.

How legal action tends to play out is also a separate question from its formal boundaries. As I have discussed, artists who make remixes and parodies tend to negotiate license agreements for expediency in managing legal risk. On the other hand, while the law technically mandates that using the mechanical license means not making significant changes, in practice there tends to be an expansive definition of what constitutes maintaining a song's fundamentals, allowing a broader set of possibilities than the law appears to provide. In a similar way, soundalikes show that what a verdict might declare infringing—i.e., intangibles like "feel"—is different from what the law formally protects—i.e., what can be written in sheet music. These patterns of interpretation are part of why legal action is unevenly distributed. However, uneven application of the law is also the product of racial inequality (in this instance as in so many others). It could be expected that mash-ups, for example, which use the same digital technology to recontextualize existing pieces of music in new songs as hip-hop samples—and, indeed, in which recombination is often the only change, unlike common transformational practices in hip-hop—would be subject to the same legal scrutiny. However, there have been no corresponding legal cases regarding mash-up, despite engaging in a fundamentally similar practice, which I argue is significantly because mash-up is racialized as white. After all, as legal scholar Anjali Vats describes, sampling has been made sense of through copyright thuggery from early in its history; "an early copyright-infringement case involving sampling, *Grand Upright Music*, showed the tendency of courts to presume criminality and bad intent on the part of Black artists, in a way that they rarely did when considering white infringers."[8]

These, then, are the specific musical instantiations of broader racially uneven protection by law. Fundamentally, property law is structured by whiteness. As Harris points out, when the United States was established through the dispossession of Indigenous people's land, only white people's occupation of territory counted.[9] In particular, only certain types of ownership were respected, as legal scholar Brenna Bhandar notes: "the nearly uniform justification for casting indigenous populations as premodern was found in the absence of private property laws."[10] Other ways of thinking about ownership, done by those without racial status, were thus overdetermined as illegitimate. This pattern with real property continues in intellectual property; as Vats argues, "intellectual property law is organized through a racial episteme that consistently protects the (intellectual) property interests of white people and devalues the (intellectual) property interests of people of color."[11] Similarly to only valuing white forms of real property, intellectual property systematically overvalues white creativity.[12] Out of this overvaluation, "over the last two centuries, copyright law has been intertwined with the construction of the so-called *Western Civilization* and the global expansion of [intellectual property rights] is still very much imagined as part of the continuous spread of civilization across the world."[13]

On the other hand, Black artists (and other artists of color, but nearly always Black artists in the context of U.S. music) are disproportionately not protected. As legal scholar Olufunmilayo B. Arewa argues, racial inequality, as reproduced by copyright, has meant that it's much easier to borrow from Black artists without compensation.[14] Although popular rejection of cultural appropriation primed a desire for Robin Thicke to be held liable for infringement of Marvin Gaye, legal scholar K. J. Greene points out that occasional protection doesn't disprove the pattern: "While individual black artists without question have benefited from the IP system, the economic effects of IP deprivation on the black community have been devastating."[15] At the same time that the work of particular *people* isn't protected, particular models of creativity aren't either. As critical legal studies scholar Boatema Boateng notes, a "sense of authorship as dependent on the work of previous authors is one that intellectual property law, almost by definition, is designed to suppress."[16] These things are of course related. Vats points out that "person of color creatorship continues to be coded as always already unoriginal or infringing as well as an inappropriate subject for court intervention."[17] Overall, the law as currently constituted is uneven both in its position and its application across similar instances, tends to favor the powerful, and in particular tends to overprotect white artists and underprotect artists of color, especially Black artists.

CONTINGENT ETHICS FOR TRANSFORMATIVE MUSICAL WORKS

Ultimately, neither the law nor popular beliefs can fully answer the question of which transformative musical works should be seen as legitimate. This insufficiency is because reuse of existing material in new works is *both* a valid way to produce creative works that should be allowed and protected *and* enmeshed in broader systems of power that produce an uneven burden for marginalized people, especially Black people. Legal and popular discourses are both logically and ethically incoherent—norms and rules don't hold in practice, there's not really an overarching theory in which they fit together, and the sense of "ought" is largely missing. To come to grips with transformative musical works, that is, it is necessary to make finer distinctions (between instances), but also different distinctions (that consider other factors). In this final section, drawing particularly on the work of Critical Race IP scholars, I lay out a normative statement of principles and use them to think through some of the examples discussed earlier in the book. I contend that this new normative model for transformative musical works would provide better criteria for legitimate and illegitimate reuse of existing creative works.

The current model of protectable and unprotectable transformative musical works has the same effect as legal scholar James Boyle argues arises from copyright structures more generally: it "leads us to have *too many* intellectual property rights, to confer them on the *wrong people*, and dramatically to undervalue the interests of both the *sources of* and the *audiences for* the information we commodify."[18] It is therefore important to move toward a system that protects the right things, in the right way. While I am sensitive to Vats's point that "intellectual property law can never be effectively reformed, even if it periodically benefits people of color, because it is too deeply intertwined with racism and racial capitalism to be redeemable,"[19] harm reduction *is* possible through rethinking the system's principles. Legal scholar Madhavi Sunder argues for seeing "intellectual property as a tool, not a right"—and therefore, this tool can be brought to bear toward producing better outcomes; she adds a reminder that the New Jersey Supreme Court declared in *State v. Shack* (1971) that "property rights serve human values."[20] Thus, the law can and should be used as a tool to serve desired values. Accordingly, she says, "what we need is a new normative vision of culture and how it matters to be incorporated into intellectual property law."[21]

In articulating such a vision, I, like legal scholar Rosemary Coombe, "advocate an ethics of contingency."[22] Who borrows from whom, on what terms, is what determines what is ethical—right and wrong are contingent on circumstance. While Sunder doesn't "advocate for a system of law that would shift continuously according to the changing political strength of either the rich or the poor in these matters,"[23] in some sense I do. Arewa argues that, on one hand, "copyright may be under-inclusive and fail to adequately protect forms of cultural production that perhaps should be protected," and on the other, "many assert that copyright is overinclusive. The key to resolving this seemingly paradoxical situation rests in better identification of the scope of acceptable copying in varied contexts with simultaneous reassessment of the assumptions about cultural production that have led to the current state of affairs."[24] That is, copyright both fails to protect some things and overprotects others, and it is only by looking at particular instances, and doing so in a different way than the current standard, that the appropriate scope of protection can be gauged.

A more just system of musical reuse has six components: It understands that unauthorized uses are not necessarily infringing. Protection is extended to not just *any* use, but transformative reuse, and particularly works that are socially valuable. Relative power between the source artist and the transformative musical work maker, particularly with regard to race, is a vital consideration. This question of relative power includes reckoning with histories of overprotecting some creativity and underprotecting other creativity. Relative power also includes taking into account the ways that some people's reuse operates from a legitimacy deficit and other people's reuse benefits from being assumed to be legitimate. Finally, equitable reuse requires careful attention to attribution, compensation, and control.

Distinguishing Unauthorized and Infringing Uses

First, I advocate, as Arewa does, "making finer distinctions with respect to unauthorized uses, and basing determinations of which uses are truly infringing on a reasonable and balanced application of copyright law."[25] This idea of peeling apart the unauthorized from the infringing is key to rethinking copyright. Assuming that unauthorized uses are inherently infringing in fact eviscerates the premise of fair use, as "in U.S. law, fair uses are stated quite clearly to be limitations on the exclusive rights of the copyright holder—uses that were never within the copyright holder's power to prohibit. The defense is . . . 'I did not trespass on your land. I walked on the public road that runs through it, a road you never owned in the first place.'"[26] Copyright does not grant complete control, and there are various ways of using someone else's work that don't infringe. Such a model would recognize, as Arewa does, that "maintaining the creative commons, leaving a sufficient public domain to provide the basis for future creations, and restocking the public domain are also important considerations"[27] that limit the control a rightsholder has.

This is not to say that there aren't cases where reuse should be seen as infringing. This is clearest with displacement covers that exactly replicate someone else's music, add nothing, and cannibalize their sales. In *Supreme v. Decca*, the distinctive artistry of the Supreme recording by Paula Watson should have been recognized and compensated when it was copied.[28] Jonathan Coulton should have been recognized and compensated by *Glee* for their use of his arrangement of "Baby Got Back" (and he should have licensed his arrangement from Sir Mix-a-Lot). The digital duplication covers that took the place of artists unwilling to sell on iTunes were likewise not legitimate. Note that every single one of these things is currently perfectly legal. In each of these instances, I'm advocating for *more* protection for source song artists. There are absolutely times when this is warranted. But at the same time, none of the cases called (or ruled) infringing that I've discussed in this book fall under this classification, as they do not meet these criteria of complete free-riding and serving as a market substitute.

Protecting Transformative and Valuable Uses

Reframing legitimate and illegitimate transformative musical works also requires moving away from the Romantic author notion that building from someone else's work is always creatively illegitimate. Existing norms about music are not the only option, which is clear from the fact that historically they were different—alluding to the work of others was a norm, until it wasn't; improvisation was a sign of musical skill, until beliefs shifted and creativity became understood as located solely in composition. As these changes happened, the idea of music as involving reuse fell out of favor. This isn't to say those practices ceased to happen after the Romantic author; as musicologist J. Peter Burkholder shows, they remain common.[29] However, their prevalence *has* been suppressed and denied under the Romantic author regime.

In place of this suppression, I advocate moving back toward recognizing the role of reuse, much as Arewa suggests that interpretations "begin with an assumption of borrowing as a norm." She adds that looking at musical forms where borrowing *is* recognized as a norm, like blues, shows "how copying can be a crucial aspect in the creation of vibrant and influential living musical forms."[30] This is to advocate for not just *any* use, but use that enables new creation—transformative reuse. It is productive to take this kind of reworking as the standard for rethinking acceptable borrowing more broadly. In such traditions, how artists rework their influences "can be as important as any 'original' contribution."[31] Recognizing this role of reuse, Arewa says, suggests that "it is often optimal to permit some type of sampling on the creation side."[32]

Accordingly, the question "what kinds of music does society value?" must be recognized as a different question than "what kinds of music *should* society value?" It is essential to take seriously that what is currently valued as creative is only one version of what could be valued. This is to argue, with Coombe, that it's essential to "recognize that juridical power is productive as well as prohibitive; the law, as discursive cultural practice, is generative of categories, distinctions, and valuations—of knowledges—spaces, identities, and subjectivities."[33] In particular, as Coombe rightly notes, when the law recognizes and protects some practices, inevitably it delegitimates others.[34] That is, drawing boundaries of acceptability inevitably marks some things as on the inside and others as outside. This is, in short, a struggle to define creativity and what's worth protecting.

It is therefore imperative to think harder about what is and isn't valued—and why. As I have shown, social beliefs about creativity, originality, and worthiness impact both legal and popular decisions about whether works are infringing or transformative, and to some extent they should. Whether the purpose of the law is to serve the public by encouraging creativity (the initial purpose) or to give what authors deserve (the contemporary purpose), it should protect what is socially valuable, creative, and an addition to culture, not just arbitrarily anything claimed by someone with the lawyers to back it up. Arewa argues that "copyright law should be constructed to permit borrowing that enables the creation of future works as well as provide compensation to creators of prior works on which such future works are based."[35] *The Grey Album* and Biz Markie's sample of Gilbert O'Sullivan's "Alone Again (Naturally)" (1972) in his "Alone Again" (1991) were both unauthorized, but that doesn't inherently make them infringing, because they were also transformative and added something to culture. They should therefore have been seen as legitimate reuses and, while compensation might be fair, prohibition is not. On the other hand, GoldieBlox's parody of "Girls" and "Blurred Lines" as riffing on Marvin Gaye, while transformative, may not be socially valuable. Much depends on how these songs are understood—critique of Beastie Boys' sexism or homage to Gaye vs. free-riding on someone else's labor to sell their own products. However, at the same time, what is socially valued is not neutral any more than the law.

Taking Relative Power into Account

Another vital consideration is relative power between the source artist and the transformative musical work maker. This is to draw on legal scholar Lateef Mtima's theory of Intellectual Property Social Justice, which "contemplates the precepts of socially equitable access, inclusion, and empowerment as both intrinsic and essential to the fulfillment of the goals of intellectual property social utility."[36] Mtima contends, and I agree, that social justice should be part of the conversation if the goals of IP are to be achieved. In fact, he points out that there is precedent for adjusting copyright on the basis of social justice; in *Authors Guild Inc. v. HathiTrust* (2014),[37] the Second Circuit explicitly took the Americans with Disabilities

Act into account, diminishing the amount of control copyright confers in order to better serve marginalized people.[38] Mtima argues that "Intellectual Property Social Justice consequently mandates that IP legal mechanisms be applied to effectuate the equitable treatment of all participants in actual practice, and not merely in theory."[39] That is, a one size fits all law might seem equitable, but doesn't play out that way, so more specific interventions are needed.

Such balancing of relative power is particularly important with regard to race. Media studies scholar Siva Vaidhyanathan, who seeks to defend sampling as a Black cultural practice with roots in African diaspora models of creativity, advocates for unauthorized sampling to be considered fair use; specifically, "if copyright law is to conform to its constitutional charge, to 'promote the progress of science and useful arts,' it should allow transgressive and satirical sampling without having to clear permission from original copyright owners." Importantly, he seeks to not only protect but expand the possibility of reuse by Black artists, particularly of stolen-back white music, so he advocates broader freedom of use: "Led Zeppelin did not 'credit' the blues masters as often as they could have," Vaidhyanathan notes, "so why should Schoolly D do anything but reciprocate? . . . repeating and reusing the guitar riff from 'Kashmir' was a transgressive and disrespectful act—a 'dis' of Led Zeppelin and the culture that produced, rewarded, and honored Led Zeppelin."[40] That is, Led Zeppelin's greater racial power let them lift from the blues, and Schoolly D's lesser power makes his re-lifting doubly legitimate, both in his own right and to correct that wrong.

In much the same way, the relative power of Biz Markie and Gilbert O'Sullivan or Danger Mouse and the Beatles matters, because these were less-established Black artists using Black musical forms being stopped by the power of white artists, and their uses should have been deemed legitimate, not infringing. Similarly from the other direction, Yankovic's use of Coolio relied on his greater power in terms of being more established in the media industry as well as his whiteness, and, as I'll discuss later in the chapter, Coolio should have had more control in the situation than he did. The relative power of Gaye and Thicke or Gaye and Williams matter too, which is why interpreting "Blurred Lines" rests significantly on which one is prioritized—Thicke as white thief should have to pay up, but Williams as reverential reuser should not. This is a model in which relative power is essential to determining whether a particular musical reuse is legitimate, which of course it already tends to be, but I turn it on its head, deliberately focusing on justice rather than unthinkingly reproducing inequality.

Drawing from this thinking provides a clue for how copyright might be reconceptualized. Arewa suggests an "Unfair Use standard," that would "address instances where borrowings become inequitable on account of the nature of the borrowings, the broader societal context within which such borrowings occur or other factors."[41] Importantly, social context—power—has to be taken into account. I argue that explicitly considering this unequal power will produce better approaches to transformative musical works. Both law and society more broadly are structured by white supremacy, and this structuration affects the popular sense of legitimate and illegitimate musical reuse. As Mtima notes, doing this kind of work, as his Intellectual Property Social Justice framework also does, is in alignment with existing ways of balancing different stakeholders, such as fair use.[42]

Reckoning with Over- and Underprotection

There is, as I've shown throughout this book, a history of underprotection of some creative works, particularly of the creations of Black, Indigenous, and other people of color. While some might want to argue for a right to sample, for instance, media industries scholar David Hesmondhalgh's analysis contends that electronica artist Moby sampling Black artists, an example where Black artistry was erased for white gain, shows how those who want to defend Black culture may not be served by expanding fair use.[43] Given these patterns, blanket claims for more freedom to reuse existing music should be greeted with skepticism. Such arguments invoke what legal scholars Chander and Sunder call the Romance of the Public Domain, an overly simplistic view that identifies the public domain as inherently better than property. As they note, such approaches "impair efforts by disempowered groups to claim themselves as subjects of property—that is, as autonomous individuals with constitutive personhood interests in property."[44] This is an argument that approaches to IP must take into account those who don't have—and haven't had—access to property, and the control and compensation it brings, before proposing to get rid of it, similar to Barbara Christian's critique that the author was conveniently declared dead just as people of color started to be more widely recognized as authors.[45] Chander and Sunder point out that advocating for expansionist visions of freedom to reuse all existing culture, justified because restrictions make it harder to create, echo an argument made by Big Pharma in favor of exploiting traditional medicinal knowledge, which should raise concerns given how clearly exploitative this latter claim is. Sunder calls for moving away from the "free culture" model of unrestricted reuse toward a "fair culture" model that takes these inequalities into account.[46]

From this angle, there's a strong argument that protection should be thought through as reparations for what has not been protected in the past. Legal scholars Vats and Keller articulate the project of Critical Race IP as "a space for creating models for the politics of reparation—not simply equal rights or distributive justice—through which oppressed groups can heal the wounds of racism and colonialism."[47] This project is about redressing past harms. Legal scholar K. J. Greene, a key proponent of a reparations model in copyright, argues for "atonement for the mass appropriation of intellectual property rights for African-American artists. An atonement model of redress, drawn from scholarship on African-American reparations, can provide needed compensation, healing, and closure to a dark chapter in American history."[48] Legal scholar Toni Lester makes an even bolder argument, saying that "Due to the legacy and contemporary ramifications of slavery, African American artists should enjoy, as a class, greater copyright protection over the actual and moral dimensions of their work."[49] Such models would be difficult to implement practically, of course, but they undoubtedly reorient the question of equity in profound and productive ways.

On the other hand, it's also important to take into account what has been overprotected. Specifically, as Vats argues, there is a consistent pattern of ascribing excessive value to the work of white creators.[50] This excessive valuation is rooted in seeing art through a model that culture is high culture is Western Civilization, as literary critic F. R. Leavis would have it.[51] Taking Western civilization as the pinnacle of what is valuable, then, combines with the ways the category "white" has traditionally relied in particular on an equation of whiteness with being controlled and "civilized," showing some of the underlying mechanics that act to produce what's seen as worth protecting by law. This convergence of what law protects with *whom* law protects means that the "normative assumptions about how new works should be creative ... discount African-American cultural production that reflects repetition and revision as a core aesthetic," as well as other traditions that are structured this way.[52]

Taking the distribution of protection seriously, it becomes clear that

Antoine Dodson and Coolio were underprotected, more vulnerable to being appropriated than they would have been were they white, and should have had more control. Correspondingly, the Beatles and Gilbert O'Sullivan were overprotected, and reuse of their works should have had more freedom. Histories of differential protection mean that Gaye and other artists of his generation were systematically underprotected, so that there was a desire from some to see this redressed through the "Blurred Lines" verdict as a form of reparations—which may well have been deserved from Thicke, but wouldn't have been from Williams.

Default and Deficit Legitimacy

Related to, but distinct from, over- and underprotection of source texts, some artists are automatically seen as illegitimately reusing someone else's work, and others are presumed legitimate by default. If intellectual property is white and Western, that is, at the point where its inviolability is challenged, racist logics dictate that the threat would be racialized as nonwhite, as in fact it is—because whiteness is also, crucially, "fundamentally a relational category" that's "defined only by reference to those named cultures it has flung out to its perimeter."[53] As Harris notes, "the right to exclude" is a fundamental characteristic of both private property and whiteness, and "whiteness in large part has been characterized not by an inherent unifying characteristic but by the exclusion of others deemed to be 'not white.'"[54] When Motion Picture Association of America president and CEO Jack Valenti "spoke of emerging civilizations threatened by unseemly hordes and villains,"[55] this rhetoric engaged the racialization of civilization as white and Western, making the threat of "hordes" not only uncivilized but nonwhite, which racist logic would insist are the same thing anyway. Speaking of intellectual property violators as "barbarians at the gate," as is quite common,[56] then, invokes the linguistic history that political theorist Wendy Brown notes—though "barbarian" in its ancient Greek context meant simply non-Greeks, it slid quickly into meaning people "unreached by civilization, beyond its canopy," and if civilization is equated to the West, then barbarism is correspondingly defined as non-Western.[57]

When intellectual property is engaged through such "colonial tropes,"[58] it activates and participates in what postcolonial theorist Gayatri Chakravorty Spivak has called "epistemic violence," the "remotely orchestrated, far-flung, and heterogeneous project to constitute the colonial subject as Other."[59] This project follows "essentialist racism, or the idea that people of color are fundamentally other than white people: different, inferior, less civilized, less human, more animal, than whites."[60] This history is whence comes what Vats calls copyright thuggery, the idea of Black people as unimaginative, lazy thieves.[61] In the end, that the threat of intellectual property violation is an all-purpose racialized folk devil[62] is clear from the slippage between different tropes—hordes, barbarians, thugs—referring to different groups whose only commonality is being racialized as not-white.

In light of this history of overprotecting whiteness and treating transformative works makers of color as barbarous thugs, "we could argue that law should put its weight on the side of those who would dissent from cultural authorities, or those who seek greater autonomy to play and share in cultural communities, in order to actively balance competing claims and interests."[63] It's important to recognize the ways law and society are both structured by racism. Black artists' transformative musical works will tend to operate from a legitimacy deficit. Danger Mouse and Biz Markie's appropriations were assumed illegitimate by default, causing legal action, but should not have been. At the same time, white extraction will tend to have a legitimacy surplus, as with Diplo and Weird Al and the Rolling Stones not being questioned for their use of artists of color and certainly not subjected to the same consequences, whereas they should have been required to compensate fairly. Adjusting for this inequality is part of how a more just ethic of intellectual property use and reuse is possible.

Attribution, Compensation, and Control

Finally, it's useful to specify the different aspects of the issue of reuse: attribution, compensation, and control. Currently, the law doesn't require attribution, but it's incredibly consistent across popular perceptions that one must give credit where credit is due. Chander and Sunder's analysis of users of Creative Commons licenses, which allow creators to select what kinds of reuse can be made of their work, found that 92% of creators required attribution.[64] Both Arewa and Hesmondhalgh advocate for an attribution requirement, with the latter saying "full and prominent credit should be given to the sampled musicians and the musical traditions to which they belong, giving indications of the cultural sources of the music, instead of mystifying the origin."[65] This norm recognizes that, while reuse within a tradition may be recognized, the source may not be known outside that community. In hip-hop, as Tricia Rose notes, sampling is often "a challenge to know these sounds, to make connections between the lyrical and musical texts. It affirms black musical history and locates these 'past' sounds in the 'present.' More often than not, rap artists and their DJs openly revere their soul forebears."[66] But these histories are quite different than intergroup borrowing. As Arewa points out, when blues music was made by Black artists for Black audiences, people knew where borrowed elements came from, which was different from borrowing from blues for rock and roll where audiences did not know and the borrower often got credit for things they didn't create.[67] Mahon similarly points out that "in the 1950s, black Americans could recognize that [Elvis] Presley borrowed his hip swivels and vocal delivery from black performers. In contrast, these styles were largely unknown to mainstream white audiences, and many took Presley to be their originator."[68] Adding attribution remedies these problems, so that, if and as the work circulates beyond those who know the origin, that source will continue to be present. I argue that attribution should always be a requirement of reuse, both because of these politics of credit and because it facilitates establishing what is new and different in a reuse—its transformation.

Whether reuse must be compensated, however, depends on context. In this, I diverge from many other thinkers. Arewa argues for blanket compensation with a "transmission-based liability rule" that would focus "on ensuring compensation and minimizing control with respect to cultural texts"[69]—this is a model in which a source artist would get paid, but wouldn't be able to stop reuse. However, relative power still matters here. Compensation from an individual artist to a corporate rightsholder, where (long experience says) it will never quite trickle down to the artist who created the work, does not have a clear benefit. Lateral compensation between corporations or between individual artists makes sense, but certainly not as exorbitant sample buyouts for using a tiny part of a song as one element in a new work rather than proportionately. The model of George Clinton's *Sample Some of Disc, Sample Some of D.A.T.* (1993) is educational here, requiring royalty payments only when copies are sold rather than up front and setting the royalty using the statutory rate for mechanical reproduction (9.1¢ per copy), as opposed to thousands of dollars up front for a standard sample buyout.

There should especially be compensation when the reuse is down a power differential. Ethnomusicologist Anthony Seeger argues for more attention to the ethical challenges of cross-cultural musical borrowing, and particularly to making sure commercial benefits flow back to the source artists, such as, in his example, Indigenous people.[70] Hesmondhalgh similarly contends about reuse of the blues that "musicians should make strenuous effort to establish ways of recompensing musicians, their descendants, or representative organizations."[71] Framing compensation as flowing this way helps avoid what might be called the "grandparent clause" problem: compensation will only flow as far back in time as people can prove that their work has been used, which will inevitably reproduce many of the same thefts from already-underrecognized Black artists that I've discussed throughout the book. Having spillover to organizations when there's not a specific, identifiable artist helps at those places where the historical record gives out. Such organizations could then fund historical research to find specific artists and their heirs, or care for artists in their old age when royalties weren't fairly apportioned to them in the beginning, or even give grants to artists just starting out who are from the same community as the source material. This norm of compensation reflects Sunder's observation that "fair culture yokes together meaning and livelihood."[72] In instances where the source materials are from members of groups who have historically gone unprotected, compensation is necessary.

Last but not least, the amount of control an artist should have is also contextual. Arewa argues that "Separating control from compensation in copyright doctrine is potentially one way to ameliorate this tendency for control of copyright to extend to control of meaning and reinterpretation and restore a potential multiplicity of possible meanings and interpretations of cultural texts."[73] Existing forms of control tend to give the powerful the ability to shut out dissent, and diminishing control can thus expand the possibility of interpretation, particularly against the grain. However, here, too, relative power matters. I say that it should be permitted to borrow laterally, as in blues—except with the addition to blues practice of overt attribution. It should be permitted to steal upward freely, as in early instantiations of sampling (before the courts decided licensing was required) and other acts of taking back from dominant culture like those of George Clinton. And, as the long and painful tradition of white extraction of Black people's music demonstrates, it should be permitted to reuse culture from those occupying positions down the social power structure only with permission.

Putting this model into practice, it's clear that the problem in many cases—Solomon Linda's "Mbube" being treated as part of the public domain and free to use in "The Lion Sleeps Tonight" (1961), Clyde Stubblefield coming up with the rhythms from James Brown records but not receiving any royalties from either the original records or the samples, and Diplo bragging that he could steal samples in Brazil without having to go through a legal or payment process—is that none of the source song artists had attribution, compensation, or control. While Antoine Dodson was eventually named and became a short-lived celebrity, gaining compensation, he never had control, which is particularly clear from the fact that he gained this attribution and compensation through mockery. Coolio was named and compensated by Weird Al from the outset, but had no control to prohibit his song from being used. Similarly, it took a lawsuit for Gaye to be attributed and compensated for his role in inspiring "Blurred Lines," but he (his estate) never had control. In all of these cases, providing attribution, compensation, and control calibrated to relative power would right the wrongs.

Ultimately, using the principles I lay out in this section will produce a more just system than the current one size fits all (but mostly powerful white people) model. The practicalities are indisputably difficult, as shown particularly well by the many different ways "Blurred Lines" could go, depending on which category it ultimately falls into. However, this case also suggests a way to think about implementation—there would be a role of fact finding in determining what the power dynamic in any given case is. Regardless, these difficulties do not mean this model cannot be an aspiration toward a more just way to make social sense of transformative musical works. It can, and should, because such a reorientation is desperately needed.

DATA APPENDIX

COVER

Case/Search Term	Type	Year
9 Best Viral Cover Videos of 2015	Event	2015
Adam Lambert Mad World	Song	2009
American Idol	TV Show	2009–2016, 2018
American Idols Live	Event	2009–2015, 2018
Annie Lennox Nostalgia	Album	2014
Anoop Desai True Colors	Song	2009
Aretha Franklin Sings the Great Diva Classics	Album	2014
Aretha Franklin Respect	Song	1967
Aubrey Logan	Artist	
Babeo Baggins	Artist	
Bette Midler It's the Girls	Album	2014
Bill St. John	Artist	
Blue & Lonesome (Rolling Stones)	Album	2016
Bobbie Nelson	Artist	
Boyce Avenue	Artist	
Brett Eldredge Glow	Album	2016
Buck 65 cover	Artist	
Carpool Karaoke James Corden	TV Show	2015–2018
Carrie Underwood Home Sweet Home	Song	2009
Cassandra Wilson Billie Holiday (Coming Forth by Day)	Album	2015
Cassandra Wilson Stylistics	Song	1993
Cassandra Wilson Tupelo Honey	Song	1993
Cassandra Wilson	Artist	
Charles Walker Band cover	Artist	
Classroom Instruments (Jimmy Fallon)	TV Show	2014–2018
Counting Crows Underwater Sunshine	Album	2012
Crystal Bowersox People Get Ready	Song	2010
Eliza Doolittle Runaway	Song	2011
Eric Clapton Clapton	Album	2010
Fallen Angels (Bob Dylan)	Album	2016
Framing Hanley Lollipop	Song	2007

Frankie Ford	Artist	
George Fest	Event	2014
George Thorogood cover	Artist	
Glen Campbell Adios	Album	2017
Glen Campbell Ghost on the Canvas	Album	2010
Groovy Kind of Love	Song	
Haley Reinhart	Artist	
Hamilton mixtape	Album	2016
Hip Pocket cover	Artist	
Jeff Buckley Hallelujah	Song	1994
Jennifer Lopez cover	Artist	
Joe Cocker cover	Artist	
John Mayer Keith Urban	Artist	
Johnny Cash American Recordings	Album	1994
Johnny Cash First Time Ever I Saw Your Face	Song	2002
Johnny Cash Redemption Song	Song	2003
Josh Kaufman	Artist	
Jukebox Mafia	Artist	
Justin Timberlake Hallelujah	Song	2010
Kane Brown	Artist	
Kennedy Center Honors	Event	2009–2018
Kina Grannis	Artist	
Lady Gaga cover	Artist	
LeAnn Rimes Lady & Gentlemen	Album	2011
Lee DeWyze The Boxer	Song	2010
Leonard Cohen cover	Artist	
Let It Be Roberta (Roberta Flack)	Album	2012
Lil Rounds Whats Love Got to Do With It	Song	2009
Little Big Town cover	Artist	
Macy Gray Covered	Album	2012
Mandy Moore Umbrella	Song	2011
Martina McBride Everlasting	Album	2014
Meet Glen Campbell	Album	2008/2012
Michael Buble	Artist	
Morgan James	Artist	
Over the Rhine Blood Oranges in the Snow	Album	2014
Pentatonix cover	Artist	
Pete Seeger's 90th birthday party	Event	2009
Peter Gabriel Scratch My Back	Album	2010
Phil Collins Going Back	Album	2010
Pitch Perfect cover	Film	2012–2017
Postmodern Jukebox	Artist	
Primus & the Chocolate Factory with the Fungi Ensemble	Album	2014

PTX Daft Punk	Song	2013
PTX Presents Top Pop Vol I	Album	2018
PTXVol IV-Classics	Album	2017
Puddles Clown (Puddles the Clown)	Artist	
Richie Havens Here Comes the Sun	Song	1971
Richie Havens	Artist	
Rosanne Cash The List	Album	2009
Rush 2112 (40th Anniversary)	Album	1976/2016
Ryan Adams 1989	Album	2015
Seal Soul 2	Album	2011
Siobhan Magnus Paint It Black	Song	2010
Smokey & Friends (Smokey Robinson)	Album	2014
The Lemonheads Varshons	Album	2009
The Night That Changed America	Event	2014
The Swon Brothers	Artist	
The Voice	TV Show	2011–2018
These Days 10000 Maniacs	Song	2004
These Days Gregg Allman	Song	1973
These Days Nico	Song	1967
Tom Jones Praise & Blame	Album	2010
Tony Lucca	Artist	
Willie Nelson American Classic	Album	2009
Willie Nelson Sheryl Crow	Artist	
Willie Nelson Stardust	Album	1978
With a Little Help from My Fwends (The Flaming Lips)	Album	2014

REMIX

Case/Search Term	Type	Year
A Millie Remix	Song	2009
Achy Breaky 2 (Billy Ray Cyrus)	Song	2014
Bale Out	Song	2009
The Bed Intruder Song	Song	2010
Bill O'Reilly remix	Song	2010
Birthday Cake remix (Rihanna)	Song	2012
Boys Remix (M.I.A)	Song	2008
Connie Francis Where the Boys Are remix	Song	2010
Cruise Nelly	Song	2013
Dee Jay Silver	Artist	
Despacito remix (Luis Fonsi)	Song	2017
DJ DU	Artist	

DJ Spankox	Artist	
Don't Taze Me, Bro	Song	2010
Frankie Knuckles	Artist	
Hotline Savesies	Song	2016
I'm Not the Only One Remix	Song	2014
Jason Aldean Dirt Road Anthem	Song	2011
Kaskade remix	Artist	
Martin Solveig Smash	Album	2011
May Mary remix	Artist	
Noy Alooshe	Artist	
Peggy Lee Why Don't You Do Right?	Song	2010
Rolling In the Heat	Song	2011
Shallow Bay Breaking Benjamin	Album	2011
Shirley Caesar Hold My Mule Remix	Song	2016
Stay With Me Remix	Song	2014
Swedish House Mafia Until Now	Album	2012
Thriller 25 (Michael Jackson)	Album	2008
Tiesto All of Me	Song	2015
Tiger Woods Voicemail Slow Jam Remix	Song	2010
will.i.am remix	Song	
Zedd	Artist	

MASH-UP

Case/Search Term	Type	Year
Bagels and Bongos	Album	1959
Beatallica	Artist	
Black Violin	Artist	
Chargaux	Artist	
CMT Crossroads	TV Show	2009–2018
Dee Jay Silver	Artist	
DJ AM	Artist	
DJ DU	Artist	
DJ Hero	Video Game	2009
DJ Z-Trip	Artist	
Found Tonight	Song	2018
Girl Talk	Artist	
Grey Album	Album	2004
Ill Submarine	Album	2013
Irving Fields	Artist	
It's a Scream How Levine Does the Rhumba	Album	2013
DJ Jazzy Jeff	Artist	

Lady Antebellum Stevie Nicks (CMT Crossroads)	TV Show	2013
Mazel Tov Mis Amigos	Album	1961
Miami Beach Rhumba	Song	1946
Robert Plant Alison Krauss (CMT Crossroads)	TV Show	2008
Sara Evans REO Speedwagon (CMT Crossroads)	TV Show	2015
Steven Tyler Carrie Underwood (CMT Crossroads)	TV Show	2012
Taylor Swift Def Leppard (CMT Crossroads)	TV Show	2008

PARODY

Case/Search Term	Type	Year
Barbra Streisand Jimmy Fallon (The Tonight Show)	TV Show	2016
Cledus T. Judd	Artist	
Dark Lord Funk	Song	2015
Goldieblox (Beastie Boys "Girls" parody)	Song	2013
Jimmy Fallon music (The Tonight Show)	TV Show	
Neil Young Fallon (The Tonight Show)	TV Show	
Shlock Rock	Artist	
Tebowie (The Tonight Show)	TV Show	2012
Timberlake Jimmy Fallon (The Tonight Show)	TV Show	
Trolls soundtrack	Film	2016
Weird Al Yankovic	Artist	

SOUNDALIKE

Case/Search Term	Type	Year
Arcade Fire Sprawl II (Mountains Beyond Mountains)	Song	2010
Blurred Lines (Robin Thicke)	Song	2013
Born this Way (Lady Gaga)	Song	2011
Daft Punk Get Lucky	Song	2013
Jason Aldean	Artist	
Justin Timberlake Suit & Tie	Song	2013
Last Nite (the Strokes)	Song	2001
Radiohead Creep	Song	1992

Sam Smith	Artist	
Stairway to Heaven (Led Zeppelin)	Song	1971
Tame Impala Feels Like We Only Go Backwards	Song	2012
Thicke Love After War	Album	2011
Uptown Funk (Mark Ronson)	Song	2014

NOTES

INTRODUCTION

1. Hugh McIntyre, "'Glee' Has More Chart Hits Than Anyone Else in History," *Forbes*, January 9, 2015, https://www.forbes.com/sites/hughmcintyre/2015/01/09 /glee-is-the-most-successful-charting-act-in-singles-history/. Though, as McIntyre notes, the data on Elvis is incomplete because his career began before the Hot 100 was invented.

2. Andrew Barker, "'Glee' Breaks New Artists and Turns Kitsch into Classics," *Variety*, March 18, 2014, https://variety.com/2014/tv/features/glee-breaks-new -artists-and-turns-kitsch-into-classics-1201137138/

3. Dee Lockett, "The 50 Best *Glee* Performances, Ranked," *Vulture*, March 20, 2015, https://www.vulture.com/2015/03/glee-best-performances-ranked.html

4. Pierre N. Leval, "Toward a Fair Use Standard," *Harvard Law Review* 103, no. 5 (1990): 1105–36, https://doi.org/10.2307/1341457

5. Campbell v. Acuff-Rose Music Inc., 510 U.S. 569 (1994).

6. See, for example, the Organization for Transformative Works, "a nonprofit organization run by and for fans to provide access to and preserve the history of fanworks and fan cultures," and the scholarly journal *Transformative Works and Cultures*, "an international, peer-reviewed journal published by the Organization for Transformative Works. *TWC* publishes articles about transformative works, broadly conceived; articles about media studies; and articles about the fan community." "About the OTW," *Organization for Transformative Works* (blog), accessed December 22, 2021, https://www.transformativeworks.org/about_otw/; "About the Journal," *Transformative Works and Cultures*, accessed December 22, 2021, https://journal.tran sformativeworks.org/index.php/twc/about

7. Anjali Vats, *The Color of Creatorship: Intellectual Property, Race, and the Making of Americans* (Stanford: Stanford University Press, 2020).

8. Thanks are due here to Netflix's feature allowing users to download their account history, which let me verify this year.

9. Jeffrey O. Valisno, "Staying In: Songbirds," *BusinessWorld*, May 20, 2011, sec. Weekender.

10. Jon Bream, "This High School Musical Usually Made the Grade," *Star Tribune*, June 2, 2011, Metro edition, sec. News.

11. Chad Berndtson, "The Year in Music: From Kanye to Cohen to Clemons to Cash, the Best (and Not So Best) of the Past 12 Months," *Patriot Ledger*, December 18, 2009, ROP edition, sec. Features.

12. Victor D. Infante, "'Glee' May Be Gone, but Songs Play On," *Telegram & Gazette*, March 20, 2015, sec. Living.

13. It seems important to note here that the excitement and enjoyment was not widely shared among the cast; in 2020, there was a series of allegations that show lead Lea Michele was abusive to her castmates, and particularly to castmates of color. For a summary, see Elizabeth Wagmeister, "Lea Michele Controversy: 'Glee' Actors and Other Co-Stars Speak Out," *Variety*, June 4, 2020, https://variety.com/2020/tv/news/lea-michele-glee-controversy-amber-riley-samantha-ware-1234625000/

14. "Pop Top: 'Glee' Falters with Priggish Madge Covers," *Salt Lake Tribune*, April 26, 2010, sec. Breaking; Features.

15. Mesfin Fekadu, "Gorillaz: We Won't Let 'Glee' Cover Our Songs," *Associated Press*, October 12, 2010, sec. Entertainment News. Of course, there is a compulsory mechanical license for recordings of someone else's composition, under which the covering artist must pay a statutory rate of 9.1¢ per copy and no permission is required.

16. "Pop Top: 'Glee' Falters with Priggish Madge Covers."

17. Valisno, "Staying In: Songbirds."

18. Bream, "This High School Musical Usually Made the Grade."

19. "CD Reviews: Underwood Expands Her Repertoire on Third Album," *Pittsburgh Tribune Review*, November 8, 2009, https://archive.triblive.com/news/cd-reviews-underwood-expands-her-repertoire-on-third-album/

20. Valisno, "Staying In: Songbirds."

21. "New Recordings," *Philadelphia Inquirer*, April 25, 2010, https://www.inquirer.com/philly/entertainment/20100425_New_Recordings.html

22. Valisno, "Staying In: Songbirds."

23. Inquirer, "CD Reviews: Underwood Expands Her Repertoire on Third Album."

24. Sandy Cohen, "'Glee' a Musical Success as Much as a Cult Success," *Associated Press*, April 12, 2010, sec. Entertainment News.

25. Cohen, "'Glee' a Musical Success as Much as a Cult Success."

26. Kembrew McLeod and Peter DiCola, *Creative License: The Law and Culture of Digital Sampling* (Durham: Duke University Press, 2011), 95.

27. Mel Stanfill, "Spinning Yarn with Borrowed Cotton," *In Media Res*, 2015, http://mediacommons.futureofthebook.org/imr/2015/05/27/spinning-yarn-borrowed-cotton, http://mediacommons.org/imr/search/site/spinning%20yarn

28. Robert Brauneis, "Copyright, Music, and Race: The Case of Mirror Cover Recordings," SSRN Scholarly Paper (Rochester, NY: Social Science Research Network, May 2, 2020), 24, 32, https://doi.org/10.2139/ssrn.3591113

29. Madhavi Sunder, *From Goods to a Good Life: Intellectual Property and Global Justice* (New Haven: Yale University Press, 2012), 97.

30. The adaptation copyright is probably why Gorillaz felt sure they would be able to deny *Glee*, because while they can't deny permission to cover their songs, they could, depending on what their recording contract looked like, be in a position to

refuse an adaptation copyright, and there's little chance a massive corporate transmedia production like *Glee* would release music without copyrighting its arrangement.

31. Francesca T. Royster, *Sounding Like a No-No: Queer Sounds and Eccentric Acts in the Post-Soul Era* (Ann Arbor: University of Michigan Press, 2012), 110.

32. Royster, *Sounding Like a No-No*, 110.

33. Bridgeport Music Inc. v. Dimension Films, 410 F.3d 792 (6th Cir. 2005).

34. Joanna Demers, *Steal This Music: How Intellectual Property Law Affects Musical Creativity* (Athens: University of Georgia Press, 2006), 122.

35. For discussions of this history of contracts as theft from Black artists, see Tricia Rose, *Black Noise: Rap Music and Black Culture in Contemporary America* (Hanover, NH: University Press of New England, 1994); K. J. Greene, "Copynorms, Black Cultural Production, and the Debate over African-American Reparations," *Cardozo Arts & Entertainment Law Journal* 25 (2008): 1179.

36. Rose, *Black Noise*, 92.

37. Demers, *Steal This Music*.

38. Sunder, *From Goods to a Good Life*.

39. Tarleton Gillespie, *Wired Shut: Copyright and the Shape of Digital Culture* (Cambridge, MA: MIT Press, 2007), 66.

40. Yochai Benkler, *The Wealth of Networks: How Social Production Transforms Markets and Freedom* (New Haven: Yale University Press, 2007), 387.

41. Susan S. Silbey and Austin Sarat, "Critical Traditions in Law and Society Research," *Law & Society Review* 21, no. 1 (1987): 172, https://doi.org/10.2307/3053389

42. Richard Delgado and Jean Stefancic, "Introduction," in *Critical Race Theory: The Cutting Edge*, 2nd ed., ed. Richard Delgado and Jean Stefancic (Temple University Press, 2000), xvi.

43. Kimberlé Crenshaw et al., "Introduction," in *Critical Race Theory: The Key Writings That Formed the Movement*, ed. Kimberlé Crenshaw et al. (New York: New Press, 1996), xxv.

44. Mari J. Matsuda, "Public Response to Racist Speech: Considering the Victim's Story," in *Words That Wound: Critical Race Theory, Assaultive Speech, and the First Amendment*, by Mari J. Matsuda, Charles R. Lawrence, Richard Delgado, and Kimberlé Crenshaw (Boulder: Westview Press, 1993), 36.

45. Crenshaw et al., "Introduction," xiii.

46. K. J. Greene, "Intellectual Property at the Intersection of Race and Gender: Lady Sings the Blues," *American University Journal of Gender, Social Policy & the Law* 16, no. 3 (2008): 368, https://digitalcommons.wcl.american.edu/jgspl/vol16/iss3/2

47. Crenshaw et al., "Introduction," xiii; Delgado and Stefancic, "Introduction," xvi.

48. Kimberlé Crenshaw, "Race, Reform, and Retrenchment: Transformation and Legitimation in Antidiscrimination Law," in *Critical Race Theory: The Key Writings That Formed the Movement*, ed. Kimberlé Crenshaw et al. (New York: New Press, 1996), 118.

49. Charles R. Lawrence III, "The Id, the Ego, and Equal Protection: Reckoning with Unconscious Racism," in *Critical Race Theory: The Key Writings That Formed the Movement*, ed. Kimberlé Crenshaw et al. (New York: New Press, 1996), 236.

50. Mari J. Matsuda and Charles R. Lawrence III, "Epilogue: Burning Crosses and the R.A.V. Case," in *Words That Wound: Critical Race Theory, Assaultive Speech, and the First Amendment* (Boulder: Westview Press, 1993), 136.

51. Cheryl I. Harris, "Whiteness as Property," in *Critical Race Theory: The Key Writings That Formed the Movement*, ed. Kimberlé Crenshaw et al. (New York: New Press, 1996), 278, 283.

52. Anjali Vats and Deidre A. Keller, "Critical Race IP," *Cardozo Arts & Entertainment Law Journal* 36 (2018): 740.

53. Vats, *The Color of Creatorship*, 2.

54. Sunder, *From Goods to a Good Life*, 12.

55. Rosemary J. Coombe, *The Cultural Life of Intellectual Properties: Authorship, Appropriation, and the Law* (Durham: Duke University Press, 1998).

56. Olufunmilayo B. Arewa, "Copyright on Catfish Row: Musical Borrowing, Porgy and Bess, and Unfair Use," *Rutgers Law Journal* 37 (2006): 281.

57. Vats, *The Color of Creatorship*.

58. For discussions of Romanticism and internal genius in the context of creation and law, see Olufunmilayo B. Arewa, "Making Music: Copyright Law and Creative Processes," in *A Companion to Media Authorship*, ed. Jonathan Gray and Derek Johnson (New York: John Wiley & Sons, 2013), 69–87; Boatema Boateng, *The Copyright Thing Doesn't Work Here: Adinkra and Kente Cloth and Intellectual Property in Ghana* (Minneapolis: University of Minnesota Press, 2011); Aram Sinnreich, *Mashed Up: Music, Technology, and the Rise of Configurable Culture* (Amherst: University of Massachusetts Press, 2010); Sunder, *From Goods to a Good Life*; Christopher M. Toula and Gregory C. Lisby, "Towards an Affirmative Public Domain," *Cultural Studies* 28, no. 5–6 (2014): 997–1021, https://doi.org/10.1080/09502386.2014.886490. The use of "his" here—which, while formerly hegemonic, is hopefully jarring to the contemporary reader—is deliberate to call attention to the default masculinization of authorship as a subject position.

59. For discussions of Romanticism and rejection of external influence on creation, see Arewa, "Making Music: Copyright Law and Creative Processes"; Martin Fredriksson, "Copyright Culture and Pirate Politics," *Cultural Studies* 28, no. 5–6 (2014): 1022–47, https://doi.org/10.1080/09502386.2014.886483; Sinnreich, *Mashed Up*; Rebecca Tushnet, "User-Generated Discontent: Transformation in Practice," *Columbia Journal of Law & the Arts* 31 (2008): 497.

60. Jack Hamilton, *Just around Midnight: Rock and Roll and the Racial Imagination*, illus. ed. (Cambridge, MA: Harvard University Press, 2016), 53.

61. Thomas G. Schumacher, "'This Is a Sampling Sport': Digital Sampling, Rap Music and the Law in Cultural Production," *Media, Culture & Society* 17, no. 2 (1995): 271, https://doi.org/10.1177/016344395017002006

62. Hamilton, *Just around Midnight*, 175.

63. Matt Stahl, *Unfree Masters: Popular Music and the Politics of Work* (Durham: Duke University Press, 2012), 4.

64. Sunder, *From Goods to a Good Life*, 87.

65. Martha Woodmansee, "The Genius and the Copyright: Economic and Legal

Conditions of the Emergence of the 'Author,'" *Eighteenth-Century Studies* 17, no. 4 (1984): 425–48, https://doi.org/10.2307/2738129

66. Jessica Litman, *Digital Copyright*, pbk. ed. (Amherst, NY: Prometheus Books, 2006), 78.

67. Roland Barthes, "The Death of the Author," in *Image-Music-Text*, trans. Stephen Heath (New York: Hill and Wang, 1978), 142–48; Michel Foucault, "What Is an Author?," in *Language, Counter-Memory, Practice: Selected Essays and Interviews* (Ithaca: Cornell University Press, 1980), 113–38.

68. Michael Awkward, *Soul Covers: Rhythm and Blues Remakes and the Struggle for Artistic Identity* (Durham: Duke University Press, 2007), 11.

69. Sunder, *From Goods to a Good Life*, 148.

70. Stahl, *Unfree Masters*, 2.

71. Rose, *Black Noise*, 213.

72. According to §101 of the Copyright Law of the United States, a work for hire is "a work prepared by an employee within the scope of his or her employment" or "a work specially ordered or commissioned for use as a contribution to a collective work, as a part of a motion picture or other audiovisual work, as a translation, as a supplementary work, as a compilation, as an instructional text, as a test, as answer material for a test, or as an atlas, if the parties expressly agree in a written instrument signed by them that the work shall be considered a work made for hire." Importantly, "if a work is made for hire, an employer is considered the author even if an employee actually created the work." Definitions, Title 17 U.S. Code § 101. Accessed December 4, 2022. https://copyright.gov/title17/92chap1.html

73. Stahl, *Unfree Masters*, 183.

74. Jane C. Ginsburg, "The Author's Name as a Trademark: A Perverse Perspective on the Moral Right of Paternity," *Cardozo Arts & Entertainment Law Journal* 23 (2005): 388.

75. Foucault, "What Is an Author?"

76. Anupam Chander and Madhavi Sunder, "The Romance of the Public Domain," *California Law Review* 92 (2004): 1335.

77. Toula and Lisby, "Towards an Affirmative Public Domain," 1005.

78. Boateng, *The Copyright Thing Doesn't Work Here*, 47.

79. James Boyle, *The Public Domain: Enclosing the Commons of the Mind* (New Haven: Yale University Press, 2008), 77.

80. Leval, "Toward a Fair Use Standard," 1111.

81. Kembrew McLeod and Rudolf Kuenzli, "I Collage, Therefore I Am: An Introduction to *Cutting Across Media*," in *Cutting Across Media: Appropriation Art, Interventionist Collage, and Copyright Law*, ed. Kembrew McLeod and Rudolf Kuenzli (Durham: Duke University Press, 2011), 1–23.

82. Julie E. Cohen, "Copyright and the Perfect Curve," *Vanderbilt Law Review* 53 (2000): 1799–1819.

83. James Boyle, "The Second Enclosure Movement and the Construction of the Public Domain," *Law and Contemporary Problems* 66, no. 1/2 (2003): 57, https://www.jstor.org/stable/20059171

84. Lewis Hyde, *Common as Air: Revolution, Art, and Ownership* (New York: Farrar, Straus and Giroux, 2010), 107.

85. Arewa, "Making Music: Copyright Law and Creative Processes," 70.

86. J. Peter Burkholder, "The Uses of Existing Music: Musical Borrowing as a Field," *Notes* 50, no. 3 (1994): 851–70, https://doi.org/10.2307/898531

87. Arewa, "Making Music: Copyright Law and Creative Processes," 76–77.

88. Greene, "Intellectual Property at the Intersection of Race and Gender," 371.

89. Greene, "Intellectual Property at the Intersection of Race and Gender," 369.

90. Anne Barron, "Introduction: Harmony or Dissonance? Copyright Concepts and Musical Practice," *Social & Legal Studies* 15, no. 1 (2006): 35, original emphasis, https://doi.org/10.1177/0964663906060972

91. Siva Vaidhyanathan, *Copyrights and Copywrongs: The Rise of Intellectual Property and How It Threatens Creativity* (New York: New York University Press, 2003), 119.

92. Coombe, *The Cultural Life of Intellectual Properties*, 240.

93. bell hooks, "Eating the Other: Desire and Resistance," in *Media and Cultural Studies: KeyWorks*, rev. ed., ed. Meenakshi Gigi Durham and Douglas Kellner (Malden, MA: Blackwell, 2006), 368.

94. Eric Lott, *Love & Theft: Blackface Minstrelsy and the American Working Class*, 20th anniversary ed. (New York: Oxford University Press, 2013), 6–7.

95. David Hesmondhalgh, "Digital Sampling and Cultural Inequality," *Social & Legal Studies* 15, no. 1 (2006): 56, https://doi.org/10.1177/0964663906060973

96. Steven Feld, "Notes on World Beat," *Public Culture* 1, no. 1 (1988): 31, https://doi .org/10.1215/08992363-1-1-31

97. Christopher M. Bingham, "Talking about Twitch: *Dropped Frames* and a Normative Theory of New Media Production," *Convergence* 26, no. 2 (2020): 269–86, https://doi.org/10.1177/1354856517736974

98. Tim English, *Sounds Like Teen Spirit: Stolen Melodies, Ripped-off Riffs, and the Secret History of Rock and Roll*, 2016 edition (2016).

99. "Nexis Uni" (LexisNexis), accessed April 10, 2022, https://www.lexisnexis.com /en-us/professional/academic/nexis-uni.page. One drawback of the database is that metadata is unevenly available. Information such as the section of the newspaper in which a story originally appeared is only sometimes present, preventing analysis of how this might be a factor in discussions.

100. See Data Appendix for the full list of transformative musical works.

101. Sheena D. Hyndman, "No Money, Mo' Problems: The Role of the Remix in Restructuring Compensation for Producers of Electronic Dance Music," *MUSICultures* 41, no. 1 (2014): 59, https://journals.lib.unb.ca/index.php/MC/article/view/22356

102. Burkholder, "The Uses of Existing Music," 854.

103. Annemarie Navar-Gill and Mel Stanfill, "'We Shouldn't Have to Trend to Make You Listen': Queer Fan Hashtag Campaigns as Production Interventions," *Journal of Film and Video* 70, no. 3–4 (2018): 85–100.

104. Mel Stanfill, *Exploiting Fandom: How the Media Industry Seeks to Manipulate Fans* (Iowa City: University of Iowa Press, 2019).

105. As feminists have long pointed out, using the masculine "Latino" universally, while grammatically correct in Spanish, is exclusionary; recently, nonbinary people have argued that "Latino/Latina" is exclusionary as well. I use Latine throughout this book as a gender-neutral option which, unlike Latinx, is pronounceable in Spanish.

106. Janez Demšar et al., "Orange: Data Mining Toolbox in Python," *Journal of Machine Learning Research* 14 (2013): 2349–53.

CHAPTER 1

1. Jon Pareles, "Peter Gabriel Says, 'I'll Sing Yours, You Sing Mine,'" *New York Times*, March 2, 2010, late edition-final edition, sec. C.

2. I use "source text" or "source song" in this chapter, on the model of "source text" from translation studies, to resist the idea that the earlier song is the only one that's "original." While Kurt Mosser's notion of a "base" performance is useful, I find that it implies addition on top rather than creating a new instance, and so is more useful to describe remixes than covers. Kurt Mosser, "'Cover Songs': Ambiguity, Multivalence, Polysemy," *Popular Musicology Online*, no. 2 (2008), http://www.popular-musicology-online.com/issues/02/mosser.html

3. Gabriel Solis, "I Did It My Way: Rock and the Logic of Covers," *Popular Music and Society* 33, no. 3 (2010): 298, https://doi.org/10.1080/03007760903523351

4. Michael Rings, "Doing It Their Way: Rock Covers, Genre, and Appreciation," *Journal of Aesthetics and Art Criticism* 71, no. 1 (2013): 55–63; Solis, "I Did It My Way"; Deena Weinstein, "The History of Rock's Pasts through Rock Covers," in *A Popular Music Reader*, ed. Richard G. King (Boston: Pearson Learning Solutions, 2012), 69–80.

5. Weinstein, "The History of Rock's Pasts through Rock Covers," 76.

6. Recordings of standards and Christmas songs don't typically respond to a particular previous recording; tribute bands don't function as standalone artists when they respond to previous works. The inclusion of these categories in cover songs is also contested within the literature: "It goes without saying that when we sing holiday songs, for example, we are not 'covering' them. When a singer sings a national anthem at the beginning of a sports event, they are not covering it either." Nadav Appel, "Pat Boone's Last Laugh: Cover Versions and the Performance of Knowledge," *International Journal of Cultural Studies* 21, no. 4 (2018): 442, https://doi.org/10.1177/1367877917692901. Including these 146 not-quite-covers would have increased the total analyzed musical texts in the book to 328.

7. These were: cover Black, cover man, cover white, cover woman, source Black, source man, source white, source woman, white cover Black source, evoke emotion, genre mixing, and originality.

8. Weinstein, "The History of Rock's Pasts through Rock Covers," 71.

9. For summaries of this history, see Olufunmilayo B. Arewa, "Blues Lives: Promise and Perils of Musical Copyright," *Cardozo Arts & Entertainment Law Journal* 27 (2010): 573; Robert Brauneis, "Copyright, Music, and Race: The Case of Mirror Cover Recordings," SSRN Scholarly Paper (Rochester, NY: Social Science Research Network, May 2, 2020), https://doi.org/10.2139/ssrn.3591113

10. Arewa, "Blues Lives," 595.

11. Eric Lott, *Love and Theft: Blackface Minstrelsy and the American Working Class*, 20th anniversary ed. (New York: Oxford University Press, 2013), 6–7.

12. Brauneis, "Copyright, Music, and Race," 20.

13. Brauneis, "Copyright, Music, and Race," 7.

14. Brauneis, "Copyright, Music, and Race," 8; Joanna Demers, *Steal This Music: How Intellectual Property Law Affects Musical Creativity* (Athens: University of Georgia Press, 2006), 51; Maureen Mahon, *Black Diamond Queens: African American Women and Rock and Roll*, illus. ed. (Durham: Duke University Press, 2020), 61.

15. Maureen Mahon, *Right to Rock: The Black Rock Coalition and the Cultural Politics of Race* (Durham: Duke University Press, 2004), 154.

16. Janet McConnaughey, "Frankie Ford, Who Sang 'Sea Cruise,' Dies at Age 76," *Associated Press*, September 29, 2015.

17. Peter Guralnick, "Elvis Presley: How Sun Records Boss Sam Phillips Discovered a Star in 1954," *Independent*, October 30, 2015, http://www.independent.co.uk/arts-en tertainment/music/features/elvis-presley-how-sun-records-boss-sam-phillips-disco vered-a-star-in-1954-a6713891.html. I describe the comment as possibly aprocyphal because the website of Phillips's label, Sun Records, claims that "Phillips long disavowed the comment," and all the references I can find say it was reported secondhand by his assistant, Marion Keisker. Jon Garelick, "Sam Phillips," Sun Record Company, accessed September 15, 2019, http://www.sunrecordcompany.com/Sam_Phillips.html

18. Mahon, *Right to Rock*, 150.

19. Demers, *Steal This Music*, 68. This history is expressed particularly clearly with blackface minstrelsy. For the foundational history of blackface minstrelsy, see Lott, *Love and Theft*.

20. Mahon, *Black Diamond Queens*, 40.

21. For a discussion of the protective tendencies of Elvis Presley Enterprises, see Demers, *Steal This Music*, 69–70.

22. Supreme Records Inc. v. Decca Records Inc., 90 F. Supp. 904 (S.D. Cal. 1950).

23. Barbara A. Ringer, "The Unauthorized Duplication of Sound Recordings," Copyright Law Revision Study 26 (Washington, DC: U.S. Copyright Office, 1957), 10, 1n3, https://www.copyright.gov/history/studies/study26.pdf

24. *Supreme Records Inc.*, 90 F. Supp.

25. K. J. Greene, "Intellectual Property at the Intersection of Race and Gender: Lady Sings the Blues," *American University Journal of Gender, Social Policy & the Law* 16, no. 3 (2008): 371, https://digitalcommons.wcl.american.edu/jgspl/vol16/iss3/2

26. *Supreme Records Inc.*, 90 F. Supp.

27. Steve Bailey, "Faithful or Foolish: The Emergence of the 'Ironic Cover Album' and Rock Culture," *Popular Music and Society* 26, no. 2 (2003): 143, https://doi.org/10 .1080/0300776032000095486

28. "Scope of Exclusive Rights in Nondramatic Musical Works: Compulsory License for Making and Distributing Phonorecords," 17 U.S. Code § 115, accessed December 10, 2022, https://copyright.gov/title17/92chap1.html#115

29. Rodney Ho, "American Idol Buzz: American Idol Recap, Top 8 Performance Show," *Atlanta Journal-Constitution*, April 7, 2009, online edition.

30. Jim Harrington, "Review: Beatles TV Special More Flop Than Fab," *Contra Costa Times*, February 10, 2014, sec. Breaking, News, Local.

31. Melinda Newman, "Album Review: LeAnn Rimes' 'Lady & Gentlemen,'" *UPROXX*, September 26, 2011, https://uproxx.com/hitfix/album-review-leann -rimes-lady-gentlemen/

32. Mosser, "'Cover Songs': Ambiguity, Multivalence, Polysemy," sec. II.b.1.

33. "Scott Bradlee's Postmodern Jukebox, Fort Myers Beach, Florida, May 11: Tickets on Sale Friday, February 3 at 10am," *Plus Media Solutions*, February 3, 2017.

34. George Varga, *San Diego Union-Tribune*, "Reinhart Wants to Party (and Sing) Like It's '69," *Telegram & Gazette*, October 26, 2017, Worcester TG edition, sec. Entertainment Life.

35. Francesca T. Royster, *Sounding Like a No-No: Queer Sounds and Eccentric Acts in the Post-Soul Era* (Ann Arbor: University of Michigan Press, 2012), 6.

36. Steven Feld, "Notes on World Beat," *Public Culture* 1, no. 1 (1988): 31, https://doi .org/10.1215/08992363-1-1-31

37. Feld, "Notes on World Beat," 31–32.

38. ABKCO Music Inc. v. LaVere, 217 F.3d 684 (9th Cir. 2000). ABKCO lost, and the decision found that the songs were not in the public domain, but what's relevant here is the reluctance to pay. For a helpful summary of the case, see Arewa, "Blues Lives," 609–11.

39. Scott Mervis, "Stealing the Show: The Singers Know That the 'Star' Slot Is Up for Grabs on 'American Idols Live!' Tour," *Pittsburgh Post-Gazette*, August 20, 2009, Sooner edition, sec. Arts & Entertainment, Music Preview.

40. Michael Bialas, "Crossover Country," *Pueblo Chieftain*, August 5, 2011, sec. Lifestyle.

41. Joe Gross, "Rogues and Stones: Movies, Books, Music and More Coming in December," *Austin American-Statesman*, November 28, 2016, State edition, sec. Life.

42. Jon Bream, "Youth Storms the Glambert Show," *Star Tribune*, September 2, 2009, Metro edition.

43. Dan Aquilante, "Grammy Grabs," *New York Post*, September 28, 2010, all editions.

44. Campbell v. Acuff-Rose Music Inc., 510 U.S. 569 (1994).

45. Scope of Exclusive Rights in Nondramatic Musical Works: Compulsory License for Making and Distributing Phonorecords.

46. Demers, *Steal This Music*, 40.

47. Mosser, "'Cover Songs': Ambiguity, Multivalence, Polysemy," sec. II.b.1.

48. Cristyn Magnus, P. D. Magnus, and Christy Mag Uidhir, "Judging Covers," *Journal of Aesthetics and Art Criticism* 71, no. 4 (2013): 364, https://doi.org/10.1111/jaac .12034

49. Jack Hamilton, *Just around Midnight: Rock and Roll and the Racial Imagination*, illus. ed. (Cambridge, MA: Harvard University Press, 2016), 53.

50. Michael Awkward, *Soul Covers: Rhythm and Blues Remakes and the Struggle for Artistic Identity* (Durham: Duke University Press, 2007), xxvi–xxvii, 12, 33.

51. Matthew Fiander, *Pittsburgh Post-Gazette*, March 29, 2012, Sooner edition, sec. Arts & Entertainment, For the Record.

52. Steve Jones, "Albums," *USA Today*, January 24, 2012, final edition, sec. Life.

53. Ruth McCann, "Tour Simmers with Whole Lotta Lambert Love," *Washington Post*, August 6, 2009, Met 2 edition, sec. Style.

54. Sean Daly, "Collins' R&B Redux Just a Wishy Wash," *Tampa Bay Times*, September 5, 2010, 4 State / Suncoast edition, sec. Tampa Bay, Review.

55. Pareles, "Peter Gabriel Says, 'I'll Sing Yours, You Sing Mine.'"

56. Jim Farber, "Praise at Last Rains o'er LaVette," *Daily News*, January 9, 2009, Sports final edition, sec. Now.

57. Sean P. Means, "Old Hits Made New: Covering the Best Cover Songs," *Salt Lake Tribune*, July 23, 2011, sec. Culture Vulture, Features.

58. Magnus, Magnus, and Mag Uidhir, "Judging Covers," 366.

59. Sean Daly, "Celebrating Her Love for Soul," *Tampa Bay Times*, January 27, 2012, sec. TBT. Flack chose the 1996 take on "Killing Me Softly" by the Fugees.

60. The data for other racial categories is so small—fewer than 100 instances—that the comparisons are noisy—e.g., the one song from a Pacific Islander source is considered positively, for 100% positive in that category, and the entire South Asian category is composed of discussions of widely criticized *American Idol* contestant Sanjaya Malakar.

61. Rings, "Doing It Their Way," 55.

62. Dan Aquilante, "The Best Secondhand Songs: When Great Singers Cover a Hit, the Results Can Be Sublime," *New York Post*, August 14, 2011.

63. Kevin C. Johnson, "Phillips Seems Destined for Stardom," *St. Louis Post-Dispatch*, July 13, 2012, second edition, sec. News.

64. Mahon, *Black Diamond Queens*, 13.

65. Scott Mervis, "Lambert, Allen Show Star Power," *Pittsburgh Post-Gazette*, August 24, 2009, Sooner edition, sec. Arts & Entertainment, Concert Review.

66. Stephen Holden, "Albums by Neil Young, Bette Midler and Miguel Zenón," *New York Times*, November 4, 2014, late edition-final edition, sec. C.

67. Aquilante, "The Best Secondhand Songs: When Great Singers Cover a Hit, the Results Can Be Sublime."

68. Aquilante, "The Best Secondhand Songs."

69. See Joane Nagel, *Race, Ethnicity, and Sexuality: Intimate Intersections, Forbidden Frontiers* (New York: Oxford University Press, 2003).

70. Aquilante, "The Best Secondhand Songs."

71. Jenée Desmond-Harris, "Annie Lennox is Singing about Lynching While Ignoring Its Horrifying History," *Vox*, October 28, 2014, https://www.vox.com/2014/10/28/7080287/annie-lennox-strange-fruit-tavis-smiley-nostalgia

72. Peter Larsen, "Lambert Dominates 'Idol' in L.A.," *Orange County Register*, July 18, 2009, sec. Arts.

73. Curtis Ross, "Gabriel Reaches beyond Covers," *Tampa Tribune*, March 5, 2010, final edition, sec. Friday Extra.

74. Jim Farber, "Roberta Flack Gets Back to the Beatles," *Daily News*, February 22, 2012, Sports final edition, sec. Now.

75. David Burger, "'American Idol' Tour Kicks Off in Utah," *Salt Lake Tribune*, July 8, 2011, sec. Friday Mix, Entertainment, Features.

76. Means, "Old Hits Made New: Covering the Best Cover Songs."

77. Ryan Nakashima, "Cover Songs: Homage or Irksome Marketing Ploy?," *Associated Press*, May 30, 2013.

78. Nakashima, "Cover Songs: Homage or Irksome Marketing Ploy?"

79. Matthias Stork, "The Cultural Economics of Performance Space: Negotiating Fan, Labor, and Marketing Practice in Glee's Transmedia Geography," *Transformative Works and Cultures* 15 (2014): para. 3.9, https://doi.org/10.3983/twc.2014.0490. Notably, *Glee* did not extend this forbearance to other fan activity such as traditional fanvids advocating relationships between characters.

80. Scope of Exclusive Rights in Nondramatic Musical works: Compulsory License for Making and Distributing Phonorecords.

81. Nakashima, "Cover Songs: Homage or Irksome Marketing Ploy?"

82. Demers, *Steal This Music*, 115.

83. Demers, *Steal This Music*, 114–15.

84. Nakashima, "Cover Songs: Homage or Irksome Marketing Ploy?"

85. Though, see Rafael Rob and Joel Waldfogel for the argument that most downloaded songs would likely not have been purchased. Rafael Rob and Joel Waldfogel, "Piracy on the High C's: Music Downloading, Sales Displacement, and Social Welfare in a Sample of College Students," *Journal of Law and Economics* 49 (2006): 29–62.

86. Patrik Wikström, *The Music Industry: Music in the Cloud*, 2nd ed. (Cambridge: Polity, 2013), 101.

87. ed condran, "Scott Brandlee and Postmodern Jukebox: Taking Modern Pop Songs and Transforming Them into Jazz," *Tampa Tribune*, November 27, 2015, sec. Friday Extra.

88. Nakashima, "Cover Songs: Homage or Irksome Marketing Ploy?"

89. Gerry Galipault, "The Boyce Are Back," *Sarasota Herald Tribune*, September 22, 2011, sec. E, Archives. The article does not explain how they got out of their record deal, though it seems rather remarkable given that, as James Boyle puts it, musicians labor under "a system of contracts . . . that makes feudal indenture look benign." James Boyle, *The Public Domain: Enclosing the Commons of the Mind* (New Haven: Yale University Press, 2008), 77.

90. Kristin M. Hall, "Kane Brown Turned Facebook Likes into a Country Music Career," *Associated Press*, December 21, 2016, sec. Entertainment News.

91. The landscape has likely changed with the rise of Tik Tok.

92. Gene Axton, "Scranton's Theater at Lackawanna College Puts a Quarter in the Postmodern Jukebox," *Times Leader*, November 9, 2015, sec. Lifestyle.

93. Limor Shifman, *Memes in Digital Culture* (Cambridge, MA: MIT Press, 2013), 58.

94. Shifman, *Memes in Digital Culture*, 124.

95. Dan Taylor, "Scott Bradlee's Postmodern Jukebox Coming to Santa Rosa," *Press Democrat*, March 26, 2018, sec. Entertainment News.

96. Tony Lacy-Thompson, "Postmodern Jukebox Wows with Talent at Stanford's Bing Concert Hall," *East Bay Times*, February 21, 2017.

97. "Scott Bradlee's Postmodern Jukebox, Fort Myers Beach, Florida, May 11: Tickets on Sale Friday, February 3 at 10am."

98. "YouTube for Press," accessed December 10, 2022, https://web.archive.org/web/20190921012619/https://www.youtube.com/about/press/

99. Kristin M. Hall, "Grammy Winners Pentatonix Finally Getting Airplay," *Associated Press*, October 16, 2015, sec. Entertainment News.

100. Carnegie Hall's website has a page devoted to "The Joke," where they note that "the earliest known written accounts are from the mid-1950s, which might suggest Borscht Belt humor from the Catskills resorts popular at the time." "The Joke," accessed December 10, 2022, https://www.carnegiehall.org/Explore/Articles/2020/04/10/The-Joke

101. *Washington Post*, May 23, 2014, every edition, sec. Weekend.

102. Solis, "I Did It My Way," 315–16.

103. Anne Barron, "Introduction: Harmony or Dissonance? Copyright Concepts and Musical Practice," *Social & Legal Studies* 15, no. 1 (2006): 26, https://doi.org/10.1177/0964663906060972

104. David Bauder, "British Singer Joe Cocker Dies of Lung Cancer," *Associated Press*, December 22, 2014, sec. Domestic News, Entertainment News.

105. Mahon, *Black Diamond Queens*, 107.

CHAPTER 2

1. Emily Yahr, "Mixing In Some Hip-Hop to the 2-Step," *Washington Post*, August 6, 2013, Suburban edition, sec. Style.

2. Joanna Demers, *Steal This Music: How Intellectual Property Law Affects Musical Creativity* (Athens: University of Georgia Press, 2006), 77.

3. Peter Manuel and Wayne Marshall, "The Riddim Method: Aesthetics, Practice, and Ownership in Jamaican Dancehall," *Popular Music* 25, no. 3 (2006): 467, 462, https://doi.org/10.1017/S0261143006000997

4. Larisa Kingston Mann, *Rude Citizenship: Jamaican Popular Music, Copyright, and the Reverberations of Colonial Power* (Chapel Hill: University of North Carolina Press, 2022), 14.

5. Demers, *Steal This Music*, 78.

6. Sheena D. Hyndman, "No Money, Mo' Problems: The Role of the Remix in Restructuring Compensation for Producers of Electronic Dance Music," *MUSICultures* 41, no. 1 (2014): 59, https://journals.lib.unb.ca/index.php/MC/article/view/22356

7. Yahr, "Mixing In Some Hip-Hop to the 2-Step."

8. Nekesa Mumbi Moody, "Connie Francis' 'Where the Boys Are' Gets Remake," *Associated Press*, May 20, 2010, sec. Entertainment News.

9. Ashley Dean, *Colorado Daily*, September 13, 2012, sec. State and Regional News.

10. Dean in *Colorado Daily*, September 13, 2012.

11. Sarah Godfrey, "Where's Wale? 10 Hot Tracks," *Washington Post*, June 3, 2009, Suburban edition, sec. Style.

12. Carl Wilson Slate, "What Is 'Achy Breaky 2'?," *Salt Lake Tribune*, February 14, 2014, sec. Features.

13. Mikael Wood, "Story behind the Song: The 'Despacito' Remix Isn't Just about Sex," *Dayton Daily News*, September 1, 2017.

14. This record was later broken by another country-hip-hop smash hit, Lil Nas X's "Old Town Road," which was at #1 for 19 weeks in 2019—and featured Billy Ray Cyrus on its four official remixes. The proliferating remixes of "Old Town Road" will be examined later in the chapter.

15. The "featuring" and dance remix genres were not coded directly, but rather these categories are emergent from the data. This means that they had to be quantified by aggregating code counts for base tracks, remixers, and featured artists, which were coded directly. The numeric range reflects the fact that I don't have the identities of both parties to a remix in all instances. Calculating by counting all instances of all codes is impacted by the generally greater fame of featured artists than remixers, producing the 24/76 split. Base track information is more consistently available, so that looking only at base tracks produces the 30/70 split, but this method inevitably undercounts some of the people doing remix work. Thus, I use both figures as a range, and in any case there are at least twice as many "featuring" remixes as dance ones in press coverage during the period this book examines.

16. Chris Talbott, "Carrie Underwood Takes Video of Year at CMT Awards," *Associated Press*, June 6, 2013, sec. Entertainment News.

17. The nomination was perceived by some to be a snub, since it did not come as part of the regular process but weeks later; it also happened in the context of MTV marginalizing the song generally, as the video "played on MTV Tres, the company's Latin channel, but MTV didn't explain why it wasn't playing the video on MTV or MTV2." Mesfin Fekadu, "'Despacito' Ties Mariah Carey's 16-Week Record at No. 1," *Associated Press*, August 28, 2017.

18. Mesfin Fekadu, "And the Grammy Nomination Goes to . . . ," *Associated Press*, December 3, 2014, sec. Entertainment News.

19. Hyndman, "No Money, Mo' Problems," 57–58.

20. Yahr, "Mixing In Some Hip-Hop to the 2-Step."

21. Mesfin Fekadu, "'Despacito' Opening Doors for Spanish Songs on English Radio," *Associated Press*, August 8, 2017, sec. Entertainment News.

22. Mesfin Fekadu, "Mary Mary Still Going Strong 9 Years Later," *Associated Press*, August 28, 2009, sec. Entertainment News.

23. Mesfin Fekadu, "Kanye West's 'Yeezus': Heaven-Sent or Weak Event?," *Associated Press*, July 20, 2013, sec. Entertainment News.

24. Mike Cidoni, "'Fever' Singer Is Hot Again," *Associated Press*, May 17, 2010, sec. Entertainment News.

25. Yahr, "Mixing In Some Hip-Hop to the 2-Step."

26. Derrik J. Lang, "Batman Goes Bale-Istic with Profane Tirade on Crew," *Associated Press*, February 4, 2009, sec. Entertainment News.

27. Lisa Orkin Emmanuel, "Tiger's Tunes: Apology Lives Online in Mashups," *Associated Press*, February 23, 2010, sec. Entertainment News.

28. Limor Shifman, *Memes in Digital Culture* (Cambridge, MA: MIT Press, 2013), 7–8, internal emphasis removed.

29. Emmanuel, "Tiger's Tunes: Apology Lives Online in Mashups."

30. Aron Heller, "Israeli Video Remix King Becomes Player in Election Campaign," *Associated Press*, January 9, 2015, sec. International News.

31. Kevin C. Johnson, "Florida Georgia Line Brings 'Good Times' to St. Louis," *St. Louis Post-Dispatch*, November 1, 2013, first edition, sec. Go!

32. Brian Kelley, "People in the News," *Dayton Daily News*, December 21, 2013, sec. Comics.

33. Scott Mervis, "'Thriller Night': Local Musicians Gather to Pay Tribute to Michael Jackson and His Blockbuster," *Pittsburgh Post-Gazette*, October 24, 2013, Sooner edition, sec. Arts & Entertainment, Music Preview.

34. Ryan Nakashima, "Apple, Labels Work on Album 'Cocktail,'" *Associated Press*, July 27, 2009, sec. Business News.

35. Hyndman, "No Money, Mo' Problems," 68.

36. Jacob Bernstein, "Postscript: Death of a Pied Piper," *New York Times*, April 6, 2014, late edition-final edition, sec. ST.

37. Chris Talbott, "Electronic DJ-Producer Zedd Blitzes the Pop World," *Associated Press*, September 26, 2013, sec. Entertainment News.

38. Demers, *Steal This Music*, 134.

39. "Show Bits: Tiesto's Birthday Gift Becomes Grammy Win," *Associated Press*, February 8, 2015.

40. Yahr, "Mixing In Some Hip-Hop to the 2-Step."

41. Hyndman, "No Money, Mo' Problems," 60–63.

42. Slate, "What Is 'Achy Breaky 2'?"

43. Chris Talbott, "Jason Derulo, John Legend among CMT Awards' VIPs," *Associated Press*, June 3, 2014, sec. Entertainment News.

44. Jon Caramanica, "The Playlist: Demi Lovato Seeks Her 'Despacito' and 9 More New Songs," *New York Times*, November 18, 2017, https://www.nytimes.com/2017/11/17/arts/music/playlist-luis-fonsi-demi-lovato-jaden-smith.html

45. Kembrew McLeod and Peter DiCola, *Creative License: The Law and Culture of Digital Sampling* (Durham: Duke University Press, 2011), 101.

46. Scott Iwasaki, "Nightclub DJ Is Proud of Utah Ties," *Deseret Morning News*, April 3, 2009.

47. Dean, *Colorado Daily*, September 13, 2012.

48. Adrian Sainz, "Lawsuits in Fla., England Related to Elvis Music," *Associated Press*, February 9, 2011, sec. Entertainment News.

49. Michael Rubinkam, "Lead Singer of Breaking Benjamin Fires Bandmates," *Associated Press*, August 2, 2011, sec. Entertainment News.

50. Jacob Bernstein, "The Queen of Quiet," *New York Times*, October 26, 2017, late edition-final edition, sec. D.

51. Mesfin Fekadu, "Shirley Caesar Isn't Cooking 'Beans, Greens' at Thanksgiving," *Associated Press*, November 19, 2016, sec. Domestic News.

52. Toni Lester, "Treating Creative Black Intellectual Property Ownership as a Human Right," SSRN Scholarly Paper (Rochester, NY: Social Science Research Network, July 6, 2020), 28–29, https://doi.org/10.2139/ssrn.3644691

53. Lester, "Treating Creative Black Intellectual Property Ownership as a Human Right," 15.

54. Boatema Boateng, *The Copyright Thing Doesn't Work Here: Adinkra and Kente Cloth and Intellectual Property in Ghana* (Minneapolis: University of Minnesota Press, 2011), 155. As people have insisted to me more than once, as a party to the Berne Convention for the Protection of Literary and Artistic Works (1886), the United States does in theory protect moral rights, but they are nevertheless not commonly considered in legal disputes. As Lester and Greene both note, moral rights only come into play with visual art. K. J. Greene, "Copynorms, Black Cultural Production, and the Debate over African-American Reparations," *Cardozo Arts & Entertainment Law Journal* 25 (2008): 1179; Lester, "Treating Creative Black Intellectual Property Ownership as a Human Right."

55. "Show Bits," *Associated Press*, February 9, 2015, sec. Domestic News, Entertainment News.

56. Ron Harris, "Review: Carly Rae Jepsen's Album 'Kiss' Is Sweet," *Associated Press*, September 17, 2012, sec. Entertainment News.

57. Alec M. Priester, "The Science and Craft of Mixology in Music," *New York Times*, February 10, 2016, late edition-final edition, sec. C.

58. Priester "The Science and Craft of Mixology in Music."

59. Scott Mervis, "Pete Townshend: Nice to Be Part of Spectacle," *Associated Press*, February 8, 2010, sec. Sports News.

60. Melanie Sims, "Asher Roth Likes Fun, but Not Just a 'Stoner Kid,'" *Associated Press*, April 28, 2009, sec. Entertainment News.

61. Christopher Holmes Smith, "'I Don't Like to Dream about Getting Paid': Representations of Social Mobility and the Emergence of the Hip-Hop Mogul," *Social Text* 21, no. 4 (2003): 82.

62. Sims, "Asher Roth Likes Fun, but Not Just a 'Stoner Kid.'"

63. Joe Coscarelli, "Where Will Latin Pop Go Next?," *New York Times*, September 7, 2017, late edition-final edition, sec. C.

64. Coscarelli, "Where Will Latin Pop Go Next?"

65. Wood, "Story behind the Song: The 'Despacito' Remix Isn't Just about Sex."

66. Alyson Shontell, "This Is the Only Person We Can Find with a Perfect 100 Klout Score," *Business Insider*, November 22, 2011, https://www.businessinsider.com/100-klout-score-2011-11

67. James McNally, "Favela Chic: Diplo, Funk Carioca, and the Ethics and

Aesthetics of the Global Remix," *Popular Music and Society* 40, no. 4 (2017): 448, https://doi.org/10.1080/03007766.2015.1126100

68. McNally, "Favela Chic," 443, 444.

69. Heller, "Israeli Video Remix King Becomes Player in Election Campaign."

70. Shifman, *Memes in Digital Culture*, 77.

71. Amber Johnson, "Antoine Dodson and the (Mis)Appropriation of the Homo Coon: An Intersectional Approach to the Performative Possibilities of Social Media," *Critical Studies in Media Communication* 30, no. 2 (2013): 156, https://doi.org/10.1080/15295036.2012.755050

72. Shifman, *Memes in Digital Culture*, 81.

73. Jorge Rueda, "'Despacito' Singers Veto Venezuelan Leader's Campaign Remix," *Associated Press*, July 25, 2017, sec. International News.

74. "Philly Police Use Drake Parody to Ward Off Parking Battles," *Associated Press*, January 21, 2016, sec. Domestic News.

75. Fisher v. Dees, 794 F.2d 432 (9th Cir. 1986).

76. "Lil Nas X, Eilish, Enlist Help in Race for No. 1," *Spokesman Review*, July 14, 2019, main edition, sec. A.

77. Jason Lipshutz, "Lil Nas X's 'Old Town Road': 5 Things the Music Industry Should Learn from Its Record-Setting Run," *Billboard*, August 21, 2019.

78. Andrew Unterberger, "It Took over 20 Years for a Song to Tie the 16-Week Hot 100 No. 1 Record—Why Now Twice in Two Years?," *Billboard*, July 25, 2019.

79. @LilNasX, "twitter please help me get billy ray cyrus on this Https://T.Co/UDo eiOZqc1," Tweet, *@LilNasX* (blog), December 5, 2018, https://twitter.com/LilNasX/status/1070125203345342464

80. Joe Levy, "How Lil Nas X Sees His Future after 'Old Town Road,'" *Billboard*, September 19, 2019.

81. Elias Leight, "Lil Nas X's 'Old Town Road' Was a Country Hit. Then Country Changed Its Mind," *Rolling Stone*, March 26, 2019, https://www.rollingstone.com/music/music-features/lil-nas-x-old-town-road-810844/

82. Chris Richards, "Lil Nas X's Horse of Any Color You Choose," *Washington Post*, April 11, 2019, Regional edition, sec. Style.

83. Ben Sisario, "Lil Nas X Added Billy Ray Cyrus to 'Old Town Road.' Is It Country Enough for Billboard Now?," *New York Times*, April 5, 2019, sec. Business, Media.

84. Namwali Serpell, "How Social-Media Meme-Makers Rescued 'Game of Thrones' from Itself: Screenland," *New York Times*, June 6, 2019, sec. Magazine.

85. Levy, "How Lil Nas X Sees His Future after 'Old Town Road.'"

86. Lipshutz, "Lil Nas X's 'Old Town Road': 5 Things the Music Industry Should Learn."

87. Lyndsey Havens, "The Summer of Cyrus: How Billy Ray, Miley & Noah Dominated the Season," *Billboard*, September 3, 2019.

88. Dee Lockett, "Billy Ray Cyrus Gives Lil Nas X's 'Old Town Road' a Ringing Endorsement with Remix," *New York Magazine*, April 5, 2019.

89. Amanda Nell Edgar, "Blackvoice and Adele's Racialized Musical Performance: Blackness, Whiteness, and Discursive Authenticity," *Critical Studies in Media Communication* 31, no. 3 (2014): 171, https://doi.org/10.1080/15295036.2013.863427

90. Lipshutz, "Lil Nas X's 'Old Town Road': 5 Things the Music Industry Should Learn."

91. Unterberger, "It Took over 20 Years."

92. David J. Gunkel, *Of Remixology: Ethics and Aesthetics after Remix*, illus. ed. (Cambridge, MA: MIT Press, 2015), xviii.

93. "Five Burning Questions: Billboard Staffers Discuss Lil Nas X's 'Old Town Road' Tying the Hot 100 Record for Weeks at No. 1," *Billboard*, July 23, 2019.

94. "Five Burning Questions: Billboard Staffers Discuss Lil Nas X's 'Old Town Road' Pursuit of Hot 100 History," *Billboard*, July 16, 2019.

95. Maeve McDermott, "Please, Pop Stars, No More Collaborations," *USA Today*, September 11, 2019, first edition, sec. Life.

96. @LilNasX, "last one i PROMISSEE," Twitter, July 24, 2019, https://twitter.com/lilnasx/status/1154227360566259713

97. Lisa Respers France, "Lil Nas X and RM of BTS Drop New 'Old Town Road' Remix," *CNN.Com*, July 25, 2019, sec. Showbiz.

98. @LilNasX, "i did not make 27 remixes to the same song to be disrespected like this," Twitter, May 12, 2020, https://twitter.com/lilnasx/status/1260255622248841216

99. Lipshutz, "Lil Nas X's 'Old Town Road': 5 Things the Music Industry Should Learn."

100. Adam Graham, "'Old Town Road' Rides into History Books," *Detroit News*, July 20, 2019, first edition, sec. Features.

101. Judith Halberstam, *In a Queer Time and Place: Transgender Bodies, Subcultural Lives* (New York: New York University Press, 2005), 6.

102. Kathryn Bond Stockton, *The Queer Child, or Growing Sideways in the Twentieth Century* (Durham: Duke University Press, 2009), 25.

103. Judith Halberstam, *The Queer Art of Failure* (Durham: Duke University Press, 2011), 3.

104. Halberstam, *The Queer Art of Failure*, 89.

105. Halberstam, *The Queer Art of Failure*, 88.

106. Judith Butler, *Bodies That Matter: On the Discursive Limits of "Sex"* (New York: Routledge, 1993), 237.

107. Halberstam, *The Queer Art of Failure*, 2.

108. Halberstam, *The Queer Art of Failure*, 20–21.

109. Aram Sinnreich, *Mashed Up: Music, Technology, and the Rise of Configurable Culture* (Amherst: University of Massachusetts Press, 2010), 16.

110. Unterberger, "It Took over 20 Years."

111. Patrik Wikström, *The Music Industry: Music in the Cloud*, 2nd ed. (Cambridge: Polity, 2013), 90.

112. Sara Ahmed, *Queer Phenomenology: Orientations, Objects, Others* (Durham: Duke University Press, 2006).

113. Jon Pareles, "The Playlist: Beyoncé Song Fit for a 'Lion King,'" *New York Times*, July 12, 2019.

114. Sinnreich, *Mashed Up*.

115. Nadia Ellis, "Out and Bad: Toward a Queer Performance Hermeneutic in

Jamaican Dancehall," *Small Axe: A Caribbean Journal of Criticism* 15, no. 2 (35) (2011): 12, https://doi.org/10.1215/07990537-1334212

116. Julie Levin Russo, "User-Penetrated Content: Fan Video in the Age of Convergence," *Cinema Journal* 48, no. 4 (2009): 126, https://doi.org/10.1353/cj.0.0147

117. Sheldon Schiffer, "Cover Song as Historiography, Marker of Ideological Transformation," in *Play It Again: Cover Songs in Popular Music*, ed. George Plasketes (London: Routledge, 2016), 82.

118. Lipshutz, "Lil Nas X's 'Old Town Road': 5 Things the Music Industry Should Learn."

119. Shifman, *Memes in Digital Culture*, 56.

120. Shifman, *Memes in Digital Culture*, 7–8.

121. Shifman, *Memes in Digital Culture*, 19.

122. Jason Lipshutz, "The 16 Best Moments from the 2019 MTV Video Music Awards," *Billboard*, August 27, 2019.

123. Serpell, "How Social-Media Meme-Makers Rescued 'Game of Thrones' from Itself: Screenland."

124. *Bernie Sanders Raps "Old Town Hall" ("Old Town Road" Parody)*, 2019, https://www.youtube.com/watch?v=PD24oApjci8

125. Harmeet Kaur, "This Third Grade Class' Remix of 'Old Town Road' Is the Only One You Need," *CNN*, May 4, 2019, sec. Showbiz.

126. *Rambo: Last Blood (2019 Movie) Teaser Trailer—Sylvester Stallone*, 2019, https://www.youtube.com/watch?v=4vWg5yJuWfs

127. *Time* Staff, "The 25 Most Influential People on the Internet," *Time*, July 16, 2019, https://time.com/5626827/the-25-most-influential-people-on-the-internet/

128. *Lil Nas X Feat. Billy Ray Cyrus, Young Thug & Mason Ramsey—Old Town Road (Area 51 Video)*, 2019, https://www.youtube.com/watch?v=aA7xDP9sQzk

129. Pareles, "The Playlist: Beyoncé Song Fit for a 'Lion King.'" "Meme recognize meme" is a snowclone of "game recognize game," a phrase describing one skilled person recognizing and respecting the skill of another person. A snowclone is a "phrase that has a standard pattern in which some of the words can be freely replaced"; other examples include "X is the new Y." "Snowclone," Macmillan Dictionary, accessed April 20, 2020, https://www.macmillandictionary.com/us/dictionary/american/snowclone

CHAPTER 3

1. Zachary Lazar, "The 373-Hit Wonder," *New York Times*, January 9, 2011, late edition-final edition, sec. MM.

2. David Tough, "The Mashup Mindset: Will Pop Eat Itself?," in *Play It Again: Cover Songs in Popular Music*, ed. George Plasketes (London: Routledge, 2016), 205–12.

3. J. Peter Burkholder, "'Quotation' and Emulation: Charles Ives's Uses of His Models," *Musical Quarterly* 71, no. 1 (1985): 3.

4. J. Peter Burkholder, "The Uses of Existing Music: Musical Borrowing as a Field," *Notes* 50, no. 3 (1994): 865, https://doi.org/10.2307/898531

5. Davis Schneiderman, "Everybody's Got Something to Hide Except for Me and My Lawsuit: William S. Burroughs, DJ Danger Mouse, and the Politics of Grey Tuesday," in *Cutting Across Media: Appropriation Art, Interventionist Collage, and Copyright Law*, ed. Kembrew McLeod and Rudolf Kuenzli (Durham: Duke University Press, 2011), 132.

6. Tough, "The Mashup Mindset: Will Pop Eat Itself?," 206.

7. Tricia Rose, *Black Noise: Rap Music and Black Culture in Contemporary America* (Hanover, NH: University Press of New England, 1994), 89.

8. Michael Serazio, "The Apolitical Irony of Generation Mash-Up: A Cultural Case Study in Popular Music," *Popular Music and Society* 31, no. 1 (2008): 80, https://doi.org/10.1080/03007760701214815

9. Sam Howard-Spink, "Grey Tuesday, Online Cultural Activism and the Mash-up of Music and Politics," *First Monday*, 2004, https://doi.org/10.5210/fm.v0 i0.1460; Liam McGranahan, "Bastards and Booties: Production, Copyright, and the Mashup Community," *Trans. Revista Transcultural de Música*, no. 14 (2010): n.p.; Schneiderman, "Everybody's Got Something to Hide Except for Me and My Lawsuit."

10. McGranahan, "Bastards and Booties."

11. Wes Woods II, "Dee Jay Silver Spins Country Mashups for Tour," *Inland Valley Daily Bulletin*, August 12, 2016, sec. C.

12. Jon Pareles, "A World of Megabeats and Megabytes," *New York Times*, January 3, 2010, late edition-final edition, sec. AR.

13. Scott Mervis, "Mashup Stage," *Pittsburgh Post-Gazette*, December 2, 2010, Sooner edition, sec. Arts and Entertainment.

14. Rose, *Black Noise*, 73.

15. Jay David Bolter and Richard Grusin, *Remediation: Understanding New Media* (Cambridge, MA: MIT Press, 2000), 45.

16. Rose, *Black Noise*, 78.

17. That is, some hip-hop producers change the sound of their samples, often to avoid lawsuits. See Kembrew McLeod and Peter DiCola, *Creative License: The Law and Culture of Digital Sampling* (Durham: Duke University Press, 2011); Joanna Demers, *Steal This Music: How Intellectual Property Law Affects Musical Creativity* (Athens: University of Georgia Press, 2006). These changes include flipping—"creatively and substantially altering material in any way"—and chopping, which, "as its name suggests, refers to altering a sampled phrase by dividing it into smaller segments and reconfiguring them in a different order" in particular. Joseph G. Schloss, *Making Beats: The Art of Sample-Based Hip-Hop*, New ed. with new foreword and afterword (Middletown, CT: Wesleyan University Press, 2014), 106. Aram Sinnreich points out that RepliCheck, "a commercial brand of production software that 'checks' CDs before they're replicated to make sure they don't contain unlicensed copyrighted material," can't detect things like pitch bending and short samples; "therefore these aesthetic decisions have become more prevalent." Aram Sinnreich, *Mashed Up: Music, Technology,*

and the Rise of Configurable Culture (Amherst: University of Massachusetts Press, 2010), 130.

18. Austin Walsh, "Z-Trip," *Eureka Times-Standard*, October 1, 2009, sec. Entertainment.

19. McLeod and DiCola, *Creative License*, 2.

20. Sinnreich, *Mashed Up*, 132.

21. Walter Benjamin, "The Work of Art in the Age of Mechanical Reproduction," in *Media and Cultural Studies: KeyWorks*, ed. Meenakshi Gigi Durham and Douglas Kellner (Malden, MA: Blackwell, 2001), 50.

22. Serazio, "The Apolitical Irony of Generation Mash-Up," 87.

23. Michel Foucault, "What Is an Author?," in *Language, Counter-Memory, Practice: Selected Essays and Interviews* (Ithaca: Cornell University Press, 1980), 113–38.

24. Mark Katz, *Capturing Sound: How Technology Has Changed Music*, rev. ed. (Berkeley: University of California Press, 2010), 192.

25. Bolter and Grusin, *Remediation*, 75.

26. Demers, *Steal This Music*, 91; Joshua Clover, "Ambiguity and Theft," in *Cutting Across Media: Appropriation Art, Interventionist Collage, and Copyright Law*, ed. Kembrew McLeod and Rudolf Kuenzli (Durham: Duke University Press, 2011), 91.

27. Demers, *Steal This Music*, 90.

28. Madhavi Sunder, *From Goods to a Good Life: Intellectual Property and Global Justice* (New Haven: Yale University Press, 2012), 36.

29. Rose, *Black Noise*, 89.

30. Lazar, "The 373-Hit Wonder."

31. Christine Boone, "Mashing: Toward a Typology of Recycled Music," *Music Theory Online* 19, no. 3 (2013): para. 8.2, https://mtosmt.org/issues/mto.13.19.3/mto.13 .19.3.boone.html

32. Ben Sisario, "A New CD That Has No Music, but Lots of Pictures," *New York Times*, June 11, 2009, late edition-final edition, sec. C.

33. Megan Gloss, "Sample Says," *Telegraph Herald*, January 22, 2010, sec. C.

34. "Danger Mouse Tries to Avoid Legal Trap," *St. Petersburg Times*, May 20, 2009, 4 State / Suncoast edition, sec. Tampa Bay.

35. Philip A. Gunderson, "Danger Mouse's Grey Album, Mash-Ups, and the Age of Composition," *Postmodern Culture* 15, no. 1 (2004), https://doi.org/10.1353/pmc.2004 .0040; Sunder, *From Goods to a Good Life*.

36. Sunder, *From Goods to a Good Life*, 36.

37. McLeod and DiCola, *Creative License*, 174.

38. McLeod and DiCola, *Creative License*, 177.

39. Schneiderman, "Everybody's Got Something to Hide Except for Me and My Lawsuit," 134.

40. Campbell v. Acuff-Rose Music Inc., 510 U.S. 569 (1994); Estate of Smith v. Graham, 799 Fed. Appx. 36 (2d Cir. 2020).

41. *Estate of Smith*, 799 Fed. Appx.; Cariou v. Prince, 714 F.3d 694 (2d Cir. 2013).

42. Kenneth Price, "Song Choices, Controllers Make 'DJ Hero' Stand apart from Cousins," *Star-News*, November 12, 2009, 1st edition.

43. Walsh, "Z-Trip."

44. Joseph Berger, "Irving Fields, Composer and Lounge Pianist, Dies at 101," *New York Times*, August 23, 2016, late edition-final edition, sec. A.

45. Carla Jimenez, "Educate, Entertain and Inspire: Black Violin Brings Their Blended Style of Classical, Hip Hop to Central Illinois," *State Journal-Register*, September 21, 2017, sec. IL Features.

46. Mara Dauber, "Grey Album Illegal, but So Worthwhile," *Santa Fe New Mexican*, April 9, 2010, sec. Generation Next.

47. *Pittsburgh Tribune Review*, September 19, 2015.

48. Chris Riemenschneider, "The Big Gigs," *Star Tribune*, October 9, 2015, Metro edition, sec. Variety.

49. Anahad O'Connor, "DJ AM, Star Disc Jockey, Found Dead in Apartment," *New York Times*, August 29, 2009, late edition-final edition, sec. A.

50. "DVD Reviews," *Oklahoman*, June 26, 2009, City edition, sec. Weekend Look.

51. Walsh, "Z-Trip."

52. Laurel Graeber, "Spare Times," *New York Times*, March 20, 2009, late edition-final edition, sec. C.

53. Chris Hewitt, "Ordway Center Announces Music and Dance from around the World," *St. Paul Pioneer Press*, April 20, 2017.

54. "Florida: Black Violin to Headline Outdoor Concert to Benefit WGCU," *Plus Media Solutions*, January 25, 2017.

55. Katz, *Capturing Sound*, 166.

56. Woods, "Dee Jay Silver Spins Country Mashups for Tour."

57. Lazar, "The 373-Hit Wonder."

58. Marco R. della Cava, "Music Lovers Take a Spin," *USA Today*, October 27, 2009, final edition, sec. Life.

59. Price, "Song Choices, Controllers Make 'DJ Hero' Stand apart from Cousins."

60. "15 Things to Do in Boulder County Today, June 10, 2016," *Daily Camera*, June 10, 2016, sec. Entertainment.

61. Walsh, "Z-Trip."

62. Graeber, "Spare Times"; "Arizona: Black Violin," *Plus Media Solutions*, November 7, 2014; Amy Scherzer, "Black Heritage Evening at the Straz," *Tampa Bay Times*, January 20, 2012, sec. City Times; Social Scene.

63. Jimenez, "Educate, Entertain and Inspire."

64. Frank Scheck, "Bach with a Beat," *New York Post*, November 10, 2012.

65. Rick de Yampert, "Rockers Stumble down Stairway to Mashups," *News-Journal*, March 19, 2010, final edition, sec. E.

66. Walsh, "Z-Trip."

67. Russell Florence Jr., "Black Violin Breaks the Mold," *Dayton Daily News*, April 27, 2014, sec. Life & Arts.

68. Florence, "Black Violin Breaks the Mold"; "Arizona: Black Violin." Recall that

R&B is the post-1949 name of what was formerly called "race music," a category which, beginning in the 1920s, "came to be used by the recording industry to describe music performed by African American musicians and marketed to an African American audience." Olufunmilayo B. Arewa, "Blues Lives: Promise and Perils of Musical Copyright," *Cardozo Arts & Entertainment Law Journal* 27 (2010): 595.

69. Lazar, "The 373-Hit Wonder."

70. bell hooks, "Eating the Other: Desire and Resistance," in *Media and Cultural Studies: Key Works*, rev. ed., ed. Meenakshi Gigi Durham and Douglas Kellner (Malden, MA: Blackwell, 2006), 373.

71. Jack Hamilton, *Just around Midnight: Rock and Roll and the Racial Imagination*, illus. ed. (Cambridge, MA: Harvard University Press, 2016), 83.

72. David Hesmondhalgh, "Digital Sampling and Cultural Inequality," *Social & Legal Studies* 15, no. 1 (2006): 56–57, https://doi.org/10.1177/0964663906060973

73. Hesmondhalgh, "Digital Sampling and Cultural Inequality," 72.

74. hooks, "Eating the Other," 369.

75. hooks, "Eating the Other," 367.

76. Marty Clear, "Keeping It Classic—and Fresh," *Tampa Bay Times*, January 13, 2012, sec. City Times; Laurel Graeber, "Spare Times: For Children," *New York Times*, November 16, 2012, late edition-final edition, sec. C.

77. Azaria Podplesky, "Black Violin's Mash Up of Classical and Hip Hop Entertaining for All Ages," *Spokesman Review*, April 3, 2017, main edition, sec. D; Graeber, "Spare Times."

78. Lazar, "The 373-Hit Wonder."

79. While in this case caricature and stereotype of Black people is most relevant, a similar formation occurs elsewhere with Indigenous people. See Anthony Seeger, "Ethnomusicology and Music Law," *Ethnomusicology* 36, no. 3 (1992): 345–59, https://doi.org/10.2307/851868; Rosemary J. Coombe, *The Cultural Life of Intellectual Properties: Authorship, Appropriation, and the Law* (Durham: Duke University Press, 1998).

80. K. J. Greene, "Intellectual Property at the Intersection of Race and Gender: Lady Sings the Blues," *American University Journal of Gender, Social Policy & the Law* 16, no. 3 (2008): 374, https://digitalcommons.wcl.american.edu/jgspl/vol16/iss3/2

81. Peter Dobrin, "Review: Black Violin Brings Strings to Hip-Hop," *Philadelphia Inquirer*, November 10, 2015, web edition, sec. Features Magazine.

82. Jeremy D. Goodwin, "Where Classical Meets Hip-Hop," *Berkshire Eagle*, May 12, 2011, sec. Weekend.

83. Dauber, "Grey Album Illegal, but So Worthwhile."

84. de Yampert, "Rockers Stumble down Stairway to Mashups."

85. Dobrin, "Review: Black Violin Brings Strings to Hip-Hop."

86. Emily Langer, "Bandleader Who Fed Postwar Mania for Yiddish Mambo," *Washington Post*, August 24, 2016, Suburban edition, sec. Metro.

87. Berger, "Irving Fields, Composer and Lounge Pianist, Dies at 101."

88. Graeber, "Spare Times: For Children."

89. Constance Gibbs, "Violin Duo Hits 'Pitch' out of Park," *New York Daily News*, November 26, 2016, Sports final edition, sec. Television.

90. Randall Roberts, "Beatles, Beastie Boys in the Mix," *Dayton Daily News*, June 27, 2013, sec. Life.

91. Mervis, "Mashup Stage."

92. de Yampert, "Rockers Stumble down Stairway to Mashups."

93. Anjali Vats, *The Color of Creatorship: Intellectual Property, Race, and the Making of Americans* (Stanford: Stanford University Press, 2020), 86, 87.

94. Vats, *The Color of Creatorship*, 90.

95. Vats, *The Color of Creatorship*, 90.

96. Grand Upright Music v. Warner Bros. Records Inc., 780 F. Supp. 182 (S.D.N.Y. 1991).

97. Vats, *The Color of Creatorship*, 90.

98. McLeod and DiCola, *Creative License*, 31; Bridgeport Music v. Dimension Films, 410 F. 3d 792 (6th Cir. 2005).

99. Henry Louis Gates Jr., *The Signifying Monkey: A Theory of African American Literary Criticism*, 25th anniversary ed. (Oxford: Oxford University Press, 2014), xxx.

100. Gates, *The Signifying Monkey*, 57.

101. Thank you to the audience member at the Association of Internet Researchers 2018 conference who asked me whether I thought mash-ups were not seen as cutting edge anymore, prompting me to do this analysis of change over time.

102. Langer, "Bandleader Who Fed Postwar Mania for Yiddish Mambo."

103. Wall Street Journal Abstracts, "Better than the Sum of Their Parts?," *Wall Street Journal*, April 6, 2012, sec. D.

104. Ben Guarino, "DNA's Alphabet Expands from Four Letters to Six," *Washington Post*, January 31, 2017, every edition, sec. Health.

105. Vats, *The Color of Creatorship*, 34.

106. Rose, *Black Noise*, 73.

107. Fisher v. Dees, 794 F.2d 432 (9th Cir. 1986).

108. Price, "Song Choices, Controllers Make 'DJ Hero' Stand apart from Cousins."

109. Sheena Barnett, "Catch Up on Some Girl Talk," *Northeast Mississippi Daily Journal*, February 5, 2009, sec. Lifestyle.

110. Lazar, "The 373-Hit Wonder."

111. David R. Roediger, *The Wages of Whiteness: Race and the Making of the American Working Class* (London: Verso, 1991), 100.

112. Charmain Z. Brackett, "Black Violin Show Will Be New, Different," *Augusta Chronicle*, April 19, 2018, all editions, sec. News.

113. Charmain Z. Brackett, "Black Violin Bridges Gaps with Classic, Modern Music," *Augusta Chronicle*, February 9, 2017, all editions, sec. Entertainment.

114. "For the Record: 'Jews on Vinyl' a Sound Exploration of History," *Daily News of Los Angeles*, May 23, 2010, Valley edition, sec. L.A. Life.

115. Dobrin, "Review: Black Violin Brings Strings to Hip-Hop."

116. Sinnreich, *Mashed Up*, 206, 205.

117. Lazar, "The 373-Hit Wonder."

118. Of course, rock music grew directly out of Black people's musical traditions, but its Black origins were suppressed as part of its popularization. For an overview of this history see Hamilton, *Just around Midnight*; Maureen Mahon, *Black Diamond Queens: African American Women and Rock and Roll,* illus. ed. (Durham: Duke University Press, 2020). For a discussion of how a group of musicians organized around gaining recognition of Black rock artists, see Maureen Mahon, *Right to Rock: The Black Rock Coalition and the Cultural Politics of Race* (Durham: Duke University Press, 2004).

119. Roberts, "Beatles, Beastie Boys in the Mix."

120. Marjorie Heins and Tricia Beckles, "Will Fair Use Survive? Free Expression in the Age of Copyright Control," A Public Policy Report (New York: Brennan Center for Justice at NYU School of Law, 2005), http://www.brennancenter.org/sites/default/files/legacy/d/download_file_9056.pdf

121. Steve Collins, "Digital Fair: Prosumption and the Fair Use Defence," *Journal of Consumer Culture* 10, no. 1 (2010): 48, https://doi.org/10.1177/1469540509354014

122. Lazar, "The 373-Hit Wonder."

123. McLeod and DiCola, *Creative License,* 176.

124. Eric Lott, *Love & Theft: Blackface Minstrelsy and the American Working Class,* 20th anniversary ed. (New York: Oxford University Press, 2013), 242.

125. Barnett, "Catch Up on Some Girl Talk."

126. Michael Machosky, "Girl Talk Pushes Listeners to Broaden Horizons," *Pittsburgh Tribune Review,* July 30, 2009; Lazar, "The 373-Hit Wonder"; Dauber, "Grey Album Illegal, but So Worthwhile."

127. Walsh, "Z-Trip."

128. Madeline Vuong, "Black Violin Will Blend Classical, Hip-Hop at the Mahaiwe," *Berkshire Eagle,* October 15, 2014, sec. Entertainment.

129. Roberts, "Beatles, Beastie Boys in the Mix."

130. "Ohio: Black Violin," *Plus Media Solutions,* March 9, 2016; Mervis, "Mashup Stage."

131. Woods, "Dee Jay Silver Spins Country Mashups for Tour."

132. Langer, "Bandleader Who Fed Postwar Mania for Yiddish Mambo."

133. Graeber, "Spare Times: For Children," November 16, 2012.

134. Chris Shott, "Lily Pond on Fire! Stereo Refugee Mike Satsky Exults in East Hampton, Trashes Greenhouse, Mum on New Manhattan Spot," *New York Observer,* May 28, 2009.

135. Dauber, "Grey Album Illegal, but So Worthwhile."

136. Wall Street Journal Abstracts, "Better than the Sum of Their Parts?"; Lazar, "The 373-Hit Wonder."

137. Edna Gundersen, "Grammys Reach for High Notes, Higher Ratings," *USA Today,* February 8, 2013, first edition, sec. Life.

138. Lazar, "The 373-Hit Wonder."

139. "For the Record: 'Jews on Vinyl' a Sound Exploration of History."

140. Billy Heller, "Oy Caramba! Lost Album Is All Mixed Up," *New York Post*, August 18, 2009, all edition.

141. "For the Record; 'Jews on Vinyl' a Sound Exploration of History."

142. Homi K. Bhabha, *The Location of Culture*, 2nd ed. (London: Routledge, 2004), 162.

CHAPTER 4

1. Randy Lewis, "'Weird Al' Marks 40 Years of Parody," *Baltimore Sun*, March 5, 2017, AdvanceBulldog edition, sec. Main News, A.

2. Sharon Hochhauser, "Take Me Down to the Parodies City," *Journal of Popular Music Studies* 30, no. 1–2 (2018): 63.

3. Walt Belcher, "Weird Al's 'Alpocolypse' Tour," *Tampa Tribune*, September 30, 2011, final edition, sec. Friday Extra.

4. Wendy J. Gordon, "A Property Right in Self-Expression: Equality and Individualism in the Natural Law of Intellectual Property," *Yale Law Journal* 102 (1992): 1535.

5. Dave Itzkoff, "Serving Pop Stars, but on a Skewer," *New York Times*, June 12, 2011, late edition-final edition, sec. AR.

6. Belcher, "Weird Al's 'Alpocolypse' Tour."

7. Itzkoff, "Serving Pop Stars, but on a Skewer."

8. Mary Ellen Wright, "'Weird Al' Yankovic Parodies Remain Relevant after 30 Years," *Sunday News*, July 10, 2011, sec. E.

9. "Weird Al" Yankovic, "The Gaga Saga," *Al's Blog* (blog), April 20, 2011, https://alyankovic.wordpress.com/the-gaga-saga/

10. Itzkoff, "Serving Pop Stars, but on a Skewer."

11. Joe Logan, "Plain Parody," *Philadelphia Inquirer*, March 19, 1996, SF edition, sec. Features Magazine: Entertainment.

12. Logan, "Plain Parody." Coolio did apparently change his mind later, saying "I was like, 'Coolio, who the f—k do you think you are? He did Michael Jackson. Michael Jackson didn't get mad'" and "I've since apologized to him. . . . That was one of the dumbest things I did in my career." "Coolio Did Not Want Weird Al to Spoof 'Gangsta's Paradise,'" August 1, 2013, https://www.yahoo.com/entertainment/bp/coolio-did-not-want-weird-al-spoof-gangsta-205954306.html

13. Itzkoff, "Serving Pop Stars, but on a Skewer."

14. Christopher R. Weingarten, "An Oral History of 'Weird Al' Yankovic's 'Smells Like Nirvana,'" *Spin*, October 11, 2012, https://www.spin.com/2012/10/weird-al-yankovic-looks-back-at-20-years-of-smells-like-nirvana/

15. Itzkoff, "Serving Pop Stars, but on a Skewer."

16. Matthew McKeague, "The Accordion Is Mightier Than the Sword: Analysing the Comedy Music Counterculture Expressed through the Works of 'Weird Al' Yankovic," *Comedy Studies* 9, no. 2 (2018): 145, https://doi.org/10.1080/2040610X.2018.1494360

17. Schuyler Velasco, "'Weird Al' Yankovic Scores His First No. 1 Album: How He Did It," *Christian Science Monitor*, July 24, 2014, sec. Business.

18. Jon Fassnacht, "Weird Al Continues to Defy the Odds," *Reading Eagle*, July 25, 2014, sec. Lifestyle.

19. Mel Stanfill, *Exploiting Fandom: How the Media Industry Seeks to Manipulate Fans* (Iowa City: University of Iowa Press, 2019).

20. Michelle Mills, "Weird Al Finds Daring to Be Stupid Pays Off," *Daily News of Los Angeles*, July 22, 2016, sec. L.

21. Henry Jenkins, Sam Ford, and Joshua Green, *Spreadable Media: Creating Value and Meaning in a Networked Culture* (New York: New York University Press, 2013).

22. Velasco, "'Weird Al' Yankovic Scores His First No. 1 Album: How He Did It."

23. Velasco, "'Weird Al' Yankovic Scores His First No. 1 Album: How He Did It."

24. John J. Moser, "Yankovic Says Next Album Is His Last," *Dayton Daily News*, June 8, 2013, sec. Comics.

25. Velasco, "'Weird Al' Yankovic Scores His First No. 1 Album: How He Did It."

26. Mills, "Weird Al Finds Daring to Be Stupid Pays Off."

27. Itzkoff, "Serving Pop Stars, but on a Skewer."

28. Heather Somerville, "Beastie Boys Sue Oakland Toy Company GoldieBlox," *Contra Costa Times*, December 12, 2013, sec. Breaking, News, Business.

29. "'Girls' Song Parody in GoldieBlox Ad Riles Beastie Boys," *Tampa Tribune*, November 28, 2013, sec. Nation & World.

30. "Goldieblox, Inc. v. Island Def Jam Music Group Complaint for Declaratory Judgment and Injunctive Relief." 2013. https://www.scribd.com/document/186402972/Beastie.

31. Sheila Marikar, "Winning Girls Over, Piece by Piece," *New York Times*, December 25, 2014, late edition-final edition, sec. E.

32. Somerville, "Beastie Boys Sue Oakland Toy Company GoldieBlox."

33. Levi Sumagaysay, "GoldieBlox Now Says It Has No Beef with the Beastie Boys," *San Jose Mercury News*, November 27, 2013, sec. News.

34. The letter is no longer available online, so I am obliged to cite the version archived by the Internet Archive's Wayback Machine: Debbie + Team GoldieBlox, "Our Letter to the Beastie Boys," November 27, 2013, https://web.archive.org/web/20131129044348/https:/blog.goldieblox.com/2013/11/our-letter-to-the-beastie-boys/

35. Sumagaysay, "GoldieBlox Now Says It Has No Beef with the Beastie Boys."

36. The letter was published in its entirety in a *New York Times* article; it's unclear whether there was ever a version posted directly by the Beastie Boys, but if there was, neither I nor the Wayback Machine can locate it now. Dave Itzkoff, "Beastie Boys Call Video Parody 'an Advertisement,'" *New York Times*, November 26, 2013, late edition-final edition, sec. C.

37. Somerville, "Beastie Boys Sue Oakland Toy Company GoldieBlox."

38. Felix Salmon, "GoldieBlox, Fair Use, and the Cult of Disruption," *Reuters Blogs* (blog), November 26, 2013, https://www.reuters.com/article/idIN312465060220131126

39. Salmon, "GoldieBlox, Fair Use, and the Cult of Disruption."

40. For examples of Uber and Airbnb resisting or even ignoring regulations, see Jim Turner, "Airbnb Has Spent at Least $1,250,000 to Prevent Local Regulation of Florida Rental Properties," *Orlando Weekly*, January 10, 2020, https://www.orlandowe ekly.com/Blogs/archives/2020/01/10/airbnb-has-spent-at-least-1250000-to-prevent-lo cal-regulation-of-florida-rental-properties; Shirin Ghaffary, "Uber and Lyft Say They Don't Plan to Reclassify Their Drivers as Employees," *Vox*, September 11, 2019, https://www.vox.com/2019/9/11/20861599/ab-5-uber-lyft-drivers-contractors-reclassify-emp loyees

41. Answer to Complaint with Jury Demand and Affirmative Defenses, Counterclaim against GoldieBlox Inc. for GoldieBlox Inc. v. Island Def Jam Music Group et al., accessed July 19, 2022. https://docs.justia.com/cases/federal/district-cour ts/california/candce/3:2013cv05428/272183/16

42. Itzkoff, "Beastie Boys Call Video Parody 'an Advertisement.'"

43. Steven Stolder, "Beastie Boys, Smashing Pumpkins Headline Tibetan Freedom Concert," *Rolling Stone*, August 8, 1996, https://www.rollingstone.com/music /music-news/beastie-boys-smashing-pumpkins-headline-tibetan-freedom-concert -183794/

44. Cihan Kaan, "Adam Yauch Was a Muslim Hero," Al Jazeera, May 9, 2012, https://www.aljazeera.com/indepth/opinion/2012/05/20125813653185358.html

45. Jacob Ganz, "MTV Loves MTV: A Bad Romance," *NPR*, September 13, 2010, https://www.npr.org/sections/therecord/2010/09/13/129833419/mtv-loves-mtv-a-bad -romance

46. Jeff Roberts, "Are the Beastie Boys Picking on Science-Loving Girls? The Copyright Case Is Not So Simple (Updated)," November 25, 2013, https://gigaom.com /2013/11/25/are-the-beastie-boys-picking-on-science-loving-girls-the-copyright-case -is-not-so-simple/

47. Itzkoff, "Beastie Boys Call Video Parody 'an Advertisement.'"

48. *Answer to Complaint* paragraph 34.

49. Kembrew McLeod and Peter DiCola, *Creative License: The Law and Culture of Digital Sampling* (Durham: Duke University Press, 2011), 210.

50. McLeod and DiCola, *Creative License*, 121.

51. Dave Itzkoff, "Beastie Boys Settle Suit over Toy Company Ad," *New York Times*, March 19, 2014, late edition-final edition, sec. C.

52. "Limitations on Exclusive Rights: Fair Use," § 107, Title 17 United States Code, http://www.copyright.gov/title17/92chap1.html#107

53. "Parody, n.2," *OED Online* (Oxford University Press), accessed December 8, 2019, http://www.oed.com/view/Entry/138059

54. "Spoof, n. (and Adj.)," *OED Online* (Oxford University Press), accessed December 8, 2019, http://www.oed.com/view/Entry/187390

55. "Satire, n.," *OED Online* (Oxford University Press), accessed December 8, 2019, http://www.oed.com/view/Entry/171207

56. Pierre N. Leval, "Toward a Fair Use Standard," *Harvard Law Review* 103, no. 5 (1990): 1111, https://doi.org/10.2307/1341457

57. Campbell v. Acuff-Rose Music Inc., 510 U.S. 569 (1994).

58. Suntrust Bank v. Houghton Mifflin Co. 268 F.3d 1257 (11th Cir. 2001).

59. Rogers v. Koons, 960 F.2d 301 (2d Cir. 1992).

60. Neil Weinstock Netanel, "Making Sense of Fair Use," *Lewis & Clark Law Review* 15 (2011): 750.

61. "Limitations on Exclusive Rights: Fair Use."

62. Dr. Seuss Enters. L.P. v. Penguin Books USA Inc., 109 F.3d 1394 (9th Cir. 1997).

63. *Suntrust Bank*, 268 F.3d.

64. Wendy J. Gordon, "Excuse and Justification in the Law of Fair Use: Transaction Costs Have Always Been Part of the Story," *Journal of the Copyright Society of the U.S.A.* 50 (2003): 174, original emphasis.

65. "Limitations on Exclusive Rights: Fair Use."

66. Rebecca Tushnet, "Scary Monsters: Hybrids, Mashups, and Other Illegitimate Children," *Notre Dame Law Review* 86, no. 5 (2011): 2139.

67. *Campbell*, 510 U.S.

68. *Rogers*, 960 F.2d.

69. *Campbell*, 510 U.S.

70. Elsmere Music Inc. v. National Broadcasting Co., 623 F.2d 252 (2d Cir. 1980).

71. *Suntrust Bank*, 268 F.3d.

72. Gordon, "Excuse and Justification in the Law of Fair Use," 174.

73. Madhavi Sunder, *From Goods to a Good Life: Intellectual Property and Global Justice* (New Haven: Yale University Press, 2012), 36.

74. *Campbell*, 510 U.S.

75. *Campbell*, 510 U.S.

76. *Elsmere Music Inc.*, 623 F2d.

77. "Limitations on Exclusive Rights: Fair Use."

78. *Campbell*, 510 U.S.

79. Lydia Pallas Loren, "Redefining the Market Failure Approach to Fair Use in an Era of Copyright Permission Systems," *Journal of Intellectual Property Law* 5 (1997): 50.

80. Sunder, *From Goods to a Good Life*, 123.

81. *Campbell*, 510 U.S.

82. *Campbell*, 510 U.S.

83. Gil Kaufman, "Watch 'Two Neil Youngs Sitting on a Tree Stump' on 'The Tonight Show,'" *Hollywood Reporter*, June 22, 2016, sec. News.

84. Craig S. Semon, "Boss, 'Tebowie' Bring Fallon Laughs," *Telegram & Gazette*, June 28, 2012, sec. Go!, Tracks.

85. "Offering Thanks for Fallon," *Tampa Tribune*, October 11, 2013, sec. Friday Extra.

86. Semon, "Boss, 'Tebowie' Bring Fallon Laughs."

87. "After Hiatus, Spoon's Back in Fine Form with New Album," *Spokesman Review*, August 8, 2014, main edition, sec. C.

88. Rod Lockwood, "Weird, Wily and Talented Al Yankovic Returning to Toledo Zoo," *Blade*, June 24, 2010, sec. Entertainment News.

89. Kaufman, "Watch 'Two Neil Youngs Sitting on a Tree Stump' on 'The Tonight Show.'"

90. Semon, "Boss, 'Tebowie' Bring Fallon Laughs."

91. Semon, "Boss, 'Tebowie' Bring Fallon Laughs."

92. Piet Levy, "'Weird Al' Yankovic Has Serious Fans—and Serious Fun," *St. Paul Pioneer Press*, July 1, 2015, sec. Entertainment.

93. McKeague, "The Accordion Is Mightier Than the Sword," 144–45.

94. "Lifeline," *Dayton Daily News*, August 10, 2017.

95. Lee Ward, "Area Comedians Team for March 8 Show at Mardi Gras Casino," *Daily Independent*, February 20, 2014, sec. Lifestyle.

96. Semon, "Boss, 'Tebowie' Bring Fallon Laughs."

97. Kai Beech, "Weird Al to Play HSU," *Eureka Times Standard*, August 16, 2010, sec. Entertainment.

98. Bay Area News Group, "Good Times: Bay Area Entertainment Guide for Nov. 3–9," *San Jose Mercury News*, November 2, 2011, sec. News; Entertainment.

99. Levy, "'Weird Al' Yankovic Has Serious Fans—and Serious Fun."

100. Rich Freedman, "King of Parodies, Weird Al Yankovic, to Hold Court at Uptown in Napa," *Vallejo Times Herald*, July 20, 2012, sec. Art.

101. Semon, "Boss, 'Tebowie' Bring Fallon Laughs."

102. David Sanjek, "Ridiculing the 'White Bread Original': The Politics of Parody and Preservation of Greatness in Luther Campbell a.k.a. Luke Skyywalker et al. v. Acuff-Rose Music Inc," *Cultural Studies* 20, no. 2–3 (2006): 279, https://doi.org/10.10 80/09502380500495742

103. Hochhauser, "Take Me Down to the Parodies City," 65.

104. Patrik Jonsson, "'Pants on the Ground' Goes Viral: Top Five Larry Platt Covers; American Idol Contestant 'General' Larry Platt's Song Mocking Contemporary Street Fashion Has Inspired Many YouTubed Versions, from Rap to Easy Listening," *Christian Science Monitor*, January 16, 2010.

105. Semon, "Boss, 'Tebowie' Bring Fallon Laughs."

106. Eric Lott, *Love & Theft: Blackface Minstrelsy and the American Working Class*, 20th anniversary ed. (New York: Oxford University Press, 2013), 6.

107. Raúl Pérez, "Racism without Hatred? Racist Humor and the Myth of 'Colorblindness,'" *Sociological Perspectives* 60, no. 5 (2017): 956–74, https://doi.org/10 .1177/0731121417719699

108. Eduardo Bonilla-Silva, *Racism without Racists: Color-Blind Racism and the Persistence of Racial Inequality in the United States* (Lanham, MD: Rowman & Littlefield, 2003), 9n55.

109. Anjali Vats, *The Color of Creatorship: Intellectual Property, Race, and the Making of Americans* (Stanford: Stanford University Press, 2020), 92.

110. Henry Louis Gates Jr., *The Signifying Monkey: A Theory of African American Literary Criticism*, 25th anniversary ed. (Oxford: Oxford University Press, 2014).

1. Jody Rosen, "Crawling from the Wreckage," *New York Times*, July 5, 2015, late edition-final edition, sec. AR.

2. Joanna Demers does use the term "sound-alike," but differently, specifically for cover songs that exactly or nearly replicate the source text, often to try to cannibalize its sales, what Robert Brauneis calls "mirror covers." Joanna Demers, *Steal This Music: How Intellectual Property Law Affects Musical Creativity* (Athens: University of Georgia Press, 2006), 40; Robert Brauneis, "Copyright, Music, and Race: The Case of Mirror Cover Recordings," SSRN Scholarly Paper (Rochester, NY: Social Science Research Network, May 2, 2020), https://doi.org/10.2139/ssrn.3591113. As discussed in chapter 1, "The exclusive rights of the owner of copyright in a sound recording under clauses (1) and (2) of section 106 do not extend to the making or duplication of another sound recording that consists entirely of an independent fixation of other sounds, even though such sounds imitate or simulate those in the copyrighted sound recording," enabling such soundalike/mirror covers. "Scope of Exclusive Rights in Sound Recordings," Title 17 United States Code § 114, accessed December 4, 2021, https://www.copyright.gov/title17/92chap1.html#114

3. J. Peter Burkholder, "The Uses of Existing Music: Musical Borrowing as a Field," *Notes* 50, no. 3 (1994): 854, https://doi.org/10.2307/898531

4. Rosen, "Crawling from the Wreckage." Others disagreed with this contention, with one story saying "Mr. Smith's song is ecstatic and soaring, and Mr. Petty's is quietly tenacious. 'Stay with Me' is far more indebted to traditional choir gospel than to Mr. Petty's meditative country-rock." Jon Caramanica, "A Verdict Based on an Old Way of Making Music," *New York Times*, March 12, 2015, late edition-final edition, sec. C.

5. Josh Terry, "7 More Songs That Were Allegedly Plagiarized," *RedEye, Chicago*, March 11, 2015, sec. Entertainment News.

6. Rosen, "Crawling from the Wreckage."

7. Rosen, "Crawling from the Wreckage."

8. Allison Stewart, "Music Review: Robin Thicke's 'Love after War,'" *Washington Post*, December 11, 2011, every edition, sec. Style.

9. Katherine Silkaitis, *Pittsburgh Post-Gazette*, December 29, 2011, Sooner edition, sec. Arts & Entertainment, For the Record.

10. Jon Bream, "Country Star Aldean Knows How to Rock It," *Star Tribune*, August 29, 2009, Metro edition, sec. News.

11. Nate Chinen, "Chipper Remnants of a Life Turned Sour," *New York Times*, December 6, 2011, late edition-final edition, sec. C.

12. James C. McKinley, Jr., "It's Happy, It's Danceable and It May Rule Summer," *New York Times*, May 30, 2013, late edition-final edition, sec. C.

13. Jim Farber, "Ronson's a Past Master," *Daily News*, January 13, 2015, Sports final replate edition, sec. Now.

14. Burkholder, "The Uses of Existing Music," 854.

15. Rosen, "Crawling from the Wreckage."

16. Marco R. della Cava, "'Finding the Funk' Excavates the Artifacts of Modern R&B: From the Bay Area to Dayton, Ohio, It's a Musical Odyssey," *USA Today*, February 4, 2014, final edition, sec. Life.

17. George Clinton, "No Sample of #Funkadelic's 'Sexy Ways' in @RobinThicke's 'Blurred Lines'—yet Armen Boladian Thinks So? We Support @RobinThicke @ Pharrell!," Twitter, August 15, 2013, https://twitter.com/george_clinton/status/368210 216828932096

18. Tim Wu, "Jay-Z versus the Sample Troll," *Slate*, November 16, 2006, https://sl ate.com/culture/2006/11/the-shady-one-man-corporation-that-s-destroying-hip-hop .html

19. Brauneis, "Copyright, Music, and Race," 22.

20. Brauneis, "Copyright, Music, and Race," 21.

21. Keith Caulfield, "Tom Petty Won't Win a Grammy for Sam Smith's 'Stay with Me,'" *Hollywood Reporter*, January 27, 2015, sec. News.

22. Brian Melley, "All That Glitters Is Gold: 'Stairway' May Be Worth Millions," *Associated Press*, June 18, 2016, sec. Domestic News.

23. Jon Caramanica, "Breezy Mien Disguised Petty's Savvy and Tenacity," *New York Times*, October 4, 2017, late edition-final edition, sec. B.

24. Farber, "Ronson's a Past Master."

25. Terry, "7 More Songs That Were Allegedly Plagiarized."

26. Caramanica, "A Verdict Based on an Old Way of Making Music."

27. Tushnet goes on to argue that this is an "indication that proper credit is an important equitable consideration in cases of copying"—that analysis should take everyday people's intuitions about copyright seriously, an argument I'll make in more depth below. Rebecca Tushnet, "Payment in Credit: Copyright Law and Subcultural Creativity," *Law and Contemporary Problems* 70, no. 2 (2007): 151.

28. Kembrew McLeod and Peter DiCola, *Creative License: The Law and Culture of Digital Sampling* (Durham: Duke University Press, 2011), 73.

29. Ben Sisario, "Songwriters Sue to Defend a Summer Hit," *New York Times*, August 17, 2013, late edition-final edition, sec. B.

30. On March 9, 2020, a panel of the Ninth Circuit Court of Appeals upheld the 2016 decision that "Stairway to Heaven" was not infringing, though the estate's lawyer suggested he might appeal to the full Ninth Circuit or to the Supreme Court. Jon Blistein, "A New Led Zeppelin Court Win over 'Stairway to Heaven' Just Upended a Copyright Precedent," *Rolling Stone*, March 9, 2020, https://www.rollingstone.com /music/music-news/led-zeppelin-stairway-to-heaven-copyright-infringement-ruling -appeal-964530/

31. Stelios Phili, "Robin Thicke on That Banned Video, Collaborating with 2 Chainz and Kendrick Lamar, and His New Film," *GQ*, May 7, 2013, https://www.gq .com/story/robin-thicke-interview-blurred-lines-music-video-collaborating-with-2-c hainz-and-kendrick-lamar-mercy

32. Caramanica, "A Verdict Based on an Old Way of Making Music." The damages were reduced to $5.3 million after the appeal. Matthew Strauss and Noah Yoo, "'Blurred Lines' Verdict Largely Upheld after Appeal," *Pitchfork*, March 21, 2018, https://pitchfork.com/news/blurred-lines-verdict-largely-upheld-after-appeal/

33. Kal Raustiala and Christopher Jon Sprigman, "Squelching Creativity: What the 'Blurred Lines' Team Copied Is Either Not Original or Not Relevant," *Slate Magazine*, March 12, 2015, https://slate.com/news-and-politics/2015/03/blurred-lines-verdict-is-wrong-williams-and-thicke-did-not-infringe-on-marvin-gaye-copyright.html

34. Tim Wu, "Why the 'Blurred Lines' Copyright Verdict Should Be Thrown Out," *New Yorker*, March 12, 2015, https://www.newyorker.com/culture/culture-desk/why-the-blurred-lines-copyright-verdict-should-be-thrown-out

35. Chris Richards, "It's Okay If You Hate Robin Thicke: But the 'Blurred Lines' Verdict Is Bad for Pop Music," *Washington Post*, March 11, 2015, https://www.washingtonpost.com/news/arts-and-entertainment/wp/2015/03/11/the-blurred-lines-of-the-blurred-lines-verdict/

36. In the Led Zeppelin case, the sheet music was also the only copyrighted element, as U.S. copyright did not protect sound recordings at all until 1972.

37. Demers, *Steal This Music*, 36.

38. Caramanica, "A Verdict Based on an Old Way of Making Music."

39. Caramanica, "A Verdict Based on an Old Way of Making Music."

40. Raustiala and Sprigman, "Squelching Creativity."

41. Supreme Records Inc. v. Decca Records Inc., 90 F. Supp. 904 (S.D. Cal. 1950).

42. Caramanica, "A Verdict Based on an Old Way of Making Music."

43. Caramanica, "A Verdict Based on an Old Way of Making Music."

44. Brauneis, "Copyright, Music, and Race," 21.

45. Rosen, "Crawling from the Wreckage."

46. Eriq Gardner, "'Blurred Lines' Appeal Gets Support from More Than 200 Musicians," *Hollywood Reporter*, August 30, 2016, https://www.hollywoodreporter.com/thr-esq/blurred-lines-appeal-gets-support-924213

47. Raustiala and Sprigman, "Squelching Creativity."

48. J. Peter Burkholder, "'Quotation' and Emulation: Charles Ives's Uses of His Models," *Musical Quarterly* 71, no. 1 (1985): 2–3; Burkholder, "The Uses of Existing Music," 854.

49. Raustiala and Sprigman, "Squelching Creativity."

50. U.S. Constitution art. I. § 8.

51. Raustiala and Sprigman, "Squelching Creativity."

52. See Mel Stanfill, "Fandom, Public, Commons," *Transformative Works and Cultures* 14 (2013): n.p., https://doi.org/10.3983/twc.2013.0530

53. Rosen, "Crawling from the Wreckage."

54. Maureen Mahon, *Right to Rock: The Black Rock Coalition and the Cultural Politics of Race* (Durham: Duke University Press, 2004), 248.

55. K. J. Greene, "Copynorms, Black Cultural Production, and the Debate over African-American Reparations," *Cardozo Arts & Entertainment Law Journal* 25 (2008): 1179; Mahon, *Right to Rock*; Maureen Mahon, *Black Diamond Queens: African American Women and Rock and Roll*, Illus. ed. (Durham: Duke University Press, 2020); Tricia Rose, *Black Noise: Rap Music and Black Culture in Contemporary America* (Hanover, NH: University Press of New England, 1994).

56. bell hooks, "Eating the Other: Desire and Resistance," in *Media and Cultural*

Studies: KeyWorks, rev. ed., ed. Meenakshi Gigi Durham and Douglas Kellner (Malden, MA: Blackwell, 2006), 373.

57. Mahon, *Right to Rock*, 148.

58. Rose, *Black Noise*, 5.

59. Matthew D. Morrison, "Race, Blacksound, and the (Re)Making of Musicological Discourse," *Journal of the American Musicological Society* 72, no. 3 (2019): 792, https://doi.org/10.1525/jams.2019.72.3.781

60. Greene, "Copynorms, Black Cultural Production, and the Debate over African-American Reparations," 1220.

61. Greene, "Copynorms, Black Cultural Production, and the Debate over African-American Reparations," 1193.

62. "The Regina Monologues," *The Simpsons*, November 23, 2003.

63. Jon Caramanica, "It's Got a Great Beat, and You Can File a Lawsuit to It," *New York Times*, January 6, 2020, sec. Arts, https://www.nytimes.com/2020/01/06/arts/music/pop-music-songs-lawsuits.html. On March 10, 2022, the Ninth Circuit found that "the eight-note pattern, known as an ostinato, consisted 'entirely of commonplace musical elements' that lacked the 'quantum of originality' needed for copyright protection." Jonathan Stempel, "Katy Perry Defeats Appeal in 'Dark Horse' Plagiarism Case," *Reuters*, March 10, 2022, sec. Lifestyle, https://www.reuters.com/lifestyle/katy-perry-defeats-appeal-dark-horse-plagiarism-case-2022-03-10/. On one hand, this decision might be seen as protecting second-comers by drawing protection narrowly. On the other, it's "musique a faire" from *Supreme v. Decca* all over again. See chapter 1.

64. Rosen, "Crawling from the Wreckage."

65. Morrison, "Race, Blacksound, and the (Re)Making of Musicological Discourse," 791.

66. Mahon, *Right to Rock*, 204.

67. Mahon, *Black Diamond Queens*, 118.

68. Greene, "Copynorms, Black Cultural Production, and the Debate over African-American Reparations."

69. Richards, "It's Okay If You Hate Robin Thicke: But the 'Blurred Lines' Verdict Is Bad for Pop Music."

70. Rose, *Black Noise*, 91–92.

71. For a side-by-side comparison of "Blurred Lines" with statements of actual rapists, see Sezin Koehler, "From the Mouths of Rapists: The Lyrics of Robin Thicke's Blurred Lines," *Sociological Images* (blog), September 17, 2013, https://thesocietypages.org/socimages/2013/09/17/from-the-mouths-of-rapists-the-lyrics-of-robin-thickes-blurred-lines-and-real-life-rape/

72. Anjali Vats, *The Color of Creatorship: Intellectual Property, Race, and the Making of Americans* (Stanford: Stanford University Press, 2020), 19.

73. "Heard," *Daily Oklahoman*, August 9, 2013, Drive edition, sec. Weekend Life.

74. *Associated Press*, "Robin Thicke's Naked 'Blurred Lines' Video Gets YouTube Ban," *Billboard*, April 1, 2013, https://www.billboard.com/articles/news/1555273/robin-thickes-naked-blurred-lines-video-gets-youtube-ban

75. Tanya Horeck, "#AskThicke: 'Blurred Lines,' Rape Culture, and the Feminist

Hashtag Takeover," *Feminist Media Studies* 14, no. 6 (2014): 1106, https://doi.org/10.10 80/14680777.2014.975450

76. Wu, "Why the 'Blurred Lines' Copyright Verdict Should Be Thrown Out."

77. Wu, "Why the 'Blurred Lines' Copyright Verdict Should Be Thrown Out."

78. Studies of mock jurors have shown that verdicts are affected by the gender and sexuality of the involved parties (see Brenda Russell, Laurie L. Ragatz, and Shane W. Kraus, "Does Ambivalent Sexism Influence Verdicts for Heterosexual and Homosexual Defendants in a Self-Defense Case?," *Journal of Family Violence* 24, no. 3 [2009]: 145–57, https://doi.org/10.1007/s10896-008-9210-7) as well as their race (see Tara L. Mitchell et al., "Racial Bias in Mock Juror Decision-Making: A Meta-Analytic Review of Defendant Treatment," *Law and Human Behavior* 29, no. 6 [2005]: 621–37, https://doi.org/10.1007/s10979-005-8122-9). The effects of race have also been shown in studies of actual verdicts (see Marian R. Williams and Melissa W. Burek, "Justice, Juries, and Convictions: The Relevance of Race in Jury Verdicts," *Journal of Crime and Justice* 31, no. 1 [2008]: 149–69, https://doi.org/10.1080/0735648X.2008.9721247).

79. Wu, "Why the 'Blurred Lines' Copyright Verdict Should Be Thrown Out."

80. Vats, *The Color of Creatorship*, 18.

81. Rose, *Black Noise*, 79.

82. Rose, *Black Noise*, 92.

83. Vats, *The Color of Creatorship*, 89.

84. Vats, *The Color of Creatorship*, 21.

85. Vats, *The Color of Creatorship*, 204.

86. Amy X. Wang, "How Music Copyright Lawsuits Are Scaring Away New Hits," *Rolling Stone*, January 9, 2020, https://www.rollingstone.com/music/music-feat ures/music-copyright-lawsuits-chilling-effect-935310/

87. Wang, "How Music Copyright Lawsuits Are Scaring Away New Hits."

88. Caramanica, "It's Got a Great Beat, and You Can File a Lawsuit to It."

89. Caramanica, "It's Got a Great Beat, and You Can File a Lawsuit to It."

90. Wang, "How Music Copyright Lawsuits Are Scaring Away New Hits."

91. Burkholder, "The Uses of Existing Music," 863.

92. James Boyle, *The Public Domain: Enclosing the Commons of the Mind* (New Haven: Yale University Press, 2008), 37.

93. Caramanica, "It's Got a Great Beat, and You Can File a Lawsuit to It."

94. Wang, "How Music Copyright Lawsuits Are Scaring Away New Hits."

95. Caramanica, "It's Got a Great Beat, and You Can File a Lawsuit to It."

96. James Boyle, "The Second Enclosure Movement and the Construction of the Public Domain," *Law and Contemporary Problems* 66, no. 1/2 (2003): 37.

97. In *Lenz v. Universal*, the Ninth Circuit held that when a DMCA takedown is filed, fair use must be considered before material is removed from the Internet. *Lenz v. Universal Music Corp.*, 801 F.3d 1126 (9th Cir. 2015).

98. James Boyle, *Shamans, Software and Spleens: Law and the Construction of the Information Society* (Cambridge, MA: Harvard University Press, 1997), x–xi, original emphasis.

99. Boyle, "The Second Enclosure Movement and the Construction of the Public Domain," 42.

100. Boyle, "The Second Enclosure Movement and the Construction of the Public Domain," 44.

101. Caramanica, "It's Got a Great Beat, and You Can File a Lawsuit to It."

102. Shyamkrishna Balganesh, "The Uneasy Case against Copyright Trolls," *Southern California Law Review* 86 (2013): 723.

103. A snowclone is a "phrase that has a standard pattern in which some of the words can be freely replaced"; examples include "X is the new Y." "Snowclone," *Macmillan Dictionary*, accessed April 20, 2020, https://www.macmillandictionary.com/us/dictio nary/american/snowclone

104. Wang, "How Music Copyright Lawsuits Are Scaring Away New Hits."

105. Caramanica, "It's Got a Great Beat, and You Can File a Lawsuit to It."

106. Wang, "How Music Copyright Lawsuits Are Scaring Away New Hits."

107. Caramanica, "It's Got a Great Beat, and You Can File a Lawsuit to It."

CONCLUSION

1. Fisher v. Dees, 794 F.2d 432 (9th Cir. 1986).

2. Rosemary J. Coombe, *The Cultural Life of Intellectual Properties: Authorship, Appropriation, and the Law* (Durham: Duke University Press, 1998), 94.

3. Maureen Mahon, *Right to Rock: The Black Rock Coalition and the Cultural Politics of Race* (Durham: Duke University Press, 2004); Maureen Mahon, *Black Diamond Queens: African American Women and Rock and Roll*, illus. ed. (Durham: Duke University Press, 2020).

4. Cheryl I. Harris, "Whiteness as Property," in *Critical Race Theory: The Key Writings That Formed the Movement*, ed. Kimberlé Crenshaw et al. (New York: New Press, 1996), 288.

5. Grand Upright Music v. Warner Bros. Records Inc., 780 F. Supp. 182 (S.D.N.Y. 1991).

6. Robert Brauneis, "Copyright, Music, and Race: The Case of Mirror Cover Recordings," SSRN Scholarly Paper (Rochester, NY: Social Science Research Network, May 2, 2020), 7, https://doi.org/10.2139/ssrn.3591113

7. This outcome is consistent with the effect of copyright-related cease and desists more broadly. A study by the Brennan Center for Justice found that nearly half of all demands for content to be removed from the Internet either made questionable claims to copyright ownership or targeted things that should be allowed under the fair use doctrine, but people still often took the content down because they didn't know the claims were illegitimate. Marjorie Heins and Tricia Beckles, "Will Fair Use Survive? Free Expression in the Age of Copyright Control," A Public Policy Report (New York: Brennan Center for Justice at NYU School of Law, 2005), http://www.brennancenter .org/sites/default/files/legacy/d/download_file_9056.pdf

8. Anjali Vats, *The Color of Creatorship: Intellectual Property, Race, and the Making of Americans* (Stanford: Stanford University Press, 2020), 90.

9. Harris, "Whiteness as Property," 278.

10. Brenna Bhandar, *Colonial Lives of Property: Law, Land, and Racial Regimes of Ownership* (Durham: Duke University Press, 2018), 4.

11. Vats, *The Color of Creatorship*, 3.

12. Vats, *The Color of Creatorship*, 16.

13. Martin Fredriksson, "Copyright Culture and Pirate Politics," *Cultural Studies* 28, no. 5–6 (2014): 1029, original emphasis, https://doi.org/10.1080/09502386.2014.88 6483

14. Olufunmilayo B. Arewa, "Copyright on Catfish Row: Musical Borrowing, Porgy and Bess, and Unfair Use," *Rutgers Law Journal* 37 (2006): 281.

15. K. J. Greene, "Intellectual Property at the Intersection of Race and Gender: Lady Sings the Blues," *American University Journal of Gender, Social Policy & the Law* 16, no. 3 (2008): 369, https://digitalcommons.wcl.american.edu/jgspl/vol16/iss3/2

16. Boatema Boateng, *The Copyright Thing Doesn't Work Here: Adinkra and Kente Cloth and Intellectual Property in Ghana* (Minneapolis: University of Minnesota Press, 2011), 47.

17. Vats, *The Color of Creatorship*, 203.

18. James Boyle, *Shamans, Software and Spleens: Law and the Construction of the Information Society* (Cambridge, MA: Harvard University Press, 1997), x–xi, original emphasis.

19. Vats, *The Color of Creatorship*, 207.

20. Madhavi Sunder, *From Goods to a Good Life: Intellectual Property and Global Justice* (New Haven: Yale University Press, 2012), 15.

21. Sunder, *From Goods to a Good Life*, 137.

22. Coombe, *The Cultural Life of Intellectual Properties*, 5.

23. Sunder, *From Goods to a Good Life*, 137.

24. Olufunmilayo B. Arewa, "Blues Lives: Promise and Perils of Musical Copyright," *Cardozo Arts & Entertainment Law Journal* 27 (2010): 618. For arguments in favor of considering context, see also Arewa, "Copyright on Catfish Row"; Olufunmilayo B. Arewa, "Making Music: Copyright Law and Creative Processes," in *A Companion to Media Authorship*, ed. Jonathan Gray and Derek Johnson (New York: John Wiley & Sons, 2013), 69–87.

25. Olufunmilayo B. Arewa, "YouTube, UGC, and Digital Music: Competing Business and Cultural Models in the Internet Age," *Northwestern University Law Review* 104 (2010): 473.

26. James Boyle, *The Public Domain: Enclosing the Commons of the Mind* (New Haven: Yale University Press, 2008), 66.

27. Arewa, "YouTube, UGC, and Digital Music," 474.

28. Supreme Records Inc. v. Decca Records Inc., 90 F. Supp. 904 (S.D. Cal. 1950).

29. J. Peter Burkholder, "The Uses of Existing Music: Musical Borrowing as a Field," *Notes* 50, no. 3 (1994): 851–70, https://doi.org/10.2307/898531

30. Arewa, "Blues Lives," 618, 576.

31. Siva Vaidhyanathan, *Copyrights and Copywrongs: The Rise of Intellectual Property and How It Threatens Creativity* (New York: New York University Press, 2003), 120.

32. Arewa, "YouTube, UGC, and Digital Music," 474.

33. Coombe, *The Cultural Life of Intellectual Properties*, 124.

34. Coombe, *The Cultural Life of Intellectual Properties*, 6.

35. Arewa, "Copyright on Catfish Row," 288.

36. Lateef Mtima, "Copyright and Social Justice in the Digital Information Society: Three Steps toward Intellectual Property Social Justice," *Houston Law Review* 53 (2015): 462.

37. Authors Guild Inc. v. HathiTrust, 755 F.3d 87 (2d Cir. 2014).

38. Mtima, "Copyright and Social Justice in the Digital Information Society," 488.

39. Lateef Mtima, "IP Social Justice Theory: Access, Inclusion, and Empowerment," *Gonzaga Law Review* 55 (2020): 420.

40. Vaidhyanathan, *Copyrights and Copywrongs*, 145, 132.

41. Arewa, "Copyright on Catfish Row," 351–52.

42. Mtima, "Copyright and Social Justice in the Digital Information Society," 465.

43. David Hesmondhalgh, "Digital Sampling and Cultural Inequality," *Social & Legal Studies* 15, no. 1 (2006): 53–75, https://doi.org/10.1177/0964663906060973

44. Anupam Chander and Madhavi Sunder, "The Romance of the Public Domain," *California Law Review* 92 (2004): 1335.

45. Barbara Christian, "The Race for Theory," *Cultural Critique*, no. 6 (1987): 51–63, https://doi.org/10.2307/1354255

46. Sunder, *From Goods to a Good Life*, 2.

47. Anjali Vats and Deidre A. Keller, "Critical Race IP," *Cardozo Arts & Entertainment Law Journal* 36 (2018): 795.

48. K. J. Greene, "Copynorms, Black Cultural Production, and the Debate over African-American Reparations," *Cardozo Arts & Entertainment Law Journal* 25 (2008): 1181.

49. Toni Lester, "Treating Creative Black Intellectual Property Ownership as a Human Right," SSRN Scholarly Paper (Rochester, NY: Social Science Research Network, July 6, 2020), 32, https://doi.org/10.2139/ssrn.3644691

50. Vats, *The Color of Creatorship*, 16.

51. F. R. Leavis, "Civilization and Minority Culture," in *Cultural Theory and Popular Culture: A Reader*, ed. John Storey (Athens: University of Georgia Press, 1998), 13–21.

52. Arewa, "Making Music: Copyright Law and Creative Processes," 40.

53. Ruth Frankenberg, *White Women, Race Matters: The Social Construction of Whiteness* (Minneapolis: University of Minnesota Press, 1993), 231.

54. Harris, "Whiteness as Property," 283.

55. Tarleton Gillespie, *Wired Shut: Copyright and the Shape of Digital Culture* (Cambridge, MA: MIT Press, 2007), 131–32.

56. Jenny Roth and Monica Flegel, "It's Like Rape: Metaphorical Family Transgressions, Copyright Ownership and Fandom," *Continuum* 28, no. 6 (2014): 901–13, https://doi.org/10.1080/10304312.2014.964175; Gillespie, *Wired Shut*.

57. Wendy Brown, *Regulating Aversion: Tolerance in the Age of Identity and Empire* (Princeton: Princeton University Press, 2006), 181–82.

58. Roth and Flegel, "It's Like Rape," 905.

59. Gayatri Chakravorty Spivak, "Can the Subaltern Speak?," in *Marxism and the Interpretation of Culture*, ed. Lawrence Grossberg and Cary Nelson (Urbana: University of Illinois Press, 1988), 271–313.

60. Frankenberg, *White Women, Race Matters*, 60–61.

61. Vats, *The Color of Creatorship*, 89.

62. Stanley Cohen, *Folk Devils and Moral Panics* (Abingdon, Oxon: Routledge, 1972).

63. Sunder, *From Goods to a Good Life*, 80.

64. Chander and Sunder, "The Romance of the Public Domain."

65. Hesmondhalgh, "Digital Sampling and Cultural Inequality," 73; Arewa, "Copyright on Catfish Row."

66. Tricia Rose, *Black Noise: Rap Music and Black Culture in Contemporary America* (Hanover, NH: University Press of New England, 1994), 89.

67. Arewa, "Making Music: Copyright Law and Creative Processes," 80.

68. Mahon, *Right to Rock*, 151.

69. Arewa, "Copyright on Catfish Row," 352.

70. Anthony Seeger, "Ethnomusicology and Music Law," *Ethnomusicology* 36, no. 3 (1992): 357, https://doi.org/10.2307/851868

71. Hesmondhalgh, "Digital Sampling and Cultural Inequality," 73.

72. Sunder, *From Goods to a Good Life*, 90.

73. Arewa, "Copyright on Catfish Row," 338.

REFERENCES

COURT CASES

ABKCO Music Inc. v. LaVere, 217 F.3d 684 (9th Cir. 2000).

Answer to Complaint with Jury Demand and Affirmative Defenses, Counterclaim against GoldieBlox, Inc for GoldieBlox, Inc. v. Island Def Jam Music Group et al. n.d. United States District Court, Northern District of California, Oakland Division. Accessed July 19, 2022.

Authors Guild Inc. v. HathiTrust, 755 F.3d 87 (2d Cir. 2014).

Bridgeport Music Inc. v. Dimension Films, 410 F.3d 792 (6th Cir. 2005).

Campbell v. Acuff-Rose Music Inc., 510 U.S. 569 (1994).

Cariou v. Prince, 714 F.3d 694 (2d Cir. 2013).

Dr. Seuss Enters. LP v. Penguin Books USA Inc., 109 F.3d 1394 (9th Cir. 1997).

Elsmere Music Inc. v. National Broadcasting Company, 623 F.2d 252 (2d Cir. 1980).

Estate of Smith v. Graham, 799 Fed. Appx. 36 (2d Cir. 2020).

Fisher v. Dees, 794 F.2d 432 (9th Cir. 1986).

"Goldieblox, Inc. v. Island Def Jam Music Group Complaint for Declaratory Judgment and Injunctive Relief." 2013. https://www.scribd.com/document/186402972/Bea stie

Grand Upright Music v. Warner Bros. Records Inc., 780 F. Supp. 182 (S.D.N.Y. 1991).

Lenz v. Universal Music, 801 F.3d 1126 (9th Cir. 2015).

Rogers v. Koons, 960 F.2d 301 (2d Cir. 1992).

Suntrust Bank v. Houghton Mifflin Co., 268 F.3d 1257 (11th Cir. 2001).

Supreme Records Inc. v. Decca Records Inc., 90 F. Supp. 904 (S.D. Cal. 1950).

WORKS CITED

Ahmed, Sara. *Queer Phenomenology: Orientations, Objects, Others.* Durham: Duke University Press, 2006.

Appel, Nadav. "Pat Boone's Last Laugh: Cover Versions and the Performance of Knowledge." *International Journal of Cultural Studies* 21, no. 4 (2018): 440–54. https://doi.org/10.1177/1367877917692901

Aquilante, Dan. "The Best Secondhand Songs: When Great Singers Cover a Hit, the Results Can Be Sublime." *New York Post*, August 14, 2011.

Aquilante, Dan. "Grammy Grabs." *New York Post*, September 28, 2010, all editions.

Arewa, Olufunmilayo B. "Blues Lives: Promise and Perils of Musical Copyright." *Cardozo Arts & Entertainment Law Journal* 27 (2010): 573–619.

Arewa, Olufunmilayo B. "Copyright on Catfish Row: Musical Borrowing, Porgy and Bess, and Unfair Use." *Rutgers Law Journal* 37 (2006): 277–353.

Arewa, Olufunmilayo B. "Making Music: Copyright Law and Creative Processes." In *A Companion to Media Authorship*, edited by Jonathan Gray and Derek Johnson, 69–87. New York: John Wiley & Sons, 2013.

Arewa, Olufunmilayo B. "YouTube, UGC, and Digital Music: Competing Business and Cultural Models in the Internet Age." *Northwestern University Law Review* 104 (2010): 431.

Associated Press. "Philly Police Use Drake Parody to Ward Off Parking Battles." January 21, 2016, sec. Domestic News.

Associated Press. "Robin Thicke's Naked 'Blurred Lines' Video Gets YouTube Ban." *Billboard*, April 1, 2013. https://www.billboard.com/articles/news/1555273/robin-thickes-naked-blurred-lines-video-gets-youtube-ban

Associated Press. "Show Bits." February 9, 2015, sec. Domestic News, Entertainment News.

Associated Press. "Show Bits: Tiesto's Birthday Gift Becomes Grammy Win." February 8, 2015.

Awkward, Michael. *Soul Covers: Rhythm and Blues Remakes and the Struggle for Artistic Identity*. Durham: Duke University Press, 2007.

Axton, Gene. "Scranton's Theater at Lackawanna College Puts a Quarter in the Postmodern Jukebox." *Times Leader*, November 9, 2015, sec. Lifestyle.

Bailey, Steve. "Faithful or Foolish: The Emergence of the 'Ironic Cover Album' and Rock Culture." *Popular Music and Society* 26, no. 2 (2003): 141–59. https://doi.org/10.1080/0300776032000095486

Balganesh, Shyamkrishna. "The Uneasy Case against Copyright Trolls." *Southern California Law Review* 86 (2013): 723–82.

Barker, Andrew. "'Glee' Breaks New Artists and Turns Kitsch into Classics." *Variety*, March 18, 2014. https://variety.com/2014/tv/features/glee-breaks-new-artists-and-turns-kitsch-into-classics-1201137138/

Barnett, Sheena. "Catch Up on Some Girl Talk." *Northeast Mississippi Daily Journal*, February 5, 2009, sec. Lifestyle.

Barron, Anne. "Introduction: Harmony or Dissonance? Copyright Concepts and Musical Practice." *Social & Legal Studies* 15, no. 1 (2006): 25–51. https://doi.org/10.1177/0964663906060972

Barthes, Roland. "The Death of the Author." Translated by Richard Howard. *Aspen* 5+6 (1967).

Barthes, Roland. "The Death of the Author." Reprinted in *Image-Music-Text*. Translated by Stephen Heath, 142–48. New York: Hill and Wang, 1978.

Bauder, David. "British Singer Joe Cocker Dies of Lung Cancer." *Associated Press*, December 22, 2014, sec. Domestic News, Entertainment News.

Bay Area News Group. "Good Times: Bay Area Entertainment Guide for Nov. 3–9." *San Jose Mercury News*, November 2, 2011, sec. News, Entertainment.

Beech, Kai. "Weird Al to Play HSU." *Eureka Times-Standard*, August 16, 2010, sec. Entertainment.

Belcher, Walt. "Weird Al's 'Alpocolypse' Tour." *Tampa Tribune*, September 30, 2011, final edition, sec. Friday Extra.

Benjamin, Walter. "The Work of Art in the Age of Mechanical Reproduction." In *Media and Cultural Studies: KeyWorks*, edited by Meenakshi Gigi Durham and Douglas Kellner, 48–70. Malden, MA: Blackwell, 2001.

Benkler, Yochai. *The Wealth of Networks: How Social Production Transforms Markets and Freedom*. New Haven: Yale University Press, 2007.

Berger, Joseph. "Irving Fields, Composer and Lounge Pianist, Dies at 101." *New York Times*, August 23, 2016, late edition-final edition, sec. A.

Berndtson, Chad. "The Year in Music: From Kanye to Cohen to Clemons to Cash, the Best (and Not So Best) of the Past 12 Months." *Patriot Ledger*, December 18, 2009, ROP edition, sec. Features.

Bernie Sanders Raps "Old Town Hall" ("Old Town Road" Parody), 2019. https://www.youtube.com/watch?v=PD24oApjci8

Bernstein, Jacob. "Postscript: Death of a Pied Piper." *New York Times*, April 6, 2014, late edition-final edition, sec. ST, 15.

Bernstein, Jacob. "The Queen of Quiet." *New York Times*, October 26, 2017, late edition-final edition, sec. D.

Bhabha, Homi K. *The Location of Culture*. 2nd ed. London: Routledge, 2004.

Bhandar, Brenna. *Colonial Lives of Property: Law, Land, and Racial Regimes of Ownership*. Durham: Duke University Press, 2018.

Bialas, Michael. "Crossover Country." *Pueblo Chieftain*, August 5, 2011, sec. Lifestyle.

Billboard. "Five Burning Questions: Billboard Staffers Discuss Lil Nas X's 'Old Town Road' Pursuit of Hot 100 History." July 16, 2019.

Billboard. "Five Burning Questions: Billboard Staffers Discuss Lil Nas X's 'Old Town Road' Tying the Hot 100 Record for Weeks at No. 1." July 23, 2019.

Bingham, Christopher M. "Talking about Twitch: *Dropped Frames* and a Normative Theory of New Media Production." *Convergence* 26, no. 2 (2020): 269–86. https://doi.org/10.1177/1354856517736974

Blistein, Jon. "A New Led Zeppelin Court Win over 'Stairway to Heaven' Just Upended a Copyright Precedent." *Rolling Stone*, March 9, 2020. https://www.rollingstone.com/music/music-news/led-zeppelin-stairway-to-heaven-copyright-infringement-ruling-appeal-964530/

Boateng, Boatema. *The Copyright Thing Doesn't Work Here: Adinkra and Kente Cloth and Intellectual Property in Ghana*. Minneapolis: University of Minnesota Press, 2011.

Bolter, Jay David, and Richard Grusin. *Remediation: Understanding New Media*. Cambridge, MA: MIT Press, 2000.

Bonilla-Silva, Eduardo. *Racism without Racists: Color-Blind Racism and the Persistence of Racial Inequality in the United States*. Lanham, MD: Rowman & Littlefield, 2003.

Boone, Christine. "Mashing: Toward a Typology of Recycled Music." *Music Theory Online* 19, no. 3 (2013). https://mtosmt.org/issues/mto.13.19.3/mto.13.19.3.boone.html

Boyle, James. *The Public Domain: Enclosing the Commons of the Mind.* New Haven: Yale University Press, 2008.

Boyle, James. "The Second Enclosure Movement and the Construction of the Public Domain." *Law and Contemporary Problems* 66, no. 1/2 (2003): 33–74.

Boyle, James. *Shamans, Software and Spleens: Law and the Construction of the Information Society.* Cambridge, MA: Harvard University Press, 1997.

Brackett, Charmain Z. "Black Violin Bridges Gaps with Classic, Modern Music." *Augusta Chronicle*, February 9, 2017, all editions, sec. Entertainment.

Brackett, Charmain Z. "Black Violin Show Will Be New, Different." *Augusta Chronicle*, April 19, 2018, all editions, sec. News.

Brauneis, Robert. "Copyright, Music, and Race: The Case of Mirror Cover Recordings." SSRN Scholarly Paper. Rochester, NY: Social Science Research Network, May 2, 2020. https://doi.org/10.2139/ssrn.3591113

Bream, Jon. "Country Star Aldean Knows How to Rock It." *Star Tribune*, August 29, 2009, Metro edition, sec. News.

Bream, Jon. "This High School Musical Usually Made the Grade." *Star Tribune*, June 2, 2011, Metro edition, sec. News.

Bream, Jon. "Youth Storms the Glambert Show." *Star Tribune*, September 2, 2009, Metro edition.

Brown, Wendy. *Regulating Aversion: Tolerance in the Age of Identity and Empire.* Princeton: Princeton University Press, 2006.

Burger, David. "'American Idol' Tour Kicks Off in Utah." *Salt Lake Tribune*, July 8, 2011, sec. Friday Mix, Entertainment, Features.

Burkholder, J. Peter. "'Quotation' and Emulation: Charles Ives's Uses of His Models." *Musical Quarterly* 71, no. 1 (1985): 1–26.

Burkholder, J. Peter. "The Uses of Existing Music: Musical Borrowing as a Field." *Notes* 50, no. 3 (1994): 851–70. https://doi.org/10.2307/898531

Butler, Judith. *Bodies That Matter: On the Discursive Limits of "Sex."* New York: Routledge, 1993.

Caramanica, Jon. "Breezy Mien Disguised Petty's Savvy and Tenacity." *New York Times*, October 4, 2017, late edition-final edition, sec. B.

Caramanica, Jon. "It's Got a Great Beat, and You Can File a Lawsuit to It." *New York Times*, January 6, 2020, sec. Arts. https://www.nytimes.com/2020/01/06/arts/music/pop-music-songs-lawsuits.html

Caramanica, Jon. "The Playlist: Demi Lovato Seeks Her 'Despacito' and 9 More New Songs." *New York Times*, November 18, 2017. https://www.nytimes.com/2017/11/17/arts/music/playlist-luis-fonsi-demi-lovato-jaden-smith.html

Caramanica, Jon. "A Verdict Based on an Old Way of Making Music." *New York Times*, March 12, 2015, late edition-final edition, sec. C.

Caulfield, Keith. "Tom Petty Won't Win a Grammy for Sam Smith's 'Stay With Me.'" *Hollywood Reporter*, January 27, 2015, sec. News.

Cava, Marco R. della. "'Finding the Funk' Excavates the Artifacts of Modern R&B: From the Bay Area to Dayton, Ohio, It's a Musical Odyssey." *USA Today*, February 4, 2014, final edition, sec. Life.

Cava, Marco R. della. "Music Lovers Take a Spin." *USA Today*, October 27, 2009, final edition, sec. Life.

Chander, Anupam, and Madhavi Sunder. "The Romance of the Public Domain." *California Law Review* 92 (2004): 1331–73.

Chinen, Nate. "Chipper Remnants of a Life Turned Sour." *New York Times*, December 6, 2011, late edition-final edition, sec. C.

Christian, Barbara. "The Race for Theory." *Cultural Critique*, no. 6 (1987): 51–63. https://doi.org/10.2307/1354255

Cidoni, Mike. "'Fever' Singer Is Hot Again." *Associated Press*, May 17, 2010, sec. Entertainment News.

Clear, Marty. "Keeping It Classic—and Fresh." *Tampa Bay Times*, January 13, 2012, sec. City Times.

Clinton, George. "No Sample of #Funkadelic's 'Sexy Ways' in @RobinThicke's 'Blurred Lines'—yet Armen Boladian Thinks So? We Support @RobinThicke @Pharrell!" Twitter, August 15, 2013. https://twitter.com/george_clinton/status/368210216828932096

Clover, Joshua. "Ambiguity and Theft." In *Cutting Across Media: Appropriation Art, Interventionist Collage, and Copyright Law*, edited by Kembrew McLeod and Rudolf Kuenzli, 84–93. Durham: Duke University Press, 2011.

Cohen, Julie E. "Copyright and the Perfect Curve." *Vanderbilt Law Review* 53 (2000): 1799–1819.

Cohen, Sandy. "'Glee' a Musical Success as Much as a Cult Success." *Associated Press*, April 12, 2010, sec. Entertainment News.

Cohen, Stanley. *Folk Devils and Moral Panics*. Abingdon, Oxon: Routledge, 1972.

Collins, Steve. "Digital Fair: Prosumption and the Fair Use Defence." *Journal of Consumer Culture* 10, no. 1 (2010): 37–55. https://doi.org/10.1177/1469540509354014

Condran, Ed. "Scott Bradlee and Postmodern Jukebox: Taking Modern Pop Songs and Transforming Them into Jazz." *Tampa Tribune*, November 27, 2015, sec. Friday Extra.

"Coolio Did Not Want Weird Al to Spoof 'Gangsta's Paradise.'" August 1, 2013. https://www.yahoo.com/entertainment/bp/coolio-did-not-want-weird-al-spoof-gangsta-205954306.html

Coombe, Rosemary J. *The Cultural Life of Intellectual Properties: Authorship, Appropriation, and the Law*. Durham: Duke University Press, 1998.

Coscarelli, Joe. "Where Will Latin Pop Go Next?" *New York Times*, September 7, 2017, late edition-final edition, sec. C.

Crenshaw, Kimberlé. "Race, Reform, and Retrenchment: Transformation and Legitimation in Antidiscrimination Law." In *Critical Race Theory: The Key Writings That Formed the Movement*, edited by Kimberlé Crenshaw, Neil Gotanda, Gary Peller, and Kendall Thomas, 103–22. New York: New Press, 1996.

Crenshaw, Kimberlé, Neil Gotanda, Gary Peller, and Kendall Thomas. "Introduction."

In *Critical Race Theory: The Key Writings That Formed the Movement*, xiii–xxxii. New York: New Press, 1996.

Daily Camera. "15 Things to Do in Boulder County Today, June 10, 2016." June 10, 2016, sec. Entertainment.

Daily News of Los Angeles. "For the Record: 'Jews on Vinyl' a Sound Exploration of History." May 23, 2010, Valley edition, sec. L.A. Life.

Daily Oklahoman. "Heard." August 9, 2013, Drive edition, sec. Weekend Life.

Daly, Sean. "Celebrating Her Love for Soul." *Tampa Bay Times*, January 27, 2012, sec. TBT.

Daly, Sean. "Collins' R&B Redux Just a Wishy Wash." *Tampa Bay Times*, September 5, 2010, 4 State / Suncoast edition, sec. Tampa Bay, Review.

Dauber, Mara. "Grey Album Illegal, but So Worthwhile." *Santa Fe New Mexican*, April 9, 2010, sec. Generation Next.

Dayton Daily News. "Lifeline." August 10, 2017.

Dean, Ashley. *Colorado Daily*, September 13, 2012, sec. State and Regional News.

Debbie + Team GoldieBlox. "Our Letter to the Beastie Boys." November 27, 2013. https://web.archive.org/web/20131129044348/https:/blog.goldieblox.com/2013/11/our-letter-to-the-beastie-boys/

Definitions, Title 17 U.S. Code § 101. Accessed December 4, 2022. https://copyright.gov/title17/92chap1.html

Delgado, Richard, and Jean Stefancic. "Introduction." In *Critical Race Theory: The Cutting Edge.* 2nd ed., edited by Richard Delgado and Jean Stefancic, xv–xix. Philadelphia: Temple University Press, 2000.

Demers, Joanna. *Steal This Music: How Intellectual Property Law Affects Musical Creativity.* Athens: University of Georgia Press, 2006.

Demšar, Janez, Tomaž Curk, Aleš Erjavec, Črt Gorup, Tomaž Hočevar, Mitar Milutinovič, Martin Možina, et al. "Orange: Data Mining Toolbox in Python." *Journal of Machine Learning Research* 14 (2013): 2349–53.

Desmond-Harris, Jenée. "Annie Lennox Is Singing about Lynching, but She Doesn't Want to Talk about It." *Vox*, October 28, 2014. https://www.vox.com/2014/10/28/7080287/annie-lennox-strange-fruit-tavis-smiley-nostalgia

de Yampert, Rick. "Rockers Stumble down Stairway to Mashups." *News-Journal*, March 19, 2010, final edition, sec. E.

Dobrin, Peter. "Review: Black Violin Brings Strings to Hip-Hop." *Philadelphia Inquirer*, November 10, 2015, web edition, sec. Features Magazine.

Edgar, Amanda Nell. "Blackvoice and Adele's Racialized Musical Performance: Blackness, Whiteness, and Discursive Authenticity." *Critical Studies in Media Communication* 31, no. 3 (2014): 167–81. https://doi.org/10.1080/15295036.2013.863427

Ellis, Nadia. "Out and Bad: Toward a Queer Performance Hermeneutic in Jamaican Dancehall." *Small Axe: A Caribbean Journal of Criticism* 15, no. 2 (35) (2011): 7–23. https://doi.org/10.1215/07990537-1334212

Emmanuel, Lisa Orkin. "Tiger's Tunes: Apology Lives Online in Mashups." *Associated Press*, February 23, 2010, sec. Entertainment News.

English, Tim. *Sounds Like Teen Spirit: Stolen Melodies, Ripped-Off Riffs, and the Secret History of Rock and Roll*, 2016 ed. Self-published, 2016 (first published, iUniverse, 2006).

Farber, Jim. "Praise at Last Rains o'er LaVette." *Daily News*, January 9, 2009, Sports final edition, sec. Now.

Farber, Jim. "Roberta Flack Gets Back to the Beatles." *Daily News*, February 22, 2012, Sports final edition, sec. Now.

Farber, Jim. "Ronson's a Past Master." *Daily News*, January 13, 2015, Sports final Replate edition, sec. Now.

Fassnacht, Jon. "Weird Al Continues to Defy the Odds." *Reading Eagle*, July 25, 2014, sec. Lifestyle.

Fekadu, Mesfin. "And the Grammy Nomination Goes to . . ." *Associated Press*, December 3, 2014, sec. Entertainment News.

Fekadu, Mesfin. "'Despacito' Opening Doors for Spanish Songs on English Radio." *Associated Press*, August 8, 2017, sec. Entertainment News.

Fekadu, Mesfin. "'Despacito' Ties Mariah Carey's 16-Week Record at No. 1." *Associated Press*, August 28, 2017.

Fekadu, Mesfin. "Gorillaz: We Won't Let 'Glee' Cover Our Songs." *Associated Press*, October 12, 2010, sec. Entertainment News.

Fekadu, Mesfin. "Kanye West's 'Yeezus': Heaven-Sent or Weak Event?" *Associated Press*, July 20, 2013, sec. Entertainment News.

Fekadu, Mesfin. "Mary Mary Still Going Strong 9 Years Later." *Associated Press*, August 28, 2009, sec. Entertainment News.

Fekadu, Mesfin. "Shirley Caesar Isn't Cooking 'Beans, Greens' at Thanksgiving." *Associated Press*, November 19, 2016, sec. Domestic News.

Feld, Steven. "Notes on World Beat." *Public Culture* 1, no. 1 (1988): 31–37. https://doi.org/10.1215/08992363-1-1-31

Fiander, Matthew. *Pittsburgh Post-Gazette*, March 29, 2012, Sooner edition, sec. Arts & Entertainment, For the Record.

Florence, Russell, Jr. "Black Violin Breaks the Mold." *Dayton Daily News*, April 27, 2014, sec. Life & Arts.

Foucault, Michel. "What Is an Author?" In *Language, Counter-Memory, Practice: Selected Essays and Interviews*, 113–38. Ithaca: Cornell University Press, 1980.

France, Lisa Respers. "Lil Nas X and RM of BTS Drop New 'Old Town Road' Remix." *CNN*, July 25, 2019, sec. Showbiz.

Frankenberg, Ruth. *White Women, Race Matters: The Social Construction of Whiteness*. Minneapolis: University of Minnesota Press, 1993.

Fredriksson, Martin. "Copyright Culture and Pirate Politics." *Cultural Studies* 28, no. 5–6 (2014): 1022–47. https://doi.org/10.1080/09502386.2014.886483

Freedman, Rich. "King of Parodies, Weird Al Yankovic, to Hold Court at Uptown in Napa." *Vallejo Times Herald*, July 20, 2012, sec. Art.

Gallpault, Gerry. "The Boyce Are Back." *Sarasota Herald Tribune*, September 22, 2011, sec. E, Archives.

Ganz, Jacob. "MTV Loves MTV: A Bad Romance." *NPR*, September 13, 2010. https://

www.npr.org/sections/therecord/2010/09/13/129833419/mtv-loves-mtv-a-bad-ro
mance

Gardner, Eriq. "'Blurred Lines' Appeal Gets Support from More Than 200 Musicians." *Hollywood Reporter*, August 30, 2016. https://www.hollywoodreporter.com/thr-esq /blurred-lines-appeal-gets-support-924213

Garelick, Jon. "Sam Phillips." Sun Record Company. Accessed September 15, 2019. http://www.sunrecordcompany.com/Sam_Phillips.html

Gates, Henry Louis, Jr. *The Signifying Monkey: A Theory of African American Literary Criticism*. 25th anniversary ed. Oxford: Oxford University Press, 2014.

Ghaffary, Shirin. "Uber and Lyft Say They Don't Plan to Reclassify Their Drivers as Employees." *Vox*, September 11, 2019. https://www.vox.com/2019/9/11/20861599/ab -5-uber-lyft-drivers-contractors-reclassify-employees

Gibbs, Constance. "Violin Duo Hits 'Pitch' out of Park." *New York Daily News*, November 26, 2016, Sports final edition, sec. Television.

Gillespie, Tarleton. *Wired Shut: Copyright and the Shape of Digital Culture*. Cambridge, MA: MIT Press, 2007.

Ginsburg, Jane C. "The Author's Name as a Trademark: A Perverse Perspective on the Moral Right of Paternity." *Cardozo Arts & Entertainment Law Journal* 23 (2005): 379–89.

Gloss, Megan. "Sample Says." *Telegraph Herald*, January 22, 2010, sec. C.

Godfrey, Sarah. "Where's Wale? 10 Hot Tracks." *Washington Post*, June 3, 2009, Suburban edition, sec. Style.

Goodwin, Jeremy D. "Where Classical Meets Hip-Hop." *Berkshire Eagle*, May 12, 2011, sec. Weekend.

Gordon, Wendy J. "Excuse and Justification in the Law of Fair Use: Transaction Costs Have Always Been Part of the Story." *Journal of the Copyright Society of the U.S.A.* 50 (2003): 149–98.

Gordon, Wendy J. "A Property Right in Self-Expression: Equality and Individualism in the Natural Law of Intellectual Property." *Yale Law Journal* 102 (1992): 1533–1609.

Graeber, Laurel. "Spare Times." *New York Times*, March 20, 2009, late edition-final edition, sec. C.

Graeber, Laurel. "Spare Times: For Children." *New York Times*, November 16, 2012, late edition-final edition, sec. C.

Graeber, Laurel. "Spare Times: For Children." *New York Times*, April 11, 2014, late edition-final edition, sec. C.

Graham, Adam. "'Old Town Road' Rides into History Books." *Detroit News*, July 20, 2019, first edition, sec. Features.

Greene, K. J. "Copynorms, Black Cultural Production, and the Debate over African-American Reparations." *Cardozo Arts & Entertainment Law Journal* 25 (2008): 1179–1227.

Greene, K. J. "Intellectual Property at the Intersection of Race and Gender: Lady Sings the Blues." *American University Journal of Gender, Social Policy & the Law* 16, no. 3 (2008): 365–85. https://digitalcommons.wcl.american.edu/jgspl/vol16/iss3/2

Gross, Joe. "Rogues and Stones: Movies, Books, Music and More Coming in December." *Austin American-Statesman*, November 28, 2016, State edition, sec. Life.

Guarino, Ben. "DNA's Alphabet Expands from Four Letters to Six." *Washington Post*, January 31, 2017, every edition, sec. Health.

Gundersen, Edna. "Grammys Reach for High Notes, Higher Ratings." *USA Today*, February 8, 2013, first edition, sec. Life.

Gunderson, Philip A. "Danger Mouse's Grey Album, Mash-Ups, and the Age of Composition." *Postmodern Culture* 15, no. 1 (2004). https://doi.org/10.1353/pmc.20 04.0040

Gunkel, David J. *Of Remixology: Ethics and Aesthetics after Remix*. Illustrated ed. Cambridge, MA: MIT Press, 2015.

Guralnick, Peter. "Elvis Presley: How Sun Records Boss Sam Phillips Discovered a Star in 1954." *Independent*, October 30, 2015. http://www.independent.co.uk/arts-enter tainment/music/features/elvis-presley-how-sun-records-boss-sam-phillips-discov ered-a-star-in-1954-a6713891.html

Halberstam, Judith. *In a Queer Time and Place: Transgender Bodies, Subcultural Lives*. New York: New York University Press, 2005.

Halberstam, Judith. *The Queer Art of Failure*. Durham: Duke University Press, 2011.

Hall, Kristin M. "Grammy Winners Pentatonix Finally Getting Airplay." *Associated Press*, October 16, 2015, sec. Entertainment News.

Hall, Kristin M. "Kane Brown Turned Facebook Likes into a Country Music Career." *Associated Press*, December 21, 2016, sec. Entertainment News.

Hamilton, Jack. *Just around Midnight: Rock and Roll and the Racial Imagination*. Illustrated ed. Cambridge, MA: Harvard University Press, 2016.

Harrington, Jim. "Review: Beatles TV Special More Flop Than Fab." *Contra Costa Times*, February 10, 2014, sec. Breaking, News, Local.

Harris, Cheryl I. "Whiteness as Property." In *Critical Race Theory: The Key Writings That Formed the Movement*, edited by Kimberlé Crenshaw, Neil Gotanda, Gary Peller, and Kendall Thomas, 276–91. New York: New Press, 1996.

Harris, Ron. "Review: Carly Rae Jepsen's Album 'Kiss' Is Sweet." *Associated Press*, September 17, 2012, sec. Entertainment News.

Havens, Lyndsey. "The Summer of Cyrus: How Billy Ray, Miley & Noah Dominated the Season." *Billboard*, September 3, 2019.

Heins, Marjorie, and Tricia Beckles. "Will Fair Use Survive? Free Expression in the Age of Copyright Control." A Public Policy Report. New York: Brennan Center for Justice at NYU School of Law, 2005. http://www.brennancenter.org/sites/default/fi les/legacy/d/download_file_9056.pdf

Heller, Aron. "Israeli Video Remix King Becomes Player in Election Campaign." *Associated Press*, January 9, 2015, sec. International News.

Heller, Billy. "Oy Caramba! Lost Album Is All Mixed Up." *New York Post*, August 18, 2009, all editions.

Hesmondhalgh, David. "Digital Sampling and Cultural Inequality." *Social & Legal Studies* 15, no. 1 (2006): 53–75. https://doi.org/10.1177/0964663906060973

Hewitt, Chris. "Ordway Center Announces Music and Dance from around the World." *St. Paul Pioneer Press*, April 20, 2017.

Ho, Rodney. "American Idol Buzz: American Idol Recap, Top 8 Performance Show." *Atlanta Journal-Constitution*, April 7, 2009, online edition.

Hochhauser, Sharon. "Take Me Down to the Parodies City." *Journal of Popular Music Studies* 30, no. 1–2 (2018): 61–78.

Holden, Stephen. "Albums by Neil Young, Bette Midler and Miguel Zenón." *New York Times*, November 4, 2014, late edition-final edition, sec. C.

hooks, bell. "Eating the Other: Desire and Resistance." In *Media and Cultural Studies: Key Works*. Rev. ed., edited by Meenakshi Gigi Durham and Douglas Kellner, 366–80. Malden, MA: Blackwell, 2006.

Horeck, Tanya. "#AskThicke: 'Blurred Lines,' Rape Culture, and the Feminist Hashtag Takeover." *Feminist Media Studies* 14, no. 6 (2014): 1105–7. https://doi.org/10.1080/14680777.2014.975450

Howard-Spink, Sam. "Grey Tuesday, Online Cultural Activism and the Mash-Up of Music and Politics." *First Monday*, 2004. https://doi.org/10.5210/fm.v0i0.1460

Hyde, Lewis. *Common as Air: Revolution, Art, and Ownership*. New York: Farrar, Straus and Giroux, 2010.

Hyndman, Sheena D. "No Money, Mo' Problems: The Role of the Remix in Restructuring Compensation for Producers of Electronic Dance Music." *MUSICultures* 41, no. 1 (2014): 57–72. https://journals.lib.unb.ca/index.php/MC/article/view/22356

Infante, Victor D. "'Glee' May Be Gone, but Songs Play On." *Telegram & Gazette*, March 20, 2015, sec. Living.

Inquirer. "New Recordings." *Philadelphia Inquirer.* April 25, 2010. https://www.inquirer.com/philly/entertainment/20100425_New_Recordings.html

Itzkoff, Dave. "Beastie Boys Call Video Parody 'an Advertisement.'" *New York Times*, November 26, 2013, late edition-final edition, sec. C.

Itzkoff, Dave. "Beastie Boys Settle Suit over Toy Company Ad." *New York Times*, March 19, 2014, late edition-final edition, sec. C.

Itzkoff, Dave. "Serving Pop Stars, but on a Skewer." *New York Times*, June 12, 2011, late edition-final edition, sec. AR.

Iwasaki, Scott. "Nightclub DJ Is Proud of Utah Ties." *Deseret Morning News*, April 3, 2009.

Jenkins, Henry, Sam Ford, and Joshua Green. *Spreadable Media: Creating Value and Meaning in a Networked Culture*. New York: New York University Press, 2013.

Jimenez, Carla. "Educate, Entertain and Inspire: Black Violin Brings Their Blended Style of Classical, Hip Hop to Central Illinois." *State Journal-Register*, September 21, 2017, sec. IL Features.

Johnson, Amber. "Antoine Dodson and the (Mis)Appropriation of the Homo Coon: An Intersectional Approach to the Performative Possibilities of Social Media." *Critical Studies in Media Communication* 30, no. 2 (2013): 152–70. https://doi.org/10.1080/15295036.2012.755050

Johnson, Kevin C. "Florida Georgia Line Brings 'Good Times' to St. Louis." *St. Louis Post-Dispatch*, November 1, 2013, first edition, sec. Go!

Johnson, Kevin C. "Phillips Seems Destined for Stardom." *St. Louis Post-Dispatch*, July 13, 2012, second edition, sec. News.

Jones, Steve. "Albums." *USA Today*, January 24, 2012, final edition, sec. Life.

Jonsson, Patrik. "'Pants on the Ground' Goes Viral: Top Five Larry Platt Covers; American Idol Contestant 'General' Larry Platt's Song Mocking Contemporary Street Fashion Has Inspired Many YouTubed Versions, from Rap to Easy Listening." *Christian Science Monitor*, January 16, 2010.

Kaan, Cihan. "Adam Yauch Was a Muslim Hero." *Al Jazeera*, May 9, 2012. https://www.aljazeera.com/indepth/opinion/2012/05/20125813653185358.html

Katz, Mark. *Capturing Sound: How Technology Has Changed Music*. Rev. ed. Berkeley: University of California Press, 2010.

Kaufman, Gil. "Watch 'Two Neil Youngs Sitting on a Tree Stump' on 'The Tonight Show.'" *Hollywood Reporter*, June 22, 2016, sec. News.

Kaur, Harmeet. "This Third Grade Class' Remix of 'Old Town Road' Is the Only One You Need." *CNN*, May 4, 2019, sec. Showbiz.

Kelley, Brian. "People in the News." *Dayton Daily News*, December 21, 2013, sec. Comics.

Know Your Meme. "Leave Britney Alone." Accessed May 30, 2020. https://knowyourmeme.com/memes/leave-britney-alone

Koehler, Sezin. "From the Mouths of Rapists: The Lyrics of Robin Thicke's Blurred Lines." *Sociological Images* (blog), September 17, 2013. https://thesocietypages.org/socimages/2013/09/17/from-the-mouths-of-rapists-the-lyrics-of-robin-thickes-blurred-lines-and-real-life-rape/

Lacy-Thompson, Tony. "Postmodern Jukebox Wows with Talent at Stanford's Bing Concert Hall." *East Bay Times*, February 21, 2017.

Lang, Derrik J. "Batman Goes Bale-Istic with Profane Tirade on Crew." *Associated Press*, February 4, 2009, sec. Entertainment News.

Langer, Emily. "Bandleader Who Fed Postwar Mania for Yiddish Mambo." *Washington Post*, August 24, 2016, Suburban edition, sec. Metro.

Larsen, Peter. "Lambert Dominates 'Idol' in L.A." *Orange County Register*, July 18, 2009, sec. Arts.

Lawrence, Charles R., III. "The Id, the Ego, and Equal Protection: Reckoning with Unconscious Racism." In *Critical Race Theory: The Key Writings That Formed the Movement*, edited by Kimberlé Crenshaw, Neil Gotanda, Gary Peller, and Kendall Thomas, 235–57. New York: New Press, 1996.

Lazar, Zachary. "The 373-Hit Wonder." *New York Times*, January 9, 2011, late edition-final edition, sec. MM.

Leavis, F. R. "Civilization and Minority Culture." In *Cultural Theory and Popular Culture: A Reader*, edited by John Storey, 13–21. Athens: University of Georgia Press, 1998.

Leight, Elias. "Lil Nas X's 'Old Town Road' Was a Country Hit. Then Country Changed Its Mind." *Rolling Stone*, March 26, 2019. https://www.rollingstone.com/music/music-features/lil-nas-x-old-town-road-810844/

Lester, Toni. "Treating Creative Black Intellectual Property Ownership as a Human Right." SSRN Scholarly Paper. Rochester, NY: Social Science Research Network, July 6, 2020. https://doi.org/10.2139/ssrn.3644691

Leval, Pierre N. "Toward a Fair Use Standard." *Harvard Law Review* 103, no. 5 (1990): 1105–36. https://doi.org/10.2307/1341457

Levy, Joe. "How Lil Nas X Sees His Future after 'Old Town Road.'" *Billboard*, September 19, 2019.

Levy, Piet. "'Weird Al' Yankovic Has Serious Fans—and Serious Fun." *St. Paul Pioneer Press*, July 1, 2015, sec. Entertainment.

Lewis, Randy. "'Weird Al' Marks 40 Years of Parody." *Baltimore Sun*, March 5, 2017, AdvanceBulldog edition, sec. Main News, A.

Lil Nas X Feat. Billy Ray Cyrus, Young Thug & Mason Ramsey—Old Town Road (Area 51 Video), 2019. https://www.youtube.com/watch?v=aA7xDP9sQzk

@LilNasX. "i did not make 27 remixes to the same song to be disrespected like this." Twitter, May 12, 2020. https://twitter.com/lilnasx/status/1260255622248841216

@LilNasX. "last one i PROMISSEE." Twitter, July 24, 2019. https://twitter.com/lilnasx/status/1154227360566259713

@LilNasX. "twitter please help me get billy ray cyrus on this Https://T.Co/UDoeiO Zqc1." Tweet. *@LilNasX* (blog), December 5, 2018. https://twitter.com/LilNasX/status/1070125203345342464

Limitations on Exclusive Rights: Fair Use, § 107, Title 17 United States Code. http://www.copyright.gov/title17/92chap1.html#107

Lipshutz, Jason. "Lil Nas X's 'Old Town Road': 5 Things the Music Industry Should Learn from Its Record-Setting Run." *Billboard*, August 21, 2019.

Lipshutz, Jason. "The 16 Best Moments from the 2019 MTV Video Music Awards." *Billboard*, August 27, 2019.

Litman, Jessica. *Digital Copyright*. Pbk. ed. Amherst, NY: Prometheus Books, 2006.

Lockett, Dee. "Billy Ray Cyrus Gives Lil Nas X's 'Old Town Road' a Ringing Endorsement with Remix." *New York Magazine*, April 5, 2019.

Lockett, Dee. "The 50 Best Glee Performances, Ranked." *Vulture*, March 20, 2015. https://www.vulture.com/2015/03/glee-best-performances-ranked.html

Lockwood, Rod. "Weird, Wily and Talented Al Yankovic Returning to Toledo Zoo." *Blade*, June 24, 2010, sec. Entertainment News.

Logan, Joe. "Plain Parody." *Philadelphia Inquirer*, March 19, 1996, SF edition, sec. Features Magazine: Entertainment.

Loren, Lydia Pallas. "Redefining the Market Failure Approach to Fair Use in an Era of Copyright Permission Systems." *Journal of Intellectual Property Law* 5 (1997): 1.

Lott, Eric. *Love and Theft: Blackface Minstrelsy and the American Working Class*. 20th anniversary ed. New York: Oxford University Press, 2013. Originally published, 1993.

Machosky, Michael. "Girl Talk Pushes Listeners to Broaden Horizons." *Pittsburgh Tribune Review*, July 30, 2009.

Macmillan Dictionary. "Snowclone." Accessed April 20, 2020. https://www.macmillandictionary.com/us/dictionary/american/snowclone

Magnus, Cristyn, P. D. Magnus, and Christy Mag Uidhir. "Judging Covers." *Journal of Aesthetics and Art Criticism* 71, no. 4 (2013): 361–70. https://doi.org/10.1111/jaac .12034

Mahon, Maureen. *Black Diamond Queens: African American Women and Rock and Roll*. Illustrated ed. Durham: Duke University Press, 2020.

Mahon, Maureen. *Right to Rock: The Black Rock Coalition and the Cultural Politics of Race*. Durham: Duke University Press, 2004.

Mann, Larisa Kingston. *Rude Citizenship: Jamaican Popular Music, Copyright, and the Reverberations of Colonial Power*. Chapel Hill: University of North Carolina Press, 2022.

Manuel, Peter, and Wayne Marshall. "The Riddim Method: Aesthetics, Practice, and Ownership in Jamaican Dancehall." *Popular Music* 25, no. 3 (2006): 447–70. https:// doi.org/10.1017/S0261143006000997

Marikar, Sheila. "Winning Girls Over, Piece by Piece." *New York Times*, December 25, 2014, late edition-final edition, sec. E.

Matsuda, Mari J. "Public Response to Racist Speech: Considering the Victim's Story." In *Words That Wound: Critical Race Theory, Assaultive Speech, and the First Amendment*, by Mari J. Matsuda, Charles R. Lawrence, Richard Delgado, and Kimberlé Crenshaw, 17–52. Boulder: Westview Press, 1993.

Matsuda, Mari J., and Charles R. Lawrence III. "Epilogue: Burning Crosses and the R.A.V. Case." In *Words That Wound: Critical Race Theory, Assaultive Speech, and the First Amendment*, 133–36. Boulder: Westview Press, 1993.

McCann, Ruth. "Tour Simmers with Whole Lotta Lambert Love." *Washington Post*, August 6, 2009, Met 2 edition, sec. Style.

McConnaughey, Janet. "Frankie Ford, Who Sang 'Sea Cruise,' Dies at Age 76." *Associated Press*, September 29, 2015.

McDermott, Maeve. "Please, Pop Stars, No More Collaborations." *USA Today*, September 11, 2019, first edition, sec. Life.

McGranahan, Liam. "Bastards and Booties: Production, Copyright, and the Mashup Community." *Trans: Revista Transcultural de Música*, no. 14 (2010): n.p.

McIntyre, Hugh. "'Glee' Has More Chart Hits Than Anyone Else in History." *Forbes*, January 9, 2015. https://www.forbes.com/sites/hughmcintyre/2015/01/09/glee-is -the-most-successful-charting-act-in-singles-history/

McKeague, Matthew. "The Accordion Is Mightier Than the Sword: Analysing the Comedy Music Counterculture Expressed through the Works of 'Weird Al' Yankovic." *Comedy Studies* 9, no. 2 (2018): 138–49. https://doi.org/10.1080/20406 10X.2018.1494360

McKinley, James C., Jr. "It's Happy, It's Danceable and It May Rule Summer." *New York Times*, May 30, 2013, late edition-final edition, sec. C.

McLeod, Kembrew, and Peter DiCola. *Creative License: The Law and Culture of Digital Sampling*. Durham: Duke University Press, 2011.

McLeod, Kembrew, and Rudolf Kuenzli. "I Collage, Therefore I Am: An Introduction to Cutting Across Media." In *Cutting Across Media: Appropriation Art, Interventionist Collage, and Copyright Law*, edited by Kembrew McLeod and Rudolf Kuenzli, 1–23. Durham: Duke University Press, 2011.

McNally, James. "Favela Chic: Diplo, Funk Carioca, and the Ethics and Aesthetics of the Global Remix." *Popular Music and Society* 40, no. 4 (2017): 434–52. https://doi.org/10.1080/03007766.2015.1126100

Means, Sean P. "Old Hits Made New: Covering the Best Cover Songs." *Salt Lake Tribune*, July 23, 2011, sec. Culture Vulture, Features.

Melley, Brian. "All That Glitters Is Gold: 'Stairway' May Be Worth Millions." *Associated Press*, June 18, 2016, sec. Domestic News.

Mervis, Scott. "Lambert, Allen Show Star Power." *Pittsburgh Post-Gazette*, August 24, 2009, Sooner edition, sec. Arts & Entertainment, Concert Review.

Mervis, Scott. "Mashup Stage." *Pittsburgh Post-Gazette*, December 2, 2010, Sooner edition, sec. Arts and Entertainment.

Mervis, Scott. "Pete Townshend: Nice to Be Part of Spectacle." *Associated Press*, February 8, 2010, sec. Sports News.

Mervis, Scott. "Stealing the Show: The Singers Know That the 'Star' Slot Is Up for Grabs on 'American Idols Live!' Tour." *Pittsburgh Post-Gazette*, August 20, 2009, Sooner edition, sec. Arts & Entertainment, Music Preview.

Mervis, Scott. "'Thriller Night': Local Musicians Gather to Pay Tribute to Michael Jackson and His Blockbuster." *Pittsburgh Post-Gazette*, October 24, 2013, Sooner edition, sec. Arts & Entertainment, Music Preview.

Mills, Michelle. "Weird Al Finds Daring to Be Stupid Pays Off." *Daily News of Los Angeles*, July 22, 2016, sec. L.

Mitchell, Tara L., Ryann M. Haw, Jeffrey E. Pfeifer, and Christian A. Meissner. "Racial Bias in Mock Juror Decision-Making: A Meta-Analytic Review of Defendant Treatment." *Law and Human Behavior* 29, no. 6 (2005): 621–37. https://doi.org/10.1007/s10979-005-8122-9

Moody, Nekesa Mumbi. "Connie Francis' 'Where the Boys Are' Gets Remake." *Associated Press*, May 20, 2010, sec. Entertainment News.

Morrison, Matthew D. "Race, Blacksound, and the (Re)Making of Musicological Discourse." *Journal of the American Musicological Society* 72, no. 3 (2019): 781–823. https://doi.org/10.1525/jams.2019.72.3.781

Moser, John J. "Yankovic Says Next Album Is His Last." *Dayton Daily News*, June 8, 2013, sec. Comics.

Mosser, Kurt. "'Cover Songs': Ambiguity, Multivalence, Polysemy." *Popular Musicology Online*, no. 2 (2008). http://www.popular-musicology-online.com/issues/02/mosser.html

Mtima, Lateef. "Copyright and Social Justice in the Digital Information Society: Three Steps toward Intellectual Property Social Justice." *Houston Law Review* 53 (2015): 459–504.

Mtima, Lateef. "IP Social Justice Theory: Access, Inclusion, and Empowerment." *Gonzaga Law Review* 55 (2020): 401–20.

Nagel, Joane. *Race, Ethnicity, and Sexuality: Intimate Intersections, Forbidden Frontiers*. New York: Oxford University Press, 2003.

Nakashima, Ryan. "Apple, Labels Work on Album 'Cocktail.'" *Associated Press*, July 27, 2009, sec. Business News.

Nakashima, Ryan. "Cover Songs: Homage or Irksome Marketing Ploy?" *Associated Press*, May 30, 2013.

Navar-Gill, Annemarie, and Mel Stanfill. "'We Shouldn't Have to Trend to Make You Listen': Queer Fan Hashtag Campaigns as Production Interventions." *Journal of Film and Video* 70, no. 3–4 (2018): 85–100.

Netanel, Neil Weinstock. "Making Sense of Fair Use." *Lewis & Clark Law Review* 15 (2011): 715–71.

Newman, Melinda. "Album Review: LeAnn Rimes' 'Lady & Gentlemen.'" *UPROXX*, September 26, 2011. https://uproxx.com/hitfix/album-review-leann-rimes-lady-gentlemen/

Nexis Uni. LexisNexis. Accessed April 10, 2022. https://www.lexisnexis.com/en-us/professional/academic/nexis-uni.page

O'Connor, Anahad. "DJ AM, Star Disc Jockey, Found Dead in Apartment." *New York Times*, August 29, 2009, late edition-final edition, sec. A.

OED Online. "Parody, n.2." Oxford University Press. Accessed December 8, 2019. http://www.oed.com/view/Entry/138059

OED Online. "Satire, n." Oxford University Press. Accessed December 8, 2019. http://www.oed.com/view/Entry/171207

OED Online. "Spoof, n. (and adj.)." Oxford University Press. Accessed December 8, 2019. http://www.oed.com/view/Entry/187390

Oklahoman. "DVD Reviews." June 26, 2009, City edition, sec. Weekend Look.

Organization for Transformative Works. "About the OTW." Accessed December 22, 2021. https://www.transformativeworks.org/about_otw/

Pareles, Jon. "Peter Gabriel Says, 'I'll Sing Yours, You Sing Mine.'" *New York Times*, March 2, 2010, late edition-final edition, sec. C.

Pareles, Jon. "The Playlist: Beyoncé Song Fit for a 'Lion King.'" *New York Times*, July 12, 2019.

Pareles, Jon. "A World of Megabeats and Megabytes." *New York Times*, January 3, 2010, late edition-final edition, sec. AR.

Pérez, Raúl. "Racism without Hatred? Racist Humor and the Myth of 'Colorblindness.'" *Sociological Perspectives* 60, no. 5 (2017): 956–74. https://doi.org/10.1177/0731121417719699

Phili, Stelios. "Robin Thicke on That Banned Video, Collaborating with 2 Chainz and Kendrick Lamar, and His New Film." *GQ*, May 7, 2013. https://www.gq.com/story/robin-thicke-interview-blurred-lines-music-video-collaborating-with-2-chainz-and-kendrick-lamar-mercy

Pittsburgh Tribune Review. "CD Reviews: Underwood Expands Her Repertoire on Third Album." November 8, 2009. https://archive.triblive.com/news/cd-reviews-underwood-expands-her-repertoire-on-third-album/

Pittsburgh Tribune Review, September 19, 2015.

Plus Media Solutions. "Arizona: Black Violin." November 7, 2014.

Plus Media Solutions. "Florida: Black Violin to Headline Outdoor Concert to Benefit WGCU." January 25, 2017.

Plus Media Solutions. "Ohio: Black Violin." March 9, 2016.

Podplesky, Azaria. "Black Violin's Mash Up of Classical and Hip Hop Entertaining for All Ages." *Spokesman Review,* April 3, 2017, main edition, sec. D.

Postmodern Jukebox. "Scott Bradlee's Postmodern Jukebox, Fort Myers Beach, Florida, May 11: Tickets on Sale Friday, February 3 at 10am." *Plus Media Solutions,* February 3, 2017.

"YouTube for Press." Accessed September 21, 2019. https://web.archive.org/web/20190 921012619/https://www.youtube.com/about/press/

Price, Kenneth. "Song Choices, Controllers Make 'DJ Hero' Stand apart from Cousins." *Star-News,* November 12, 2009, first edition.

Priester, Alec M. "The Science and Craft of Mixology in Music." *New York Times,* February 10, 2016, late edition-final edition, sec. C.

Rambo: Last Blood (2019 Movie) Teaser Trailer—Sylvester Stallone, 2019. https://www .youtube.com/watch?v=4vWg5yJuWfs

Raustiala, Kal, and Christopher Jon Sprigman. "Squelching Creativity: What the 'Blurred Lines' Team Copied Is Either Not Original or Not Relevant." *Slate Magazine,* March 12, 2015. https://slate.com/news-and-politics/2015/03/blurred-li nes-verdict-is-wrong-williams-and-thicke-did-not-infringe-on-marvin-gaye-cop yright.html

Richards, Chris. "It's Okay If You Hate Robin Thicke. But the 'Blurred Lines' Verdict Is Bad for Pop Music." *Washington Post,* March 11, 2015. https://www.washingtonp ost.com/news/arts-and-entertainment/wp/2015/03/11/the-blurred-lines-of-the-bl urred-lines-verdict/

Richards, Chris. "Lil Nas X's Horse of Any Color You Choose." *Washington Post,* April 11, 2019, Regional edition, sec. Style.

Riemenschneider, Chris. "The Big Gigs." *Star Tribune,* October 9, 2015, Metro edition, sec. Variety.

Ringer, Barbara A. "The Unauthorized Duplication of Sound Recordings." Copyright Law Revision Study 26. Washington, DC: U.S. Copyright Office, 1957. https://www .copyright.gov/history/studies/study26.pdf

Rings, Michael. "Doing It Their Way: Rock Covers, Genre, and Appreciation." *Journal of Aesthetics and Art Criticism* 71, no. 1 (2013): 55–63.

Rob, Rafael, and Joel Waldfogel. "Piracy on the High C's: Music Downloading, Sales Displacement, and Social Welfare in a Sample of College Students." *Journal of Law and Economics* 49 (2006): 29–62.

Roberts, Jeff. "Are the Beastie Boys Picking on Science-Loving Girls? The Copyright Case Is Not So Simple (Updated)." November 25, 2013. https://gigaom.com/2013 /11/25/are-the-beastie-boys-picking-on-science-loving-girls-the-copyright-case -is-not-so-simple/

Roberts, Randall. "Beatles, Beastie Boys in the Mix." *Dayton Daily News,* June 27, 2013, sec. Life.

Roediger, David R. *The Wages of Whiteness: Race and the Making of the American Working Class.* London: Verso, 1991.

Rose, Tricia. *Black Noise: Rap Music and Black Culture in Contemporary America.* Hanover, NH: University Press of New England, 1994.

Rosen, Jody. "Crawling from the Wreckage." *New York Times*, July 5, 2015, late edition-final edition, sec. AR.

Ross, Curtis. "Gabriel Reaches beyond Covers." *Tampa Tribune*, March 5, 2010, final edition, sec. Friday Extra.

Roth, Jenny, and Monica Flegel. "It's Like Rape: Metaphorical Family Transgressions, Copyright Ownership and Fandom." *Continuum* 28, no. 6 (2014): 901–13. https://doi.org/10.1080/10304312.2014.964175

Royster, Francesca T. *Sounding Like a No-No: Queer Sounds and Eccentric Acts in the Post-Soul Era*. Ann Arbor: University of Michigan Press, 2012.

Rubinkam, Michael. "Lead Singer of Breaking Benjamin Fires Bandmates." *Associated Press*, August 2, 2011, sec. Entertainment News.

Rueda, Jorge. "'Despacito' Singers Veto Venezuelan Leader's Campaign Remix." *Associated Press*, July 25, 2017, sec. International News.

Russell, Brenda, Laurie L. Ragatz, and Shane W. Kraus. "Does Ambivalent Sexism Influence Verdicts for Heterosexual and Homosexual Defendants in a Self-Defense Case?" *Journal of Family Violence* 24, no. 3 (2009): 145–57. https://doi.org/10.1007/s10896-008-9210-7

Russo, Julie Levin. "User-Penetrated Content: Fan Video in the Age of Convergence." *Cinema Journal* 48, no. 4 (2009): 125–30. https://doi.org/10.1353/cj.0.0147

Sainz, Adrian. "Lawsuits in Fla., England Related to Elvis Music." *Associated Press*, February 9, 2011, sec. Entertainment News.

Salmon, Felix. "GoldieBlox, Fair Use, and the Cult of Disruption." *Reuters Blogs* (blog), November 26, 2013. https://www.reuters.com/article/idIN312465060220131126

Salt Lake Tribune. "Pop Top: 'Glee' Falters with Priggish Madge Covers." April 26, 2010, sec. Breaking, Features.

Sanjek, David. "Ridiculing the 'White Bread Original': The Politics of Parody and Preservation of Greatness in Luther Campbell a.k.a. Luke Skyywalker et al. v. Acuff-Rose Music Inc." *Cultural Studies* 20, no. 2–3 (2006): 262–81. https://doi.org/10.1080/09502380500495742

Scheck, Frank. "Bach with a Beat." *New York Post*, November 10, 2012.

Scherzer, Amy. "Black Heritage Evening at the Straz." *Tampa Bay Times*, January 20, 2012, sec. City Times, Social Scene.

Schiffer, Sheldon. "Cover Song as Historiography, Marker of Ideological Transformation." In *Play It Again: Cover Songs in Popular Music*, edited by George Plasketes, 77–97. London: Routledge, 2016.

Schloss, Joseph G. *Making Beats: The Art of Sample-Based Hip-Hop*. New ed., with new foreword and afterword. Middletown, CT: Wesleyan University Press, 2014.

Schneiderman, Davis. "Everybody's Got Something to Hide Except for Me and My Lawsuit: William S. Burroughs, DJ Danger Mouse, and the Politics of Grey Tuesday." In *Cutting Across Media: Appropriation Art, Interventionist Collage, and Copyright Law*, edited by Kembrew McLeod and Rudolf Kuenzli, 132–51. Durham: Duke University Press, 2011.

Schumacher, Thomas G. "'This Is a Sampling Sport': Digital Sampling, Rap Music and the Law in Cultural Production." *Media, Culture & Society* 17, no. 2 (1995): 253–73. https://doi.org/10.1177/016344395017002006

Scope of Exclusive Rights in Nondramatic Musical Works: Compulsory License for Making and Distributing Phonorecords, Title 17 U.S. Code § 115. Accessed December 10, 2022. https://copyright.gov/title17/92chap1.html#115

Scope of Exclusive Rights in Sound Recordings, Title 17 U.S. Code § 114. Accessed December 4, 2021. https://www.copyright.gov/title17/92chap1.html#114

Seeger, Anthony. "Ethnomusicology and Music Law." *Ethnomusicology* 36, no. 3 (1992): 345–59. https://doi.org/10.2307/851868

Semon, Craig S. "Boss, 'Tebowie' Bring Fallon Laughs." *Telegram & Gazette*, June 28, 2012, sec. Go!, Tracks.

Serazio, Michael. "The Apolitical Irony of Generation Mash-Up: A Cultural Case Study in Popular Music." *Popular Music and Society* 31, no. 1 (2008): 79–94. https://doi.org/10.1080/03007760701214815

Serpell, Namwali. "How Social-Media Meme-Makers Rescued 'Game of Thrones' from Itself: Screenland." *New York Times*, June 6, 2019, sec. Magazine.

Shifman, Limor. *Memes in Digital Culture*. Cambridge, MA: MIT Press, 2013.

Shontell, Alyson. "This Is the Only Person We Can Find with a Perfect 100 Klout Score." *Business Insider*, November 22, 2011. https://www.businessinsider.com/100-klout-score-2011-11

Shott, Chris. "Lily Pond on Fire! Stereo Refugee Mike Satsky Exults in East Hampton, Trashes Greenhouse, Mum on New Manhattan Spot." *New York Observer*, May 28, 2009.

Silbey, Susan S., and Austin Sarat. "Critical Traditions in Law and Society Research." *Law & Society Review* 21, no. 1 (1987): 165–74. https://doi.org/10.2307/3053389

Silkaitis, Katherine. *Pittsburgh Post-Gazette*, December 29, 2011, Sooner edition, sec. Arts & Entertainment, For the Record.

Sims, Melanie. "Asher Roth Likes Fun, but Not Just a 'Stoner Kid.'" *Associated Press*, April 28, 2009, sec. Entertainment News.

Sinnreich, Aram. *Mashed Up: Music, Technology, and the Rise of Configurable Culture*. Amherst: University of Massachusetts Press, 2010.

Sisario, Ben. "Lil Nas X Added Billy Ray Cyrus to 'Old Town Road.' Is It Country Enough for Billboard Now?" *New York Times*, April 5, 2019, sec. Business, Media.

Sisario, Ben. "A New CD That Has No Music, but Lots of Pictures." *New York Times*, June 11, 2009, late edition-final edition, sec. C.

Sisario, Ben. "Songwriters Sue to Defend a Summer Hit." *New York Times*, August 17, 2013, late edition-final edition, sec. B.

Slate, Carl Wilson. "What Is 'Achy Breaky 2'?" *Salt Lake Tribune*, February 14, 2014, sec. Features.

Smith, Christopher Holmes. "'I Don't Like to Dream about Getting Paid': Representations of Social Mobility and the Emergence of the Hip-Hop Mogul." *Social Text* 21, no. 4 (2003): 69–97.

Solis, Gabriel. "I Did It My Way: Rock and the Logic of Covers." *Popular Music and Society* 33, no. 3 (2010): 297–318. https://doi.org/10.1080/03007760903523351

Somerville, Heather. "Beastie Boys Sue Oakland Toy Company GoldieBlox." *Contra Costa Times*, December 12, 2013, sec. Breaking, News, Business.

Spivak, Gayatri Chakravorty. "Can the Subaltern Speak?" In *Marxism and the Interpretation of Culture*, edited by Lawrence Grossberg and Cary Nelson, 271–313. Urbana: University of Illinois Press, 1988.

Spokesman Review. "After Hiatus, Spoon's Back in Fine Form with New Album." August 8, 2014, main edition, sec. C.

Spokesman Review. "Lil Nas X, Eilish, Enlist Help in Race for No. 1." July 14, 2019, main edition, sec. A.

Stahl, Matt. *Unfree Masters: Popular Music and the Politics of Work.* Durham: Duke University Press, 2012.

Stanfill, Mel. *Exploiting Fandom: How the Media Industry Seeks to Manipulate Fans.* Iowa City: University of Iowa Press, 2019.

Stanfill, Mel. "Fandom, Public, Commons." *Transformative Works and Cultures* 14 (2013): n.p. https://doi.org/10.3983/twc.2013.0530

Stanfill, Mel. "Spinning Yarn with Borrowed Cotton." *In Media Res,* 2015. http://medi acommons.org/imr/search/site/spinning%20yarn

Stempel, Jonathan. "Katy Perry Defeats Appeal in 'Dark Horse' Plagiarism Case." *Reuters,* March 10, 2022, sec. Lifestyle. https://www.reuters.com/lifestyle/katy-pe rry-defeats-appeal-dark-horse-plagiarism-case-2022-03-10/

Stewart, Allison. "Music Review: Robin Thicke's 'Love after War.'" *Washington Post,* December 11, 2011, every edition, sec. Style.

Stockton, Kathryn Bond. *The Queer Child, or Growing Sideways in the Twentieth Century.* Durham: Duke University Press, 2009.

Stolder, Steven. "Beastie Boys, Smashing Pumpkins Headline Tibetan Freedom Concert." *Rolling Stone,* August 8, 1996. https://www.rollingstone.com/mu sic/music-news/beastie-boys-smashing-pumpkins-headline-tibetan-freedom-con cert-183794/

Stork, Matthias. "The Cultural Economics of Performance Space: Negotiating Fan, Labor, and Marketing Practice in Glee's Transmedia Geography." *Transformative Works and Cultures* 15 (2014). https://doi.org/10.3983/twc.2014.0490

St. Petersburg Times. "Danger Mouse Tries to Avoid Legal Trap." May 20, 2009, 4 State / Suncoast edition, sec. Tampa Bay.

Strauss, Matthew, and Noah Yoo. "'Blurred Lines' Verdict Largely Upheld after Appeal." *Pitchfork,* March 21, 2018. https://pitchfork.com/news/blurred-lines-verd ict-largely-upheld-after-appeal/

Sumagaysay, Levi. "GoldieBlox Now Says It Has No Beef with the Beastie Boys." *San Jose Mercury News,* November 27, 2013, sec. News.

Sunder, Madhavi. *From Goods to a Good Life: Intellectual Property and Global Justice.* New Haven: Yale University Press, 2012.

Talbott, Chris. "Carrie Underwood Takes Video of Year at CMT Awards." *Associated Press,* June 6, 2013, sec. Entertainment News.

Talbott, Chris. "Electronic DJ-Producer Zedd Blitzes the Pop World." *Associated Press,* September 26, 2013, sec. Entertainment News.

Talbott, Chris. "Jason Derulo, John Legend among CMT Awards' VIPs." *Associated Press,* June 3, 2014, sec. Entertainment News.

Tampa Tribune. "'Girls' Song Parody in GoldieBlox Ad Riles Beastie Boys." November 28, 2013, sec. Nation & World.

Tampa Tribune. "Offering Thanks for Fallon." October 11, 2013, sec. Friday Extra.

Taylor, Dan. "Scott Bradlee's Postmodern Jukebox Coming to Santa Rosa." *Press Democrat*, March 26, 2018, sec. Entertainment News.

Terry, Josh. "7 More Songs That Were Allegedly Plagiarized." *Chicago Tribune, Redeye*, March 11, 2015, sec. Entertainment News.

"The Joke." Accessed September 14, 2019. https://www.carnegiehall.org/Explore/Artic les/2020/04/10/The-Joke

"The Regina Monologues." *The Simpsons*, November 23, 2003.

Time Staff. "The 25 Most Influential People on the Internet." *Time*, July 16, 2019. https:// time.com/5626827/the-25-most-influential-people-on-the-internet/

Tough, David. "The Mashup Mindset: Will Pop Eat Itself?" In *Play It Again: Cover Songs in Popular Music*, edited by George Plasketes, 205–12. London: Routledge, 2016.

Toula, Christopher M., and Gregory C. Lisby. "Towards an Affirmative Public Domain." *Cultural Studies* 28, no. 5–6 (2014): 997–1021. https://doi.org/10.1080/09 502386.2014.886490

Transformative Works and Cultures. "About the Journal." Accessed December 22, 2021. https://journal.transformativeworks.org/index.php/twc/about

Turner, Jim. "Airbnb Has Spent at Least $1,250,000 to Prevent Local Regulation of Florida Rental Properties." *Orlando Weekly*, January 10, 2020. https://www.orlan doweekly.com/news/airbnb-has-spent-at-least-1250000-to-prevent-local-regulati on-of-florida-rental-properties-26617620

Tushnet, Rebecca. "Payment in Credit: Copyright Law and Subcultural Creativity." *Law and Contemporary Problems* 70, no. 2 (2007): 135–74. https://www.jstor.org/st able/27592184

Tushnet, Rebecca. "Scary Monsters: Hybrids, Mashups, and Other Illegitimate Children." *Notre Dame Law Review* 86, no. 5 (2011): 2133–56.

Tushnet, Rebecca. "User-Generated Discontent: Transformation in Practice." *Columbia Journal of Law & the Arts* 31 (2008): 101–20.

Unterberger, Andrew. "It Took over 20 Years for a Song to Tie the 16-Week Hot 100 No. 1 Record—Why Now Twice in Two Years?" *Billboard*, July 25, 2019.

Vaidhyanathan, Siva. *Copyrights and Copywrongs: The Rise of Intellectual Property and How It Threatens Creativity.* New York: New York University Press, 2003.

Valisno, Jeffrey O. "Staying In: Songbirds." *BusinessWorld*, May 20, 2011, sec. Weekender.

Varga, George, *San Diego Union-Tribune.* "Reinhart Wants to Party (and Sing) Like It's '69." *Telegram & Gazette*, October 26, 2017, Worcester TG edition, sec. Entertainment Life.

Vats, Anjali. *The Color of Creatorship: Intellectual Property, Race, and the Making of Americans.* Stanford: Stanford University Press, 2020.

Vats, Anjali, and Deidre A. Keller. "Critical Race IP." *Cardozo Arts & Entertainment Law Journal* 36 (2018): 735–95.

Velasco, Schuyler. "'Weird Al' Yankovic Scores His First No. 1 Album: How He Did It." *Christian Science Monitor*, July 24, 2014, sec. Business.

Vuong, Madeline. "Black Violin Will Blend Classical, Hip-Hop at the Mahaiwe." *Berkshire Eagle*, October 15, 2014, sec. Entertainment.

Wagmeister, Elizabeth. "Lea Michele Controversy: 'Glee' Actors and Other Co-Stars Speak Out." *Variety*, June 4, 2020. https://variety.com/2020/tv/news/lea-michele-glee-controversy-amber-riley-samantha-ware-1234625000/

Wall Street Journal Abstracts. "Better than the Sum of Their Parts?" *Wall Street Journal*, April 6, 2012, sec. D.

Walsh, Austin. "Z-Trip." *Eureka Times-Standard*, October 1, 2009, sec. Entertainment.

Wang, Amy X. "How Music Copyright Lawsuits Are Scaring Away New Hits." *Rolling Stone*, January 9, 2020. https://www.rollingstone.com/music/music-features/music-copyright-lawsuits-chilling-effect-935310/

Ward, Lee. "Area Comedians Team for March 8 Show at Mardi Gras Casino." *Daily Independent*, February 20, 2014, sec. Lifestyle.

Washington Post, May 23, 2014, every edition, sec. Weekend.

Weingarten, Christopher R. "An Oral History of 'Weird Al' Yankovic's 'Smells Like Nirvana.'" *Spin*, October 11, 2012. https://www.spin.com/2012/10/weird-al-yankovic-looks-back-at-20-years-of-smells-like-nirvana/

Weinstein, Deena. "The History of Rock's Pasts through Rock Covers." In *A Popular Music Reader*, edited by Richard G. King, 69–80. Boston: Pearson Learning Solutions, 2012.

Wikström, Patrik. *The Music Industry: Music in the Cloud.* 2nd ed. Cambridge: Polity, 2013.

Williams, Marian R., and Melissa W. Burek. "Justice, Juries, and Convictions: The Relevance of Race in Jury Verdicts." *Journal of Crime and Justice* 31, no. 1 (2008): 149–69. https://doi.org/10.1080/0735648X.2008.9721247

Wood, Mikael. "Story behind the Song: The 'Despacito' Remix Isn't Just about Sex." *Dayton Daily News*, September 1, 2017.

Woodmansee, Martha. "The Genius and the Copyright: Economic and Legal Conditions of the Emergence of the 'Author.'" *Eighteenth-Century Studies* 17, no. 4 (1984): 425–48. https://doi.org/10.2307/2738129

Woods, Wes, II. "Dee Jay Silver Spins Country Mashups for Tour." *Inland Valley Daily Bulletin*, August 12, 2016, sec. C.

Wright, Mary Ellen. "'Weird Al' Yankovic Parodies Remain Relevant after 30 Years." *Sunday News*, July 10, 2011, sec. E.

Wu, Tim. "Jay-Z versus the Sample Troll." *Slate*, November 16, 2006. https://slate.com/culture/2006/11/the-shady-one-man-corporation-that-s-destroying-hip-hop.html

Wu, Tim. "Why the 'Blurred Lines' Copyright Verdict Should Be Thrown Out." *New Yorker*, March 12, 2015. https://www.newyorker.com/culture/culture-desk/why-the-blurred-lines-copyright-verdict-should-be-thrown-out

Yahr, Emily. "Mixing In Some Hip-Hop to the 2-Step." *Washington Post*, August 6, 2013, Suburban edition, sec. Style.

Yankovic, "Weird Al." "The Gaga Saga." *Al's Blog* (blog), April 20, 2011. https://alyankovic.wordpress.com/the-gaga-saga/

INDEX

ABKCO Music, 31
ABKCO v. LaVere (2000), 31
AC/DC, 41, 103, 115
"Achy Breaky Heart," 64
"Achy Breaky 2," 55
Aerosmith, 4
Ahmed, Sara, 66
"Air That I Breathe, The," 114
Akon, 53
Aldean, Jason, 51, 115
Alice in Chains, 32
"All Day," 71
Allen, Lily, 3
"All of Me," 54
"All the Way Up," 63
"Alone Again," 83, 148
"Alone Again (Naturally)," 83, 148
Alpert, Herb, 70
AM (DJ), 77
"American Girl," 118
American Idol, 4, 30, 31, 32, 36, 39, 110
American Idols Live! Tour, 39
Americans with Disabilities Act, 148–49
"Amish Paradise," 96
"Angel on Each Arm," 115
Aphex Twin, 78
appropriation, 6, 16, 21–22, 28, 31, 38, 55,
    58, 80–81, 103, 105, 126–28, 131, 133,
    140, 143, 151–53
Arewa, Olufunmilayo B., 9, 15, 143, 145–
    48, 150, 153–55
A$AP Rocky, 50
attribution, 146, 153–56
aura function, 21, 71–76, 80, 139
authenticity, 10, 31, 45, 62, 73–74
Authors Guild Inc. v. HathiTrust, 148

authorship, 9–13, 15, 17, 20, 26, 33, 44, 79,
    90, 130, 144. *See also* Romanticism
Awkward, Michael, 12, 33

"Baby Got Back," 4, 146
Bach, Johann Sebastian, 38, 79
Bad Hair Day, 111
Bagels and Bongos, 88
Bale, Christian, 52, 59
"Bale Out," 52
Baptiste, Jean, 123
Barron, Anne, 44
Barthes, Roland, 12
Beastie Boys, 18, 88, 90, 99–104, 112, 148
Beatles, 1, 17, 30, 39, 41, 45, 75–77, 79, 82,
    88, 90, 103, 149, 152
"Bed Intruder Song, The," 59
Beethoven, Ludwig van, 38
Benjamin, Walter, 73
Berlin, Irving, 93
Beyonce, 43, 79
Bhabha, Homi, 91
Bhandar, Brenna, 143
Bieber, Justin, 49, 50–51, 55, 58
Biggie Smalls, 69
Billboard, 61–62, 75
Billboard Hot 100, 1, 61, 63, 65
Bjork, 53
Black Album, The, 17, 75, 79
Black Crowes, 123
Black Eyed Peas, 57
blackface, 27–28, 89, 111
Blackness, 21, 28, 31, 36, 71, 79–84, 89
Black Sabbath, 69
Blacksound, 127
Black Violin, 77–79, 82, 87, 90–91

223